TO SPEND

ETERNITY ALONE

The Trial of Jesse Billings Jr.

First Edition

COMPILED AND WRITTEN

BY

DR. HOLLIS A. PALMER

Deep Roots Publications,
Saratoga Springs, N. Y.

To Spend Eternity Alone
The Trial of Jesse Billings Jr.

Published by:

Deep Roots Publications
Post Office Box 114
Saratoga Springs, NY 12866

Library of Congress Number 99-90440

Printed in the United States of America

ISBN 0-9671713-7-7

Palmer, Hollis Albert.
    To spend eternity alone : the trial of Jesse
Billings Jr. / Hollis A. Palmer. -- 1st ed.
    p. cm.
    Includes bibliographical references and index.
    ISBN: 0-9671713-7-7

    1. Billings, Jesse--Trials, litigation, etc.
    2. Trials (Murder)--New York (State)--Saratoga
County.   I. Title.

KF223.B53P35 1999   345.73'02523
                        QBI99-570

**I have been fortunate to have had many mentors.
This book is dedicated to them.**

Family mentors:
  Lawrence Palmer   father
  Ernest Palmer   grandfather
  Albert Wooddell   grandfather
  Donald Wooddell   uncle

Non-family in the order of their appearance in my life and what each taught me:
  Lenny Moss- horse owner and neighbor   patience
  Johnny Hart- cartoonist and neighbor   culture
  Jerry Murphy- principal   about people and analysis
  Cal Peterson-superintendent   about people and synthesis
  Bill Moran- retired superintendent *if all else fails, act Irish*

**Special thanks to
Sharon Mitchell
for suffering through the editing
of my thoughts.**

vi

Part I

The Storm

Late in the afternoon of June 4, 1878, a severe summer storm moved across Saratoga County. Emanating from the southwest corner of the county, the storm moved northeast, passing across the numerous open farm fields and building in intensity as it progressed. At about 5:00 p.m., the tempest reached the small canal hamlet known as Fort Miller's Bridge. The savage storm washed out crops, blew dead limbs off trees, and loosened rail fences. More important, to the lives of those who lived in this community, it softened the soil which had hardened during the recent drought. The havoc of this storm was but a prelude to the ravages on the social structure that were to be created just a few hours later by the murder of the wife of the settlement's most prosperous citizen.

1

The Murder

As a soft breeze pushed dusk slowly west, a shot was fired through a window into the sitting room of the home of the wealthy Billings family. Mrs. Mary Eliza Billings was seated with her daughter and maid when, without any sound except the discharge of the gun and the shattering of the window pane, her head drooped to her left shoulder. Within critical moments, the maid and daughter ran from the room. The maid, Maggie Mahoney, ran screaming out the door on the west side of the largest house in town. Jennie Billings, the daughter, thought that, after the gun shot, she had seen a figure running past the broken window toward the street in front of the house. Instinctively, Jennie ran out through the front door screaming for help.

Moments later, in a time when people helped their neighbors and before the yellow tape of modern investigations, numerous persons were at the scene. Most of those who came to the house did so to aid eighteen year old Jennie. The form of this aid varied based on the person. A few, as in all times of crisis, were there to help either by assisting the injured or by calming the fears of the innocent. Some, probably a larger number than the first group, would be described as curious wanting to see what had occurred. At least one, following Jennie's description of the events, went to the lumber pile across the street in search of the perpetrator. The remaining adult residents of Fort Miller Bridge gathered in groups throughout the small community. Few would understand until much later how greatly their memories of those first few minutes would effect the outcomes of their own and many other peoples' lives.

Within half an hour, Jesse Billings, Jr., husband of the victim, arrived by carriage at the murder scene. Upon seeing the body of his wife, he fell to the floor and held her foot to his chest. Fifteen minutes later, with the help of two of his friends, Billings was brought to his feet. His only child, the beautiful Jennie, looked at him and said something to the effect "three tries and out." With these words she cast her vote with those who would hold to her father's guilt.

In 1878, Jesse Billings Jr. was the wealthiest citizen in the area holding on at least one occasion that he was wealthier than any "four other families in the town." He was in fact one of the wealthiest persons in that part of the State of New York. It is claimed that he had at least seventy-two canal boats (the true number may have exceeded 100), forty farms, a store, a boat yard employing twenty men, and, next to his house, a large personal bank. It was also believed that he had a mistress living in the apartment above the bank, at the time of his wife's murder.

The account you are about to read is true. The story has been carefully collected, sequenced and transcribed from the various newspapers that covered the events in incredible detail. On the surface, this is the tale of a man of means being tried for the murder of his wife. Beneath that level, it is the tale of a community divided into distinct camps before, during and after the trial. At a still deeper level, we learn of the life style, work ethic, social values and family values of the late 1870's. Excavating to the bottom, this is a tale of how well those who descended from Revolutionary war veterans accepted people who were not like themselves.

Time and Place

In 1878 the president of the United States was Ohio's native son and former governor, Rutherford B. Hayes. Hayes had won the highly disputed and totally corrupt election of 1876 by one electoral vote 185 to 184. He actually lost the popular vote by over 3%. To add to the calamity, Hayes's administration followed an even more scandal ridden presidency, that of Ulysses S. Grant. It would appear that the country, if not the county, was used to disreputable conditions existing among those in power.

Over the previous twenty years life had changed radically. Fortunes had been made and lost during the Civil War thirteen years earlier. Anyone over fifty could remember a period when society moved at four miles an hour. Now, with the advent of railroads and telegraphs, life was hurtling along at twenty-five miles an hour. In every community there were living reminders of the past: the disabled veterans who had given their health during the war and the widows of the soldiers.

In some ways it was a time of great equality. There was no electricity and only rarely was there natural gas in homes. Everyone, regardless of wealth, used an outhouse. Without air-conditioning, everybody was hot in the summer, and without central heat, everyone was cold in the winter. Men who weren't farmers usually worked seasonal jobs or as day workers. Many farmers also had other part-time work to

3

provide cash for the necessities of their families. The mills closed when they ran out of raw material or water power. People went to bed at dark rather than use candles or oil lamps. For almost everyone, life ran in periods of have or have not. If you had a job that actually paid a salary, it often came with either a home or board. Residing in the Billings house at various times were his numerous workers and the "girls" who helped Mrs. Billings "keep house."

Without media, the men folk met in the evening at the local store or tavern to exchange the news of the day. This intense degree of social contact resulted in deep friendships and even deeper rivalries. Communities were like families with strict rules of conduct and clearly defined, even if ever- changing, relationships.

This was a time before the concept of political correctness. The ethnicity of people often followed their names if they should be so unfortunate as to have them appear in the paper. During this time, one did not speak unkindly of the dead. Newspapers often told people how they should be treating their neighbors or behaving in public. In short, it was a confusing time to live.

Businesses were owned by individuals, not corporations. If you owned the enterprise, as Jesse Billings, Jr. did, you were expected to provide for your employees. Billings was unique in the provisions he made for his employees. Since he owned diverse operations, he often employed the same people in various jobs all year long.

Fort Miller's Bridge, now know as Northumberland, is on the Champlain Canal less than two miles north of Schuylerville, New York. Today the hamlet is marked only by a speed limit sign that restricts drivers to 40 miles per hour. This area is part of a county rich in history. Schuylerville, originally named Saratoga, is the site of Burgoyne's surrender after the Battle of Saratoga. Someone once noted that a small town is one where you don't need to use your turn signals because everyone already knows where you are going. By that definition, Fort Miller's Bridge, at the time of the murder, was a place where no turn signals were needed. Even with the official change of designation, the hamlet remains today a small community where everyone, at the very least knows everyone else, if not where they are going. Annually, thousands of wayfarers on the section of highway where Routes 4 and 32 are joined, pass the site of the Billings tragedy unaware that they were

4

traveling past the location of the most mysterious moment in the history of Saratoga County.

To provide insight into the temperament of the times, several articles were taken directly from the local papers and included in the first section of this text.

The First Reports

In 1878, there were no national news services. Each paper, whether weekly or daily, had its own pool of reporters. Those reporters, as today, strived to break the news before their competition. The first day, the various papers in the region reported only the factual information. By the second day, the papers pushed their reporters in an effort to get the lead story. The reporter for the Daily Saratogian arrived at 11:00 a.m.; by 1:00 p.m. he was able to telegraph the following article to the paper for publication that afternoon. [The transcription is exact.]

The Daily Saratogian June 5, 1878

Later Account

At about half past eight o'clock last evening one of the most terrible murders was perpetrated at the small village known as Fort Miller, ever recorded in the vicinity. Today the whole eastern part of the county is in a state of unprecedented excitement. The victim of the tragedy is Mrs. Eliza Billings wife of Jesse Billings a well known speculator and owner of canal boats

The Scene of the Murder

The house where the murder occurred is situated on the main road on the west side of the Fort Miller Dam, about half a dozen rods (100 feet) from the river's edge. It is a large, comfortable mansion, surrounded with trees, and ample grounds and outhouses. About 200 feet north of the house is a new two-story new brick building erected last year by Jesse Billings, nominally for a banking-house, but really a private institution and office for Billings's use in his extensive business. Jesse Billings, his wife, Jennie Billings his daughter, and a servant girl, lived in the house. In the upper part of the bank building lived Weller Curtis and his wife, a young lady of 21 years of age, pretty and vivacious. All that ample means could furnish seemed supplied for a comfortable and even a luxurious country life.

The Parties

5

Jesse Billings is a shrewd business man who has made money-getting the end and aim of his life. If reports are true he is rich. He owns a great deal of real estate, houses, lands and a large fleet of canal boats. He is the big man of the section and is about fifty years of age, tough, hard build, iron gray hair and beard, medium height, and countenance indicating worldly wisdom, energy and great nerve. His moral character is not above suspicion. Indeed the people we met today, almost without exception, spoke unfavorably of his character as a man, an old and evil report about the suspicious death of his brother a number of years ago being revived by some and freely commented on. He is about 50 years of age. His family consisted of his wife, Eliza, daughter of Mrs. Mary C. Harris, of Fort Miller Falls, a daughter, Jennie, about 18 years of age, and a servant girl. The household has been the scene of unhappiness for many years, and last night's fearful act was the climax of the wretchedness.

The Murder

The shooting was done through the sitting room window on the south side of the house. Mrs. Billings was sitting in a rocking chair, not over three feet from one window, and her daughter opposite her on the other side of a table which stood against the wall. The hired girl was sitting further back in the room. A lamp stood on the table. At about 8 1/2 o'clock the sharp report of a pistol was heard from outside the closed window, the blinds being open, and simultaneously Mrs. Billings sank back in her chair without a word and expired almost instantly. Miss Jennie sprang to her mother's side and as she did so the blood ran down the carpet. Horrified and frightened, she ran to the door shrieking for help and crying out

"O, Mother is Shot!"

The whole neighborhood which consists of twenty houses, a couple of stores, mills, blacksmith shop, etc. was instantly alarmed, and in a few moments the house was filled with horror- stricken neighbors. Mrs. Billings sat in her chair dead, the shot having been fired with fatal accuracy, penetrating her head just over the ear and lodging in her brain. Death must have been almost instantaneous. In the lower pane of glass was

A Round Bullet Hole,

6

and the glass outside, and on some parts of the frame were grains of burned powder, showing that the assassin had held the weapon almost against the glass. On the outside, between the walk and the house, a space of some three feet, the border was grown full of yellow June roses in full blossom, amongst which the person who fired the murderous shot could have concealed himself from view if he desired. The windows are low, the window sill not being more than four feet from the ground, so a person standing on the beaten path could, by extending his arm, almost touch the window pane with his hand. The murderer, whoever he was, stood breast amid the blooming roses, cruelly leveled his weapon at the mother's head and fired, shooting her dead in the presence of her family. It was the work of a relentless hand prompted by a heart as pitiless as that of a tiger.

The Morning in the Household

When we reached the house at eleven o'clock this morning, the body had been laid out in the parlor, the daughter was closeted upstairs with District Attorney Ormsby and John Foley. In the front chamber was Mrs. Mary C. Harris, mother of the murdered woman, and some other friends. Mr. Billings was at his office in the Bank building, and did not, while we were there, approach his daughter or his wife's relatives. He remained quietly in his office. From conversation, we learned that the relations of Mr. and Mrs. Billings had never been amicable since they were married. They had disagreed about the wife's property, and lately a most bitter quarrel had grown out of the relations of Mr. Billings with the handsome young woman, Mrs. Curtis, who occupied rooms over the Billings's office. It is freely alleged that Billings had attempted to throw his wife into the river, and she and the daughter both asserted that Mrs. Billings considered her life unsafe. Billings, they said, had tried to make that his wife was crazy. So passionate accusations of Billings are mingled with tears and sobs over the murdered woman.

Who Fired the Fatal Shot?

Of course speculation was rife over the case. The general feeling, as indicated by the remarks of the people who gathered about, was adverse to Billings, and he has doubtless been both arrested ere this. Where was Billings when the murder was committed? He was not in the house. He had been absent all day, departing before Mrs. Billings and her

7

daughter had risen in the morning, and returning late in the afternoon. It is for him to show where he was when the murderous shot was fired, and he will need to make the case very plain, for suspicion points with sullen finger at him and at his record for months and years as furnishing the only clue to the dreadful mystery.

He Visits His Mother-In-Law.

Mrs. Harris will testify, when she is examined, that Billings came to her house at Fort Miller Falls about noon yesterday, the first time he had been there in two years, and called for his dinner. He talked bitterly about his family, and told Mrs. H. that he wanted her to get the d---d Harrisses out of his house, as they were the curse to him. Some sharp language was used by him against Mrs. Harris yesterday. He returned home late in the afternoon, and after the heavy wind and rain, which came about five o'clock, had passed over, he went out to visit his farm back on the hills. That was the last the family saw of him till a short time after the murder, when he came into the room and threw himself on the floor, ejaculating some words expressive of grief. He was at a Mr. Washburn's about an eighth of a mile from his own house, when word was brought in of the shooting of his wife. Whether he had been there long enough to cover the period of the tragedy is yet to be proved.

What Mr. Billings Says.

We found Mr. Billings in his small private office in the Bank building. He said he could tell no more about it than anybody else outside. They were after him sharp, he said, and he supposed that he ought to be careful what he said. The case was one of willful murder, and the circumstances were very unfortunate for him. He had trouble with his family, but knew of no one whom he would suspect of doing such an act. He thought there might be others implicated some way, and supposed that "the whole batch of us ought perhaps to be arrested." He said he was at Washburn's when he first heard of the shooting. He had been out looking after his stock on the farm, and had stopped at Washburn's on some business. He manifested no special grief, but he is not a man who would show much feeling.

Mrs. Emma Curtis's Statement

Mrs. Emma Curtis has pleasant chambers over the Billings's Bank building. She is a very bright, chatty and prepossessing young woman of twenty-one years. She has sued Mrs. Billings for slander and, in the course of conversation told us how shamefully Mrs. Billings had treated her, applying opprobrious epithets to her from her open window across the open yard. She had never had words with Mrs. Billings except once or twice, and Mr. Billings had never said much about his wife to her except to tell her not to mind what Mrs. Billings said, as he thought she was crazy. She has lived over the bank since last October. Her husband is away a good deal of the time, but that night at the time of the murder, was sitting on the steps of the store, next door to the bank. Mrs. Curtis talked in a straightforward way, and gave out no indications of murder, malice or wickedness. The only thing against her that we could learn was that she is pretty and lives over Billings's office. Her own and her husband's reputations are both good so far as we could learn.

The Daughter's Grief

Miss Jennie Billings is a young lady evidently well bred and educated. She has been at school at Mechanicville, Fort Edward, and Hudson. She was of course over-whelmed with grief, but like others, her sympathies were all with her mother's side of the case.

No Clue

Up to one o'clock to-day, when we left Schuylerville, no clue to the murder had been obtained other than such as arose for the circumstances detailed above, if we except alone the finding of a hat on the road some distance south of the house. The coroner's jury was to have met this afternoon, the results of which we shall present to-morrow. The case is remarkable as well as horrible in its strange circumstances and incidents.

The afternoon of June 5th, the coroner convened a jury to determine what had occurred. The district attorney, Ormsby, as well as the coroner were there. As the coroner's inquest was held in one of the local stores, Jesse Billings sat in the office of his bank with his father, Dr. Jesse Billings, a man of 84 years.

The newspaper considered to be local by those residing in Fort Miller Bridge, was a weekly journal published in Schuylerville entitled the Saratoga County Standard. The reports of the Billings tragedy carried by this periodical were far more personal than those of their competition. In reading the articles related to the case, it doesn't take great detective skills to determine who was interviewed for the story. There were two articles pertinent to this case published in the Standard shortly after the murder. The first appeared two days after the crime and the second one week later. Both of these articles are reprinted in their entirety so the reader can experience the temperament of the community at the time.

The Saratoga County Standard   June 6, 1878

MURDER

The Wife of a Well Known Citizen Assassinated.

A strange fatality of death coming with violence and with awful suddenness seems to haunt the life of Mr. Jesse Billings, Jr. of Fort Miller Bridge. Many years ago, while a lad of eighteen, himself and an older brother Hugh were out hunting, and the latter was shot instantly dead by Jesse, a ball having gone clean through his heart. The deed was acknowledged by Jesse, who said it was an accidental shot. Hugh was a handsome, talented lad of 22, and his untimely death was much mourned.

Again on Tuesday evening last was Mr. Billings one of the chief sufferers in an appalling tragedy which has stunned the community and startled the county, as the family is one of the highest and most widely known in this section. At about 8:30 o'clock on that evening, his wife, Mrs. Eliza Billings, was shot instantly dead while sitting quietly in her own home, the ball entering the left ear and remaining in her head. She had just returned from the wedding ceremonies of the brother, John Harris, of Saratoga Springs, and was sitting in a sofa rocking chair within a yard of a window that looked out upon a lawn at the south of the house. In her company were her daughter, Miss Jennie Billings, a young lady of 17, and the servant girl. Mr. Billings was absent from the house salting his cattle. Suddenly a loud report was heard, a ball crashed through the window, and the doomed lady gave one slight gasp and fell foreword dead. The daughter immediately ran out of the house, and saw a man dodge behind a lumber pile. The report of the gun startled the whole settlement, and her screaming told the citizens where the point of disturbance was. A crowd immediately gathered, but the good people of Fort Miller are not sufficiently used to tragedies of this sort to instantly develop into keen detectives, and the assassin escaped.

The antecedent circumstances of the case are peculiar. Mr. and Mrs. Billings have led an unfortunate and unhappy married life. For several years the mutual crimination had been so violent that the parties had not used marital relations, and had scarcely spoken a kind word to each other. Within a short time a Mrs. Curtis, living over Mr. Billings's bank and employed by him to take care of his business rooms in it, had caused Mrs. Billings much uneasiness, and she accused her husband of scandalous conduct with her. The matter had culminated in a suit for slander by Mrs. Curtis, and Mrs. Billings had been arrested, and the suit was to have commenced on the next day after the evening that proved so fatal.

Rumors without number are flying through the air with reference to the affair. As we write, the coroner's jury is in session investigating the whole thing. These things are evident:

The murder was not for plunder.

It was no haphazard crime committed by a tramp.

It was done for pure hatred to the woman

It was a cold, deliberate murder, and whoever is found to be the criminal can plead no insanity, no sudden flaring up of uncontrollable anger. It is scarcely possible that the principal of so open a crime, committed as it was in the first of the evening, in a well settled community, can go undetected. Murder will almost always out, and the avenging halter hovers about the neck of the assassin, unseen as yet, but surely tightening to its dreadful task.

Mrs. Eliza Billings was born Sept. 10, 1832. Her maiden name was Harris. She leaves one child, a daughter, to frantically mourn her tragic death.

One week later The <u>Standard</u> in its June 13, 1878 edition, published a follow-up article that tried to encapsulate what was happening in the hamlet north of its offices.

The Northumberland Murder

On Sunday June 2, Mrs. Eliza Billings of Northumberland attended devine service at the M. E. church in this village. On Sunday, June 9, her lifeless body was laid in the cemetery at Bacon Hill. The six intervening days had wrought an awful change in the pleasant Billings home in the little hamlet.

The life of its mistress had been extinguished with the terrible suddenness of a lightning stroke; its master had been seized by the law on the awful charge of murder; it had been deserted, perhaps forever, by the only child, upon whom was forced by one cruel blow the fearful inheritance of a memory indelibly stamped with the misfortunes of one parent and the disgrace of the other.

It is with a shudder that we uncover to the gaze of the public the worse than witch's caldron, which "like a hell-broth boiled and bubbled" in that home for years and years until, with a convulsion that shook the social world around it, upheaved the foul mess in the fatal catastrophe we recorded last week. In this fuller account we give now of the affair and its antecedents, we shall endeavor to give the exact truth, knowing that the truth can harm nobody. The fatal shot that rang out upon the still air of the beautiful valley of the Hudson on the evening of Tuesday, June 4, will reverberate unceasingly in the memory of every inhabitant of the quiet community around, and as he who is now a prattler tells the grandchild who clings shudderingly to his knee of the bloody tragedy that startled his youth, of the deep damnation of the victim's taking off," he will utter, too, words of warning against the recklessness and wickedness that brewed the deadly draught.

We give below in full the testimony taken by the coroner's jury. Reports have been given in some of the papers that the coroner, Dr. Gow, was careless in the selection of his jury and had selected several who were in the employ of Mr. Billings and dependent upon him for a livelihood. There is no truth in this. Not a member of the jury was in any way connected with him, as will be seen by its composition, which is as follows:

A. B. Baucus, foreman; S. Winney, James Matthews, John Matthews, James Fake, James Wilson, L. Gorham, E. W. Downs, R. Woodworth.

The verdict was given on Friday afternoon and is as follows, and a careful examination of the testimony will convince any one that no other could possibly in fairness have been given:

The body of the said Mrs. Mary Eliza Billings was found sitting dead in her chair, in her residence in Northumberland, and that the said body, when so found as aforesaid, appeared to have been pierced with a bullet fired from a gun or pistol by some person to

12

the said jury unknown, and the said jurors upon their oaths aforesaid do say that the said Mrs. Mary Eliza Billings came to her death by the said wound appearing upon her body, as aforesaid, and not otherwise, but who inflicted said wound is to the jury unknown.

From the first moment of the crime it was almost a universal belief that Mr. Billings himself was the assassin who had shot his wife. He had left the house about an hour before the deed was done, prowling about the fields of his farm; had returned to the house a half hour after the shooting and had instantly been confronted by his own daughter with an accusation of the murder, crouched in these words: "You are my father; but you are the one that killed my mother. This is the third time you have tried and now you have done it."

It was not, however, until Friday that the damning clue was found that seemed to clinch the fast-gathering proofs of his guilt. In giving an account of the findings of the clue, we want to call attention to one of two parties who have not had sufficient credit given them for their skill and energy in working it up. On Thursday Marcus Cary and David Prosser were strolling over the Billings farm, examining the footmarks and horse tracks spoken of in the testimony of Mr. Billings, when they happened upon an old long disused well not far from where he had hitched his team on that Tuesday evening. It was covered with a couple planks and was full of water to within a yard of the surface. There was also a single track visible in the grass in the direction of where the horse had stood. One said instantly to the other: "If any gun is found it will be found in that well." They then went down to the inquest and informed officer Gilbert of their theory, who, however did not seem to pay any attention to the matter. In the evening Cary met officer Alanson Chase in the village and told him about the well, and they made an appointment to go up the following morning and dredge it. Early the next morning they repaired to the well, and for more than two hours officer Chase worked hard with a patent spring grappling iron, to find out what story that old well could tell. At last, when just about to give it over in despair, he struck the tell tale weapon, and soon it was brought up and identified as the one that had stood for years in Billings's store.

The instant result was the formal arrest of Billings on the charge of murder, and on the same day he was taken to Ballston to await the action of the grand jury which meets on Monday next. As he was taken away he seemed to break down with grief, and sobbed out a sorrowful "good-bye, good-bye my home." The whole merit of the finding of the gun – thorough detective skills.

Jesse Billing, Jr., was a boy and has been a man of very peculiar characteristics. What education he received more than the learning of the district school was the result of a brief attendance in an academy at Poultney, Vt.

As a boy he was jealous of his older, handsomer and more talented brother, Hugh, and was often heard to mutter that "that business should be changed." When about 18 years of age he shot his brother while they were out together squirrel hunting. They both aimed at the same squirrel sitting on the branch of a high tree; but while Hugh shot the animal above, Jesse shot Hugh. He did not instantly die, but lived a few moments after his father and a neighbor arrived at the scene. Although not able to speak, he motioned away every approach of his brother. Jesse's version of the accidental shooting was received at the time, but there are rumors that he has been charged by both his father and mother, in moments of petulance, with having murdered Hugh.

Mr. Billings seems to have been a man of unusual ability and force; indeed, no other kind of man could have built up, in so quiet and diminutive a hamlet as Northumberland village, the splendid business which will now fall to pieces if its master is taken from it. His property consists of a greater or less interest in 78 canal boats, running mainly on the Champlain Canal; a store well stocked with goods; his cozy homestead, and his fine farm of 500 acres of choice land. His method of procedures as to his boats was to build or buy them cheap, and then sell them on time at a large advance upon cost, taking a cash payment down, and putting a mortgage on the boat to secure the balance. He would usually reserve, too, the right to send a load for the trip in the fall, which he would sell to some potato buyer at a round sum. In very many cases it would happen that the parties who had bought the boat, after making greater or less payments, would default on the balance, and the craft would fall back into his hand to be sold again. In this way his profits were large, and his wealth is at present estimated at a quarter of a million.

At the time not long ago that he proposed to start a bank in Northumberland, he suggested that he would put up $30,000 cash into the stock of the concern. We cannot find that Mr. Billings was an unjust or even ungenerous man to deal with. He had the habit, unpardonable in these graceless days, of insisting upon collecting 100 cents on every dollar that was due him, and he had the energy to enable him to succeed in doing it. We cannot find a single instance where he was not willing to pay the full number of cents on the dollar.

He was a robust, active, driving man of great energy and of violent passions. Some years ago he attacked a neighbor, Mr. A. L. Finne, with a shovel which he had procured for the express purpose, as he declared, of "laying Finne cold." The attack was unsuccessful but cost him $500.

He was the Mogul of the hamlet where he lived, and ruled it with a rod of iron. He was perfectly lawless as to the rights of others, going through fields and tearing down fences as though all farms were his own.

When a young man, he became acquainted with Miss Eliza Harris, of Fort Miller, a smart, likely, somewhat plain daughter of a well-to-do doctor. Her he courted six long years and finally wedded, despite the objections of her parents. They ran away to be married but went home immediately after, where they remained about a year. Within a few weeks after they were married, they had quarreled violently, and Jesse, Jr. had struck her on the head. Mrs. Harris, his mother-in-law, asserts that they were so much afraid of him that they used always to lock the stair door upon him when he had gone to his room for the night.

About four years after their union, a daughter was born to them, the only child of their union, who now survives her mother's awful death - a dark eyed, rich-lipped beauty of 18, who will, if the course of true love runs smooth, be united in marriage at the proper time to Mr. John Sherman, late confidential clerk for her father, and estimable young man of Argyle, Washington Co. The birth of children sometimes heals dissentions, but it was not so in this case. Bad became worse.

15

Whether justly or unjustly cannot be known; Mrs. Billings's name was scandalously associated with one Congdon, now dead. Mr. Billings was far from choice in his own infidelities while in New York and even in his own home. The couple criminated and recriminated each other fiercely. About eight years ago he attempted to stifle his wife with chloroform; about four years ago he saturated the bed clothes where she was sleeping with kerosene, and set them on fire.

Mrs. Billings had premonitions of her approaching death, and a few days before it came upon her, said mother: "If anything happens to me take care of Jennie yourself. The third attempt to kill me will be fatal. Bury me in the cemetery at Bacon Hill and have Mr. Cochrane preach the sermon. Don't bury me in the rain." Her wishes were carried out. The funeral was held on Saturday, but the storm was so violent that the burial was deferred until Sunday, when the last obsequies were performed over the remains of Mrs. Eliza Harris Billings, and the spirit which found life so stormy and troubled was forever at rest in the peace of the grave.

One act of the ghastly tragedy is complete; man has sundered the lives that God joined in holy wedlock: what will be the denouncement? A powerful public opinion points to Mr. Billings as the assassin. He was by his own acknowledgment prowling about in an aimless way back and forth not far from the house when the murder occurred. His gun was found empty in the old well in 17 feet of water. Evidence accumulates that he attempted the deed before. On Sunday last the prints of tell-tale rubber boots that had been across the garden were observed on the threshold of the front door of the old Metcalf office near his house, a door which had not before been opened for years. The daughter saw a man disappear behind the woodpile, just after the shooting, but does not at all connect him with the affair. There are few who do not believe Mr. Billings to be the guilty man, but when asked a plausible theory of the murder are unable to do so. THE ADEQUATE MOTIVE FOR THE DEED CLINGS TO ONE PERSON ONLY. The ill feeling of years between the husband and wife had culminated of late because of the scandal connecting Mr. Billings's name with the Mrs. Curtis who lives over the bank. Of this woman the Whitehall *Chronicle* says:

Mrs. Curtis is the daughter of a Mr. Foster, formerly of Sandy Hill; keeps a boarding house at L.

Thompson's saw mill, opposite the Billings residence, across the river. She (Mrs. Curtis) did not bear a good character before she married Curtis. She is well known as is her husband in this locality.

Mrs. Billings had openly accused Mrs. Curtis of being a woman of vile character, and the latter had retaliated by bringing a suit for slander against the former. This suit was to have come off soon and members of the Harris family had threatened to reveal Mr. Billings's attempts to kill his wife.

The rupture between Billings and his wife was not complete until January last, when he told her that he had inoculated her with venereal diseases and she thereupon left his bed but not his board. The sequel of this whole vile mess is that Eliza Harris is in the Grave; Jesse Billings, Jr. is in jail; the unfortunate daughter is a refugee among friends.

An indictment by the grand jury is a matter of certainty. The trial will be the most intensely dramatic that has ever shaken the county. The defendant has energy and wealth; the prosecution will be backed by money and desire for revenge. Whatever the out-come, two fortunes will be shattered in the contest. In this trial there can be no intermediate results. Mr. Billings will be hung or he will be entirely acquitted. He may be the victim of a series of sinister circumstances. Let us hope that the absolute truth will be found out, and pure justice be the only result.

The newspapers of the day provide a wealth of understanding as to the feelings of those who lived in the various communities. The following article demonstrates that by June 14th the <u>Daily Saratogain</u> was able to indicate the effect of the murder charge on Billings's business. The implication was clear, the problems were just beginning.

The Billings Tragedy

On Wednesday James H. Lloyd, the Waterford photographer, was at Fort Miller Bridge, the home of Billings, the suspected murderer, and took pictures of the house where the tragedy occurred and the surroundings. Billings's home is now deserted; the house is locked up, the domestics discharged, and the unfortunate daughter is at the residence of her grandmother, Mrs. Harris. The store that was wont to be the scene of so much business activity is also closed. John C. Sherman, the former clerk, has gone

17

to the home of friends in Connecticut. Another clerk has been engaged to take charge of affairs, but when he opened the store the early part of the week there were so many that wished to close their accounts that he was compelled to close the store until he could balance the books and get in readiness for the rush.

On June 18th the grand jury was already addressing the case. It was widely reported that a great many witnesses had been sworn. Unlike the coroner's inquest and the trial that followed, the testimony was not in the public record. The Daily Saratogain, which by now was immersed in the case, had one report about the grand jury. In order to serve on a jury at this time in Saratoga County you were required to be male and a property owner. These requirements limited the pool of candidates for jurors. As might be anticipated in a rural county, Jesse Billings's case was almost immediately impacted by these limits.

Composition of the Jury.
    It turns out that four or five of the grand jurors, before whom the Billings case is being examined are relatives of his- within the ninth and prohibited degree. An effort was made this morning to see if the they could not be challenged by the People, but on examination it was found that under the statute a challenge for this cause does not lie with the People. The indictment, when found, will be the vitiated, as the prisoner has made no challenge.

It took until June 20th, sixteen days after the murder, for substantive news regarding the status of the Billings case to be reported. From the brevity of the Daily Saratogian's report it appears that the news was anticlimactic.

Indictment of Billings
    At 11 o'clock a vote was taken in the Billings case, and the grand jury by unanimous vote found a bill for murder in the first degree and at 12:30, noon, filed the indictment which contains 28 counts and 16,200 words. The name of Mary Eliza Billings, the murdered woman, occurs 420 times and that of Jesse Billings, Jr. 140 times.
    The friends of Jesse Billings, Jr. (probably expecting that no bill would be found,) appear to be considerably taken back at the finding of a bill of indictment. They are unusually quiet and reticent.

Billings is said to maintain his characteristic bearing.

Deputy Sheriffs D. S. Gilbert of Saratoga Springs and Wm. Wolf of Waterford deserve credit for the efficient manner in which they have served the interest of the people by the thorough manner in which they have worked up the case.

Miss Billings this noon visited her father in his cell in the county jail.

After the indictment had been found, several of the grand jurors called on the prisoner in his cell.

Those grand jurors who are related to Billings are: Simeon D. Arnold, dentist, of Milton; Ezra T. Golden, farmer, of Wilton; James M. Gailor, of Saratoga Springs, and George Holmes, farmer, of Saratoga. Holmes is the only blood relation, the others being relatives by marriage only. The fact of their being relatives did not seem to have any effect on the finding, and it is stated here as a fact that one of the above claims to have never heard that he had a distant relative by the name of Billings until after the tragedy took place.

As one becomes immersed in this case, all pieces of evidence seem to take on some degree of relevance. One example is the small article carried on June 21st in the Daily Saratogain. The significance is in the way the actions could be interpreted, not in the acts themselves.

One of Jesse Billings, Jr.'s Buildings Burned.
About five o'clock yesterday afternoon, a story and half wooden building located one mile east of Sandy Hill, in the town of Kingsbury, and owned by Jesse Billings, Jr., was entirely destroyed by fire. It was situated on the Glens Falls feeder. It was uninsured and the loss is placed at eight hundred dollars. The building was occupied by Simeon French, who succeeded in saving a portion of his effects. He states his loss to be one hundred and fifty dollars, which is covered by an insurance of four hundred dollars. Some four of five years ago this house was kept as a canal grocery by one Lewis Perry, who committed suicide by hanging.

The Saratoga County Standard, as the newspaper of Schuylerville, the community closest to Fort Miller, felt compelled to keep its citizens informed. The June 25th edition carried some interesting social commentary on the events of that week.

Billing Matters;

Mr. Geo. Halm, an artist from Frank Leslie's, stopped at Ballston Spa with a view of obtaining a sketch of Jesse Billings, but he refused to be seen, and the artist, after taking a sketch of the jail and the cell, came here to look for a photograph, and also with a view of getting a sketch of Miss Jennie Billings, expecting to go over to Fort Miller to get it. Learning that the young lady was in this place, he awaited an opportunity of seeing her and was soon rewarded, as she passed him on Broadway and entering the Arcade. Mr. Halm, to whom she had been pointed out, addressed the young lady in the Arcade and asked permission to sketch her features. Miss Billings .instantly hung her head down, pulling her veil over her face, saying she preferred not to allow her portrait to appear as "the paper wouldn't sell well with a copy of her face in it." "I beg to differ with you," said Mr. Halm. "I think it would sell very well." " Well, I would rather be excused," said the young lady. "Very well," said Mr. Halm, "I have it." Miss Billings raised her face, and the artist again asked permission to sketch her. "Well, I would rather not," said she. "Very Well," said Mr. Halm, "I have got it perfectly," and bowed himself out of her presence.

- Much sympathy is felt for Mrs. Curtis, who has been charged with complicity in the Billings tragedy, and the public generally look upon the matter as an attempt to implicate the woman for the purpose of misleading the public for the guilty one. A few days ago a drummer entered a certain grocery store, there being present at the same time a third party who remained quiet during a conversation between the proprietor and the drummer, until the latter came to the subject of the Billings tragedy, and gave the startling information that "Mrs. Curtis had confessed," when the silent man blurted out, "You lie!" The drummer, rather nonplused at the bluntness of the man, endeavored to explain that he only made the assertion as based upon reports he had heard during the day, when again came in tones of thunder, "You are a liar, sir: I would have you understand that I am the uncle of the Mrs. Curtis, and you lie when you say she has made a confession, for she done no such thing." The commercial man was silenced while the proprietor smiled audibly, and thus was a false report "nipped in the bud." The drummer had no more business to transact at the store, it is said and quietly "slid off on his ear," to use a vulgar expression. The people of this place are unanimously agreed in acquitting Mrs. Curtis of all complicity in this terrible crime, and those who know the lady (and she has many acquaintances and true friends in this village) speak of her in terms of highest praise. But gossiping tongues never cease their deviltries, which they practice alike upon the innocent and guilty.

At the time of the murder, Glens Falls was the next community of significant size north of Fort Miller Bridge. There were several papers in Glens Falls at the time. The Glens Falls Republican carried a very different article on June 25th. The articles in the Republican were inconsistent as to their perception of Billings's guilt. In some they were supporting Billings, while in others the editor condemned him.

Interview with Miss Jennie Billings
While the whole community has been aroused and excited by the terrible scene enacted at Northumberland, no one can understand the emotion nor sympathize fully with the distress of the daughter, Miss Jennie Billings, who is now left, not only alone, but forced to leave her beautiful home with the thrilling circumstances ever in her mind: her mother in the grave, and her father enveloped in suspicion awaiting his trial as a criminal.
The young lady is a blonde of full habit, dark eyes, and a general air of one who has had but little of the responsibilities of life upon her shoulders, vivacious and quite prepossessing in appearance. She has been the idol of her parents and been allowed all the privileges and pleasures money could procure or a fond parent devise. Her face has now a deathly pallor that is painful to look upon. While she showed where her mother was sitting, and where the round hole through the large glass intensifies the recital of the circumstances, she would start and clench her hands, glancing quickly behind her, while a cold tremor seemed to convulse her frame, and the silent tears were continually streaming down her cheeks. Occasionally she would exclaim, "Oh, my beautiful home: I never knew how to prize it before. It cannot

be my mother is not coming back, although her dead body lay in the house four days, and I saw it buried: yet it must be she will come and be with me again!" Meeting her grandfather, Dr. Billings, she said, "Oh, I once had a father who supplied all my needs, and a mother who took the full charge of me. Now they are both gone and the responsibility all rest upon me. I have never done anything, and it weighs upon me so heavily!" Then, completely overcome, she turned and sobbing piteously, while strong men unused to tears did not attempt to hide those which now filled their eyes at the sight of another's woe. Miss Billings is now staying with her grandmother, Mrs. Harris, having locked up the house and superintended the arrangement of the furniture. Her aunt is constantly with her. She says Jennie will scream in her sleep and seems to imagine some one is trying to shoot her.

Public opinion is changing in regard to the guilt of Jesse Billings, Jr., as, according to the testimony of Justice Washburn and family, he was at their house at or near the time the fatal shot was fired. Several persons have run and driven over the course he must have taken from the house to the old well and down the lane to the road, and thence to Washburn's house, and find it cannot be done in the time he must have done it. An effort will doubtless be made to impeach their testimony as regards time, but it seems almost impossible. People in that vicinity are taking strong sides for and against the supposed assassin, and while some evidently would be glad to have him suffer the full penalty of the law, whether guilty or otherwise, many people there are who say they will not believe he fired the gun even though it is proved against him in court, unless he should make a confession of having committed the act himself. Those who have visited the prisoner in his cell say he seems perfectly natural, and they can detect no appearance of guilt whatever. He looks every one square in the eye and converses freely. Certain if the whole proceeding shows a deep laid plot, well executed in its diabolical intention, and we await with much interest the final unraveling of the threads of evidence pro and con.

Jesse Billings Jr.

The true personality of Jesse Billings, Jr. is difficult to establish. The tale of Billings's fortune is not one of 'rags to riches'; his father was a prosperous physician, yet, at the time of the trial, he was wealthier than his father. Living in a time when it was the practice for employers to lay off their help during slow seasons, those who worked for Jesse Billings Jr. enjoyed year-round work and income. If his workers were not needed in the boat yard, he would have them work on the various farms that he owned, fixing fences, cutting brush or cutting the trees to be used as lumber in boats he would build the next season. In contrast there are reports that if someone failed to make payments on their boat loans, he would literally have their possessions removed from the boat and leave them and often their families on the shore as he repossessed the boats. He was known to supervise his own workers to be sure that everyone he paid did a full day's work.

Billings was not an overly educated man. He first attended the district school which is characterized today as the old one-room school. Later he briefly attended the academy at Poultney, Vermont. His boyhood friends described him as a hard worker who was honest if not patient. In many reports he is described as jovial or jolly.

Billings was considered tight with his money and in fact demonstrated his self control on several occasions. One New York newspaper reported that when he was very sick in that city the hotel management was worried about their tenant and insisted on calling a doctor. Billings would not let the physician examine him until he had agreed to the fee. He had a fine home, but it was in no way palatial or in keeping with his wealth.

The Billings boat building business was across the "highway" from his house. He built canal shipping boats for his own use and to sell to others. Wooden boats are framed so that the exterior boards run from the bow to the stern. To facilitate in the identity of his boats, he had the decks laid across the boat, the reverse of other boat builders. With this construction, even if someone painted and renamed the boat, he could easily identify his property. In some years he built over ten boats which would sell for about $2,000 each.

Billings owned numerous farms in both Saratoga and Washington Counties. His primary crop was potatoes which he would ship to New York City on his own boats. To insure freshness and to guarantee that he would not be forced to wait to unload his various cargoes, Jesse owned his own pier in New York. Billings did not restrict himself to shipping only the potatoes he raised. He was a speculator buying the harvests of numerous farmers in Washington County and shipping the produce to the city for a huge profit. A true merchant, Jesse could not allow his boats to return empty; so while in New York he would buy coal to be brought back and sold in the Saratoga region. On his numerous farms, he also raised beef cattle and hogs. He is said to have supplied virtually all the meat used in the hotels of Saratoga. At the time Billings was in business, refrigeration was an issue, so beef was shipped live and prepared at the stock yards outside Saratoga. When it appeared that a change in taste would allow western producers to take over the business, Billings took a train west and purchased live beef, bringing a train load home to graze on his farms. He then notified the hotels he could provide whatever kind of beef they preferred.

Another of Billings's businesses was the sale of ice. In the days before refrigeration, the only way to keep fresh products from spoiling was to store them in "the ice box." At this time ice was a natural product which was harvested by cutting it from frozen lakes and rivers. New York City was the largest market for ice in the world. The state raised revenue by selling the rights to harvest the winter's ice on the Hudson and Mohawk Rivers. Early one spring, Billings began building a huge ice house near his home in Northumberland. Neighbors thought Jesse was finally making a bad business decision as there were long term contracts in effect on all the ice from Fort Edward south to New York. The ice above Fort Edward could not be brought to Billings's warehouse without melting. In the dead of winter Jesse ordered the ice in his contracted area cut. He then started cutting a lane in the ice from his contracted area south to the warehouse. Those who held the contracts for the sections Billings was cutting through protested in court. The judge ruled that, although they had the sole right to harvest the ice, they did not have the right to obstruct navigation; so Billings could cut the lane and move his ice through their sections. One year when the river failed to freeze below Troy, Billings is reported to have made a profit of over $80,000. This at a time when a laborer was fortunate to make an annual income of $700 and a well equipped farm, including its barns, house, and equipment, would sell for $3,500.

Billings owned a general merchandising store named "Cheap Side." The store was the second building north of his house. It is reported that he had over $100,000 in inventory in the store. In this one store a customer could buy everything from safety pin to a canal boat.

One of the more unusual businesses Billings owned was his own bank. It is said that anyone he knew could borrow from $1,000 to $2,000 with very little collateral.

Yet with all that he owned and all that he had loaned, Billings only needed a part-time clerk. He literally kept the books in his head. He could tell anyone exactly what they owed him from memory.

Not all memories of Billings are flattering. There is a story still told of how he got the bridge replaced. The plank bridge which crossed the canal and river north of Billings's house had fallen into a state of disrepair. Despite petitions, the State refused to make the necessary restorations. One night after Jesse had nearly lost a wagon through a break in the planking, a burning barrel floated down the river and lodged against the support to the wooden bridge. In minutes the dry wooden structure of the bridge was fully engulfed in flames. The State subsequently replaced the structure.

The Attorneys

By June 29th it was reported that the defense and prosecution teams had selected their respective membership. The various newspapers in the area were reporting that the defense would be comprised of W. A. Beach of New York City, Hon. Charles Hughes of Sandy Hill, Messrs. L'Amoreaux of Ballston and W. Butler of Saratoga Springs. The prosecution's team included District Attorney Ormsby, Pike and Foley of Saratoga and N. C. Moak of Albany. Despite the threat of a defense team member being a celebrated attorney from New York City, W. A. Beach was not involved in the trial.

Attorneys for the defense

All of the numerous attorneys for both the defense and prosecution had regional backgrounds. The attorneys all knew that this would be one of, if not the most, important trial of their careers. Naturally there existed a rivalry between the various members of the defense team throughout the trial.

The defense team was comprised of the best, or at the very least the most colorful, attorneys available. The four men selected by Billings were: J. S. L'Amoreaux of Ballston Spa, Charles Hughes of Sandy Hill, J. P. Butler of Saratoga, and D. S. Potter of Schuylerville. The two lead attorneys, L'Amoreaux and Hughes, competed for press on different planes. Hughes was by nature boisterous, jovial and social. The serious, studious professional was L'Amoreaux. Hughes was always showing his rapid wit, while L'Amoreaux was seeking the opportunity to demonstrate the depth of his knowledge.

L'Amoreaux, the intellectual leader, was paid the princely sum of $2,000 for his services. Over his career, L'Amoreaux had already distinguished himself for his attention to detail and thorough presentation of cases. Senator Hughes was a successful criminal attorney, having served as the defense in four previous murder trials, each of which ended in an acquittal. For his experience and political influence, Hughes was paid the kingly sum of $5,000.

Senator Charles Hughes was the politician of the Billings team. He had been a member of the law firm of Hughes and Northrup since 1850. Fifty-eight at the time of the trial, he had served in the United States Congress in 1852. During the Civil War, Hughes had been instrumental in organizing the 123rd New York Volunteers. During the time of the Civil War, units were mustered locally; the group of soldiers in the 123rd were primarily from Hughes's home, Washington County. His militia, which continued after the war, lead to Hughes being referred to as "General" throughout the trial. One year before this trial he was elected State Senator; during the intervening winter term, Hughes had been recognized by the state senate as its most versatile and humorous member.

Jesse L'Amoreaux was a contemporary of Jesse Billings both in age and ambition. A native of Wilton, he had attended the Fort Edward Collegiate Institute. He taught for two years in Schuylerville before reading for the bar. He studied for the bar from 1856-58 when he moved to Ballston Spa and began the practice of law. He was a serious man whose deep-set eyes could look into the soul of a person. Although primarily a corporate attorney, L'Amoreaux had been involved in one other major murder defense (Robinson) in Saratoga County. Among the defense team; he would be considered the student of the law. L'Amoreaux was noted for the thoroughness of his work and his commitment to insure that all aspects of the case were presented. In 1865, he married Ellen Holbrook of Ballston Spa. They had no children.

The third member of Billings defense team was Walter Butler, who was 62 at the time of the trial. Butler had served as the District Attorney of his native Essex County. He relocated to Saratoga Springs in 1857, twenty-one years before the trial. In Saratoga Springs, he remained politically active, serving as a trustee and supervisor. Butler's political position is unclear. He had been a Captain in the Civil War serving as provost marshal for the eighteenth district of New York (Schenectady) from 1863 until 1865 . He had served in public office as a Whig and Republican. Despite his conservative leanings, Butler was proud of the fact that he had enlisted the first African-American to serve for New York State in the Civil War.

Attorneys for the Prosecution
The prosecution had a team of five attorneys officially led by District Attorney I. C. Ormsby, of Waterford. Serving with Ormsby was the real leader of the team an Albanian, Nathaniel C. Moak. Moak was the true "rags to riches" story. Born in 1833, Moak was forty-five at the time of the trial. His father was a farmer in central New York.

Isaac Ormsby was fifty eight at the time of the trial. He was aided by his twenty one year old son, Charles, who was reading for the bar under his father. The senior Ormsby, born in Greenfield, was a native of Saratoga County. His professional practice was in Waterford, where he had completed his law studies. He was known among his peers as a brilliant lawyer, an able orator and a man of sterling integrity.

The remaining three members were L. B. Pike, John Foley both of Saratoga, and P. C. Ford of Schuylerville. Lemuel B. Pike, although a native of the small community of Fort Ann in Washington County, was trained for the law in New York City. While studying the law, Pike became friends with Chester A. Arthur, the future president. Aged fifty-eight at the time of the trial, Pike had established himself as one of the top criminal lawyers in eastern New York State.

John Foley, only 30 years of age at the time of the trial, was an associate of Pike. Foley, a bachelor and native of Ireland, had been retained by Mrs. Billings prior to her murder to collect a note she held against her husband for $1,000. Foley's prominence in the trial related to the testimony of Jennie Billings. He became her confidant and support. Both Foley and Ormsby had been involved with the case since the convening of the Coroner's Jury. All three teams had worked hard to prepare for the struggle that was to ensue.

The news continues all summer

The Saratoga County Standard continued to cover the occurrences in the Billings matter throughout the summer of 1878. Real news was not always happening as evidenced by these two "shorts" that appeared in the July 21st edition.

The excitement over the Billings Murder has subsided, but will probably be revived with greater intensity than ever in September when the trial begins.

Later in the same paper there appeared a second brief article which would be very different today in a time when the paparazzi rush to sell their pictures to the highest bidder.

It is said that James Lloyd, a photographer of Waterford, has a complete duplicate set of pictures of the Billings family: husband, wife and daughter. He is besieged by the artist of the illustrated papers for copies, but has firmly refused to furnish any except by order of Jesse Billings, Jr.

Not all the news of the day dealt with Jesse Billings's case. Another article appeared in the same newspaper edition as the two above. This article shows how society viewed certain other behaviors at the time.

The Harrigan lassies returned from their thirty days in jail in Ballston on Tuesday evening last, and immediately celebrated their release with one of their old-fashion pow-wows.

On July 30th, the Republican, which was published by a man named Harris, was still doing its part providing an appetizer for the public's craving in the "Billings Matter."

The Billings Case
The Ballston Correspondent of the Albany Knickerbocker says: Messrs. Hughes, Butler and L'Amoreaux, of counsel for Jesse Billings, Jr., the latter of this place. We understand that they claim they will be able to produce a man who will testify that he

28

discharged in an accidental manner the gun which caused the death of Mrs. Billings. We learn that they will also be able to prove that this gun found in the well was placed there subsequent to the evening of the shooting of Mrs. Billings.

There are two possible explanations for the following report that appeared in early August, in the <u>Republican</u>. Either the editor had developed for himself the strategies to be used by the defense in the September trial or, as would be alleged in the trial, he had a source among the defense attorneys.

Here are some pills for people to swallow who have already tried, convicted and hung Jessie Billings for the murder of his wife: In the first place, the gun found in the well was not the gun that fired the shot. The hole through the window pane is much smaller than the ball that fits the gun. The ball taken from the head of Mrs. Billings is not half the size of the ball required to fit the carbine. Again, if Billings put the gun in the well, it had been there over sixty hours before it was taken out, and it was not rusty at all. In warm weather, iron will rust in water in half that time: yes, in a third of that time; and it is an impossibility for the gun to have been in the well sixty hours without being rusty at all; and besides two men will swear the covering of the well was not disturbed until 24 hours after the murder.

Again, Jennie Billings states that on the night of the murder, just before the shot was fired, she saw someone back of the house near the window through which the shot was fired, and that, immediately after the shot was fired, she saw someone running across the road toward the river. On being questioned by Dr. Gow as to how the man she saw was dressed, she said he had on a hat like his (Dr. Gow's) hat. Dr. Gow's hat was a soft, black felt hat. Mr. Billings that evening wore a straw hat, light colored. Mr. J. A. Wilson, one of the coroner's jury, with others, on hearing this statement of Jenny's, looked for tracks across the road, and they measured four and one half feet apart and were of course made by some one running in an opposite direction for the course alleged to have been taken by Billings.

Again Mr. George Washburn says he looked at his watch that evening on leaving Billings's store and it lacked twelve minutes of nine o'clock, and that in less than one minute thereafter, the shot was fired. He heard the outcry from Billings's house and went to see what the matter was, and then started immediately for Mr. Finney's and his own home for help. He stopped at Finney's and told them what had happened and walked immediately home- the whole distance being about eighty rods - and when he got home it was two minutes after nine, and he has walked the same ground over since at his usual gait in six minutes. Mr. Isaac Washburn says that Billings came to his father's house at twenty minutes to nine o'clock and wanted his father so as to get a summons of execution of someone, and that he told Billings to sit down; Billings said, "no", he would go down to the store and see him there; but that he finally persuaded Billings to come in and sit down, and that Billings was in no way nervous or excited, and acted as usual; that when his father came in, it was two minutes after nine o'clock, and that Billings had been there over twenty minutes, and his mother and sister corroborate this story, and the clock and the watch run together and alike in keeping time.

A respectable man who was fishing near Washburn's house that night will swear that he saw Billings drive up there and hitch his horse and heard the shot while Billings was hitching his horse. Two young men who had recently had their watches repaired at Schuylerville were looking at their watches together to see how they ran at the very moment the shot was fired, and it lacked seven and one half minutes of nine by each of them. A woman living near the bridge was winding her clock at the instant the shot was fired and it was fifteen minutes to nine by her clock.

Now, remembering that, if Billings fired the shot he was standing on the south side of his house and had to go up on the hill and unhitch the horse, then go to the well and drop in the gun, then travel around that road nearly a mile, and go down a steep clay hill right after a rain, then go up the river to Washburn's house and hitch his horse, and then go in the house and wait twenty minutes till Washburn came - all within seven minutes and a half! No man on earth could do that business in half an hour! No jury on earth, if they ever look at that road, will convict Billings, unless they first find, as a matter of fact, that Billings was in two places at one time.

Who did kill Mrs. Billings? We don't know. Could any one else have killed her? Yes. Did any one else have a motive? Yes. Would any person frenzied at the base calumnies heaped by Mrs. Billings upon the head of Mrs. Curtis, have a motive for killing? Yes. Does Billings act like a guilty person? No; he is cheerful during his confinement and has gained twenty pounds of flesh since he has been there. When men charged with murder never grow fat.

FINAL PREPARATIONS

The justice of the Supreme Court selected to preside over the most important murder trial in the State, was Judge Jordan S. Landon of Schenectady. Although only in his fifth year on the bench, this was Judge Landon's eleventh murder trial. Prior to the Billings trial, he had sentenced three men to be hanged, two were acquitted, four sent to prison for life and two for lesser terms. In 1878, a judge was assisted by other justices when presiding over a case. The three associate justices were John W. Crane, W. C. Talmadge, and J. C. Bogart. John Crane, 51, was a native of Saratoga County: as a lawyer had specialized in real estate law. By the time of the Billings trial, Crane had been active in politics for over fifteen years, serving previously as county judge, building commissioner, and supervisor of the town of Saratoga. John W. Crane was noted throughout the county for his honesty and integrity.

The court room in Ballston was not built for the onslaught of people that would want to experience an event of the magnitude of the Billings trial. The poorly ventilated chamber would not hold the four hundred plus people who would want to get in each day. Those who were serious in their intent for seats would arrive hours before the court opened. Devotees of the trial would bring with them hampers containing their lunches so they would not lose their seats to get refreshments. Among the case groupies were several ladies from Saratoga who made the trip each day. As the trial progressed, these Saratoga ladies slowly moved their seats closer and closer to the defendant. Reporters remarked on how this contingent often flirted with the witnesses, especially John Sherman. The trial was such a spectacle that those in attendance started to bring opera glasses to view the witnesses more clearly.

Ever the devoted father and benefactor of his son, Dr. Billings, had reserved the entire Eagle Hotel in Ballston Spa to house the defense witnesses. As the trial opened, the women were told to expect a stay of three weeks. To demonstrate how hale he was, Dr. Billings, 84 years old would travel home each night. The trip was twenty miles each way. The reason he provided the press was his desire for "a good night's rest." The reality was probability his concern for Mary, his disabled daughter, who still lived at home.

The prosecution housed the women they had subpoenaed at the San Souci Hotel in Ballston Spa. The women who were considered most important to the prosecution's case were: Mrs. Harris, the murdered woman's mother, whom Jesse had visited earlier the day of the murder, and Jennie Billings. Among the ladies called by the prosecution were two maids who had worked in the Billings household. Also in residence at the San Souci were several of the women who were first on the scene, including Mrs. Amanda Palmer, Mrs. Passnow, and Mrs. Reed. The most colorful potential witness was Mrs. Susan B. Durkee. The Troy Times carried this article about Mrs. Durkee:

Mrs. Susan Durkee has known Mr. Billings for over 40 years, also his wife since childhood, and always lived as neighbor to them. This lady has been conversant with their domestic dissensions, and has been somewhat taken in by Billings during a few business transactions. She was at the scene of the murder during the succeeding day, and has some very important revelations to make when placed on the stand, which is thought will have material bearing.

Mrs. Durkee is a widow lady of prepossessing appearance, has a flow of speech and repartee equal to the force of a 90 foot waterfall. She alleges that the prisoner defrauded her out of several thousand dollars, and she has told him that the time would come for retribution. Some friends of Billings have since approached her and hinted at a return of the money, and given her to understand that she might attend the Paris exposition as a pleasure trip if the same was desirable.

Mrs. Durkee thinks that Charley Hughes, who will examine the witnesses is "a saucy scamp", but she has no fears of him - at least of his cross examination - and expects to "give him as good as he sends." She will enact the Mrs. Jencks of this case, and her appearance in the chair will create a large amount of interest. Her face had figured in several cases of which one was held in this court house, in a breach of promise suit, when her evidence was the raciest kind imaginable.

Jesse Billings Jr., as the prisoner of the county, had spent the summer in what was called the murderer's cell on the northeast corner of the court house. The room was one floor below the court room where the trial was to be held. Jesse's cell had earned its nickname by having been used several times before to house those charged with murder. The cubicle was described as being tolerably well furnished. The ambiance of Billings's space was different from the other austere cells in the building. On the day before the trial, a female relative from Syracuse had sent him two bouquets of flowers. Throughout the summer, flowers were sent by several "lady friends." On the day before the trial, the reporter from the Troy *Times* visited Billings. In the cell were a table and six chairs, a writing desk and a place for his business papers. The reporter took this desk to be an indication that Billings had continued to run his extensive business holdings even while in confinement.

Saratoga County's budget was saved a minor expense as Billings was permitted to have his meals provided by the American Hotel, at his own expense. Throughout the summer, Billings shunned company taking his meals in private.

Despite the leniency afforded by the sheriff, Billings had aged rapidly during the long hot summer. This could be attributed to his unaccustomed confinement with its lack of activity combined with the trepidation inevitable when one knows he is to be tried for his life. At one point during the summer, he was reported to have been seriously ill. He was comforted during his confinement by his many friends including his pastor, Reverend Ford, of Bacon Hill. It was reported that Billings had professed a religious conversion during the summer.

Jennie spent the summer living with her mother's family. Immediately after the murder, she resided with her grandmother, Mrs. Mary Harris. During the summer, she moved in with her mother's brother and his new wife. As the trial was about to commence, Jennie was thought to be the conspicuous figure in the whole trial. To save her from the choosing whether to testify, she was subpoenaed by the prosecution.

They wanted to be sure she would testify against her own father. As the trial approached, Jennie's position was unclear. Her uncle, John Harris, claimed Jennie was "hostile" toward her father and would be "merciless in her testimony." At the same time, newspapers carried articles stating that she was determined to be impartial in her testimony. If the case were to go as the prosecution planned, she would help her mother's soul to rest, by generating the words that would condemn her father to death.

Jesse had written the court asking that Jennie be spared the painful ordeal of publicly testifying on the stand. He suggested that her testimony from the coroner's jury be read into the record. The defense asserted that this request was prompted by a humane desire to prevent the embarrassment of Jennie having to testify against her father. The prosecution held that the request to avoid her testimony was a shrewd hope by the defense that they could prevent key evidence from being admitted into the trial.

The entire community waited to see Mrs. Curtis, the paramour so compelling and charming that just the idea of being with her would cause a man to murder his wife. Who would not want to see such a beauty?

Contrary to the report in the <u>Saratoga County Standard</u>, Jesse Billings, although 52 years of age, had no white hair. His dark hair was more dramatic because he had a full beard and mustache. Each day, Billings would appear in court in his black business coat, a white vest and dark pantaloons.

The Billings trial was the twenty fifth capital offense trial in the eighty five year history of Saratoga County. Of the twenty four previous trials, only two had resulted in the execution of the defendant.

In early September, the papers reported that the case for Billings rested on the testimony of the Washburn family. If the Washburns stood up to cross examination, it was felt that Billings would be acquitted. Those following the case, which was virtually everyone at the time, were nearly evenly divided on the issue of Billings's guilt; yet, virtually no one believed he could be convicted.

The judge tried to expedite the trial by announcing a change in the traditional court hours. Sessions were usually Monday through Friday from 10 a.m. to 5 p.m.; to keep the pressure on both sides, the judge changed the hours to 9 a.m. to 6 p.m. Monday through Saturday.

Part II

Testimony

Day 1

The murder trial of Jesse Billings, Jr. began on Tuesday September 10, 1878. Ironically, this was the same day on which the late Mrs. Billings would have turned 46.

Based on the extensive newspaper coverage over the summer, no one anticipated that the jury would be selected on the first day. Without an expectation of witnesses, day one was one of the easiest occasions to be part of the throng of people seeking to experience the events that would transpire in the courtroom.

Shortly after dawn the first train arrived at the Ballston Spa station carrying numerous people directly connected to the Billings trial. For the next month, early morning trains to the county seat would convey passengers destined to be part of the trial. The first morning and the second day the train carried the men who had been summoned as potential jurors. After the jury was selected, their train seats were occupied by a group that was to grow considerably throughout the trial; this was the group of curiosity seekers or court groupies. Each day the gawkers sought a glimpse of the accused, the soon-to-be famous attorneys, and the key witnesses. Throughout the testimony, the early morning trains carried those who were to be witnesses

Although the court was crowded every day of the Billings trial, the number of observers fluctuated based on who was to be called to the stand. For the next month, seeing a witness embarrassed by an attorney was considered the highest form of entertainment in Saratoga County. The duels between attorney and witness actually attained the level of raucous fun when the witness, through glib answers or deep-seated belief, outwitted an examining attorney.

On September 10, at 10:15, the crier opened the court. District Attorney Ormsby moved that the trial of Jesse Billings, Jr. be opened. The judge so ordered and Billings, wearing the same black coat he had worn the night of the murder, entered the room lead by Sheriff Winney and followed by the Jailer, N. T. Howland. The coat which, at the time, was in many ways the measure of the man, was worn and shabby. Billings had recently shaved a portion of his cheeks. The newly exposed skin was white and wrinkled, giving him an appearance much older than on the day he was arrested three months before. If it were the intent of the defense to dispel the image of Billings as a rich womanizer capable of killing his wife to be in the arms of another, the effect of his appearance that day would seem to have succeeded.

Seated nearest Billings, to his right, were his four attorneys. On Billings's left was his minister, twenty-nine year old Reverend Ford of Bacon Hill. Dr. Billings, Jesse's father, sat immediately behind him. Other friends were clustered in his immediate vicinity. There was one person whose constant presence throughout the trial was considered intriguing. Mr. P. B. Middler, a wealthy contractor from Syracuse, was in the court as one of Billings's sponsors. Each day Middler occupied a chair next to Dr. Billings. Mr. Middler's appearance each day of the long trial was very significant, since he was the uncle of Billings's murdered wife. By his attendance, Middler was publicly demonstrating support for Billings.

Since the court had summoned two hundred men as possible jurors, each one of the four hundred seats in the courtroom was filled. The weather was unusually warm for mid September, so even when the court doors opened at 9:10, the room was oppressive. General Hughes began the debate arguing with fervor that since the jury was selected when the court was not in session, the selection of the jury was not done according to the law. After listening to logic expressed by both sides, the judge ruled against Hughes. Hughes's vehemence on such a minor point clarified, even to those most hopeful of a speedy trial, that the defense was intent on making the matter long and bitter.

Of the two hundred called to be potential jurors, only 173 responded when their names were read by the court. The court allowed those who were present to provide excuses/reasons for not serving. After listening to their reasons, thirty six men were excused. Extenuating circumstance accepted by the court were: deafness (3), ill health (19), over age (5), physician (1), relationship (2). One of those excused for relationship was the brother of the victim. Other reasons included: member of the grand jury that heard the case (1), witness previously in the case (2), fireman (1), foreman of mills (2).

The court then began to question the remaining potential jurors to assure that they were suitable. Questioning took an average of fifteen minutes for each man. The court's questions related to: the location of their residence, any relationships to the prisoner, the extent to which they had read accounts of the case in the papers, and whether they had formed an opinion on the case. The potential jurors were also asked if they belonged to a religious sect that would prevent them from finding a verdict of guilty in a capital case. Those in attendance that day agreed that, overall, Jesse Billings Jr. had regained his bearing. Frequently, Billings would smile as the various potential jurors gave their frivolous reasons not to serve. Once again Billings looked like a dispassionate man who had made a fortune but would still fix his own fences. In front of the press and the crowd, he calmly picked at his teeth with a quill as the various lawyers argued over points of law.

By the end of the day only four jurors had been selected.

Day 2

It only took until three in the afternoon of the second day for a jury of twelve men to be seated. One of the primary reasons that potential jurors had been set aside was their scruples against capital punishment. The prosecution was going for a complete victory; they sought the death penalty. In 1878, the death penalty as a punishment was under criticism from religious sects. The prosecution knew that to have a juror who would withhold a guilty verdict to avoid the burden of having been morally accountable for someone being hanged, could remove any chance for a conviction.

On the second day, the unbridled enthusiasm of the gallery was already evident. As the attorneys were arguing over whether a potential juror was a freeholder, an unnamed person in the audience shouted out, "he owns property, he is taxed on lots of estates." Clearly, Judge Landon had not yet established his total authority over the room.

Throughout the case the prosecution appeared to be afraid that Billings would use his fortune to influence the jury. At one point, a potential juror from Hadley, in northern Saratoga County, claimed that the deputy sheriff who served his summons had tried to influence him with a promise of some financial benefit. The court immediately called the deputy sheriff, John Kathan, to defend his actions. To describe Kathan as a character would be to understate the obvious. He was the father of ten children, a tavern owner, and a farmer on some of the roughest terrain in the State. When he appeared on the stand, he wore a black velvet vest with a heavy gold chain hanging from the pockets. Kathan sported a two foot long curly beard and long hair which he had pulled back slightly for the court appearance. His towering presence and menacing stare provided a truly threatening experience for the sophisticated city attorneys. No one asked as second time when he denied approaching the potential juror.

Of the twelve men who were ultimately selected for the jury eleven were farmers; the twelfth was a civil engineer. None of those selected were from the town of Northumberland where the crime occurred. Those selected to perform the task of determining Billings's guilt or innocence are listed below in the order they were chosen:

Charles M. Corp, farmer: town of Ballston.

George Perkins, farmer: town of Saratoga.

Henry P. Perry, farmer: town of Edinburg.

Edwin R. Abbott, farmer: town of Ballston.

Ansel Olmsted, farmer: town of Edinburg.

Nelson W. Grippen, farmer: town of Corinth.

Charles D. Burrows, civil engineer: Ballston Spa.

Edward S. Hubbs, farmer: town of Clifton Park.

Charles Wiswall, farmer: town of Ballston.

George Burr, farmer: town of Ballston.

William H. Blood, farmer: town of Stillwater.

Henry D. Kellogg, farmer: town of Moreau

It took only minutes for the word to get out to the streets of Ballston Spa that the jury had been named. Immediately, a crowd consumed with anticipation rushed to the courtroom to gaze at those selected. The gapers had come to the courtroom to scrutinized the twelve upright men. The reporters in the court noted that the faces of those in attendance demonstrated a genuine gratification that generally comes when inordinate curiosity is satisfied. Meeting the eyes of the spectators were the faces of twelve hard-working, apparently honest, men. Based on the criteria of the period, which emphasized physical appearance, initial examination of those on the jury revealed fair minded, intelligent men, impartial regarding the profound consideration before them.

An examination was done of those accepted by both sides to serve on the jury and of those for whom an exception was offered. It appeared that the defense wanted jurors from Billings's region, people who would recognize his standing in the area and the potential effect of the loss of his business on the economy. Conversely, the prosecution sought jurors who resided well away from the scene of the murder. The large number of jurors from the town of Ballston reflect its location in the middle of the county.

At 3:15, before a packed court room, Saratoga County's District Attorney Ormsby, a lifelong acquaintance of the prisoner, rose to present the People's case against Jesse Billings Jr. Ormsby's voice was unable to contain the emotions at conflict within him. "I have known the accused since he was a boy. His father was my father's doctor. In checking, I found that we are distant relatives. Jesse Billings knew the girl I married before I did. Jesse Billings, his father, and I have been lifelong friends; naught but the most imperative sense of duty could force me to occupy my present position." Ormsby then paused to regain his composure.

Ormsby set the stage for the murder. "Billings lives in one of the grandest houses in Northumberland. His house is not on a hill on the outskirts of the community. No, not Jesse Billings, Jr.; he lives a life that would most accurately be called that of a mogul. His house, although on his farm, is in the center of the village. He is the economy of this, his own, canal hamlet; a community consisting of twenty to thirty homes. His house is across the highway from his boat-building business. There is only one building between his home and his store; that building is his personal bank."

"On the night of June fourth last, through the window of this pleasant house, a shot was fired into the sitting room. In that comfortable room were a devoted mother, her beloved daughter and constant servant girl. They were talking graciously about the wedding of the mother's brother, when the bullet shattered the glass and entered the head of Mrs. Billings. In an instant their world had changed." Ormsby, by visualizing what had happened, had fully regained his composure. "Half an hour afterwards; Billings entered and groveled at the dead woman's feet. One of those present that night will state how he only behaved like he was 'because he was trying to act like he knew nothing about the murder.'"

"The marital relations in the Billings house were virtually in a state of war. The motive for this murder was simple; it was the notorious troubles between his wife and himself. On previous occasions, Mr. Billings had tried to get rid of his wife through the use of poison, kerosene, water and an insane asylum." Ormsby let the jury ingest the full measure of his theory as to a cause before proceeding. It was not enough that Billings had a motive; Ormsby knew he needed to erase the possibility of others having one. As he spoke the next person's name, he pointed to her so all would see that she was an unusually attractive woman. "It has been bruited that Mrs. Curtis, the woman who lived over the bank, and of whom Mrs. Billings was jealous, had a motive because of the wife's accusation against her. This could not be so, for Mrs. Curtis sued Mrs. Billings for slander and had the possibility of collecting."

"The prosecution has the difficult task of proving a case where there are no eye witnesses who can name the guilty party." Examining the eyes of each of the new jurors, Ormsby explained, "The circumstantial evidence in this case will erase any doubt from a reasonable person's mind. We come today prepared to prove nine points that all lead to a verdict of guilty. In addition to the ample motive we are ready to exhibit, Billings had reached the end of a short rope in his relations with his in-laws."

"Billings and Billings alone had the motive. He had called on his mother-in-law the day of the murder asking her to take her daughter off his hands. This was the first time Billings had been to her house in over two years. Billings's excuse for this visit was that his wife was injuring his business." While taking this opportunity to establish motive, Ormsby used the word "injury" with respect to the wife and Billings's business in an effort to reinforce the obvious physical injury she would receive later that fateful night. Both sets of attorneys were careful in their vocabulary. They wanted the words to set the stage.

To demonstrate the extensive planning Billings had made for his escape from the crime scene, Ormsby noted, "We will also prove that night, Billings drove his wagon into the lane behind his home, turned the horse around so he could jump into the wagon on the instant and then dash down the lane."

"We will show that nobody saw Billings on the night of the murder from the time he left the house with the avowed purpose of salting his cattle until after the shot was fired. During those two hours, he crept around his farm waiting for God to shroud the scene with a mantle of twilight. Darkness was needed so he could do his hellish work." The defense was not required to furnish a list of their witnesses to the

41

prosecution. If they had, Ormsby might have changed the words he had just uttered.

"We will show that a horse was hitched to the fence near the old well where the gun that was used to commit this horrible crime was found. The gate was left open to expedite the escape, but by being left open all night it showed he did escape."

"Fifth, we will show that the tracks leading back from where the wagon had been hitched to the abandoned storeroom were made by the man who fired the fateful shot. In his own testimony before the coroner's jury Billings said he went into the wood shed that night to get a measure. He said the storm had blown open the door. He went to the door and closed it."

"We will show that the door to the storeroom had not been opened before in a long time, and the next morning the door thereof was found open. This storeroom has a window that has an unobstructed view of the window through which Mrs. Billings was shot." Ormsby hammered home the point. "The door had not, could not, and never blew open. We will show it was held closed by a nail."

"The people will show that the tracks leading back from the house were made by the same person who fired the shot."

It was imperative that the prosecution demonstrate access to the murder weapon. "Most important, we will prove that the rifle found in the old well, the weapon that killed Mrs. Billings, belonged to Mr. Billings."

Ormsby concluded his remarks with a brief summation of his belief in the simplicity of the process of this murder. "He probably had his carbine hid in the woodhouse, used it, ran over the farm to his wagon, jumped the fence, threw the carbine in the well, untied his horse and dashed down the lane for Washburn's."

When Ormsby finished, two of his partners in the trial, Mr. Moak and Mr. Pike asked for permission to speak to the court. They told the judges that they had heard some unpleasant rumors regarding the conduct of Sheriff Winney. "It is well known he is notoriously in sympathy with the prisoner. Your honor, when Mr. Winney has disposition of the jury, he may well be able to afford the jurymen the opportunity to be corrupted." Moak requested Winney not be allowed near the jury. As Moak started his remarks, Winney stepped from his position behind the clerk and moved to a place in front of the bench. He glared unflinchingly at the prosecutor's table until Moak's barrage ended.

With a grace he would show throughout the trial, Messrs. L'Amoreaux calmly disclaimed any impropriety. He pointed out, "The corruption of a jury could happen by the prosecution as well as the defense. I, however, have total confidence in the integrity of the good sheriff."

Both sides continued their arguments for several minutes. Judge Landon was polite, but after the major points had been made he eventually interrupted L'Amoreaux. The Judge was eloquent in his first major ruling, "I have permitted this discussion because I believe that a suspicion secretly entertained is often relieved by open expression. No harm had resulted in this case. The court considers it its duty to treat the Sheriff as the Sheriff of the county should be treated - as a high-minded, honest, intelligent gentleman. The court has no further instructions to give him but will leave him to discharge his duties under the oath he took when he assumed them, and he will discharge them until proof of improper conduct on his part - and I do not anticipate any such proof - may be adduced." Court was adjourned early because of the excessive heat.

Day 3

It was Thursday morning, the third day of the trial, when the first witness was called to the stand. To most court watchers, having a witness this early demonstrated that the trial was going to be more expeditious than had been expected. Those following the case, which was just about everyone in the county, thought the selection of the jury would monopolize a week. On the morning of the previous day there had been open chairs in the courtroom. Today, despite the anticipated extreme heat, the promise of testimony by witnesses to the murder resulted in every seat being occupied.

The first to be called to the witness stand was Maggie Mahoney, the Irish house keeper. Maggie was sitting near Mrs. Billings at the time of the murder. Ms. Mahoney was rather plain looking, very thin and seventeen years old. Her lightly freckled pale skin contrasted with her dark auburn hair. Before the session began she had been the center of attention in the courtroom. In her new dress, bought just for the occasion, Maggie had thrived on her fifteen minutes of fame.

Maggie Mahoney

Direct. District Attorney Ormsby began questioning the witness by asking "Where were you on the evening of June 4th last?"

Before the court had opened, Maggie had relished the attention focused on her. Now on the witness stand, in a situation for which she was not emotionally prepared, her voice was weak as she responded. "Jennie, myself and Mrs. Billings were in the sitting room at the Billings house."

"Can you, please, describe the room and where each person was seated?"

"Mrs. Billings was seated in a rocking chair beside the window on the south side of the house. Jennie was sitting opposite to her mother. A small stand stood between the windows on which there was a lighted lamp. I was seated on the sofa on the east side of the room." Her speech was so soft the people in the back had to strain to hear what she was saying.

"Were the curtains and blinds open or closed?"

"I cannot remember."

"What do you remember about that night?" Ormsby had prepped the witness and knew exactly what she would respond to next series of questions.

"I heard the report of a rifle. I looked up and saw the hole in the window. Mrs. Billings had been struck in the side of the head." Wrenching her hands on a handkerchief, Maggie continued. "I saw the blood running down the side of her head."

"Which side was the blood running from?"

"The blood was on the side toward the window." Maggie looked anxiously at the jury as she continued. "She did not rise or make any noise, her head just dropped toward the window."

"What did you do next?"

"I ran from the room. I was scared. I went out through the west door."

"Were you there when Mr. Billings came into the room after the shooting?"

"No."

44

"When was the last time you saw Mr. Billings before the shooting?"

"It was just after supper, about 6 o'clock. I would guess about ten minutes after dinner. He asked me to get him a hammer."

"And did you get him the hammer?"

"I think I got one from the pantry and delivered it to him."

"Was there anything distinctive about the hammer?"

"No, it was just an ordinary old hammer."

"Did he have on rubber boots after supper?"

"Yes."

"Have you ever seen him wear the rubber boots before?"

"Yes, several times when it was wet outside."

"Do you still work for the Billings?"

"No, I left right after the funeral."

"When did you see Mr. Billings after the shooting?"

"It was Wednesday afternoon or night. He was in the dining room."

"Did you say anything to him?"

"Yes, I said I was afraid to pass that window."

"And how did he respond?"

"Mr. Billings said, 'Maggie, you need not be afraid. Whoever fired that shot hit the one they wanted to. They did not mean it for you'. "

"Did you have any other conversations with Mr. Billings between the shooting and your leaving the employment of the Billings?"

"At the inquest I said to Mr. Billings, 'You ought to have got rid of Mrs. Curtis'. Don't think I said anything further on that subject."

"Did Mr. Billings respond?"

"He asked to see Jennie. And he wanted to know when the funeral was to be."

"What did he do then?"

"He walked into the parlor where the corpse was laying. He placed his hand on Mrs. Billings head and said. 'Too bad, too bad'."

"Did Mr. Billings say anything else?"

"He said he wished he could die as she had died, because she never knew what struck her."

"Did he say anything about the death being an easy one?"

"Not that I remember. My memory is very uncertain. I was very nervous at the time." Watching Maggie's actions on the witness stand, none in the courtroom questioned that she was nervous on the night of the shooting.

"Have you had any conversation around the village with a young man named Washburn concerning the murder?"

"No."

"I have nothing further." With those words the chalice was passed from prosecution to defense.

State Senator, former Congressman and General in the State Militia, Charles Hughes was chosen to carry out the cross examination of each of the prosecution's witnesses. Despite his well earned reputation for attacking the oppositions witnesses, Hughes was tempered when he began questioning young Maggie. His tone was gentle, more like a patient grandfather than an attack dog. He started with a series of questions about the hired help in the Billings house. Maggie answered, "I was the only female help. I did general house work. Sam Philo was the man employed about the house. He did some general indoor work also."

Cross: "Was Sam Philo working there at the time of the murder?"

"Philo was discharged some time before the murder by Mr. Billings." Maggie had been told of Hughes's reputation and appeared very anxious. At points early in the cross examination she almost appeared as if she was afraid that he was going to strike her.

"When was the last time you saw Philo before the murder?"

"He was about the premises the morning that the shooting happened."

"Do you know what he was doing there?"

"His business was with Mrs. Billings."

"Where did he meet with her?"

"He came in through the kitchen where I was and went into the sitting room."

"Do you know what happened when he met with Mrs. Billings?"

"No. I did not see the two of 'em together."

"How long were they together?"

"I would say about five minutes, not much longer."

"Did you get along with Philo?"

"There had been trouble between myself and Philo before he left."

46

"Did you see him again that day?"

"Yes he walked up and down past the windows."

"Did you see any other strangers that day?" Hughes continued to use a uniform mild tone while addressing this vulnerable young girl.

"I do not remember any strangers about the house that day."

"Were there any other visitors that day?"

"Mrs. Billings's mother and sister came by the house that day between 4 and 5 o'clock."

"How long were they there?"

"They remained to tea and left between 7 and 8 o'clock."

"Was Mr. Billings in the house when her family was there?"

"No, he took his tea and left."

For reasons unknown, Hughes did not follow up on the conflicting statements that Maggie claimed Billings was in the house for dinner at six and that Mrs. Billings's family was there from 5 until at least 7, yet they were not in the house together.]

"How many windows are there in the sitting room?" [

"There are two about 8 feet apart."

"What, if anything, was between the windows on the night of the murder?"

"There is a table between the windows with the lantern on it that I brought in."

"Was anyone else in the room when you brought the light in?"

"No one else. Just Jennie and Mrs. Billings."

"Where exactly were each of you when the shot was fired?"

"Mrs. Billings was seated in front of the south easterly window. Jennie was about in front of the other one. I was seated on the lounge on the east side of the room."

"What were each of you doing when the shot was fired?"

"Jennie was sewing. Mrs. Billings wasn't doing much of anything. She was juss sitting in the rocking chair not moving. I was looking at Mrs. Billings when the shot was fired."

"Were you in the line of fire of the window?"

"I would say our heads were about in a line."

"How long after you brought in the lamp was the shot fired?"

"I would say about ten minutes."

"What did you and Jennie do after the shot was fired?"

"There is a west door that goes on to the back porch. I ran out through that door. Jennie ran out into the hall and out the front door. I started screaming 'murder'."

"Did you see anyone on either the south side of the house or behind the house?"

"No. I didn't see anybody."

"What did you do next?"

"I ran back into the house and met Jennie in the hall as she was coming back in."

"What did she say?"

"She said 'I saw a man run across the road behind the lumber pile.'"

"Did she describe the man?"

"She said he had a high hat and broad brim.'"

"Was there lumber there?"

"There was pile of lumber across from the house on the river bank."

"Were there any other inmates staying at the house on the day of the murder?"

"John Sherman, Charley Cramer, and John Terhune were staying in the house."

"When and where did you see Mr. Billings after he left the house?"

"Mr. Billings left the table while John Sherman was having dinner. A little later I saw him coming to the house from the lane behind the house."

"Did he come back into the house?"

"He did not."

"Maggie, I want you to think real hard. Was it afternoon or evening when Mr. Billings asked for the hammer? Before you answer, remember you swore to God you would tell the truth." By pointing to the deity, Hughes, for the first time in this trial, was using his ability to manipulate people by hitting at their weak point.

Hands clasped on her lap, Maggie's eyes rolled briefly toward the ceiling as if heaven really was concerned about her words at this moment. "No sir, I cannot swear it was in the afternoon or evening."

Voice soft, Hughes held the emotional attack. "Maggie, can you swear that it was the day of the murder when Mr. Billings asked for the hammer?"

"No sir, it may have been another day. But I think it was the day of the murder." Her eyes were held down as if she had disappointed someone in the audience and didn't want to face him or her.

"Are you sure that it was the Wednesday after the murder in the dining room the first time you spoke to Mr. Billings about your fear that the bullet was meant for you?"

"No. I had spoken to him the night before."

"Did anyone else hear you the first time you spoke to him?"

"No. The ladies were all upstairs together."

"Who planned for the funeral?"

"After the shooting, Mrs. Billings's sister and mother and other relatives came to the house and took charge of the corpse. The arrangements were all made by the relatives."

"Was Mr. Billings at the funeral?"

"Mr. Billings was arrested and taken away before the body was buried."

"Have you seen Mr. Billings since that day in the dining room?"

" I have not seen Mr. Billings since he was arrested until he was brought into the courtroom this morning."

"No further questions at this time."

The prosecution's pitbull was Nathaniel Moak a red-haired-full-bearded Albanian. He rose and walked slowly into the small space in front of the witness. He walked with his hands clasped behind his back, chest fully exposed. Like Hughes, Moak started his examination by trying to relax the witness. "Maggie, have you spoken to any of the defense counsel before today?"

Re-direct: "No sir. I have not seen any of them."

"Who have you talked to about the case?"

"Patsey Moak and Mr. Wolf called to see me and talked to me about the case."

"Why did Mr. Wolf call on you?"

"He called on me twice to subpoena me."

"Have you talked to anyone else about what you know?"

"I have talked to several people since coming here, about what I know."

"Can you tell who they were."

"I don't remember any of them. They are sitting in the audience; maybe you should ask them." Maggie wasn't being sarcastic, just innocently honest.

Moak ignored the offer of assistance. "Were there many people about the Billings house after the murder?"

"There were 'bout forty-'leven people around the house all the time, and I could not keep it in order."

"Maggie, were the blinds and curtains usually left open or closed at night."

"The widows were usually left open at night in the summer 'cause of the heat."

"When did Mr. Billings come back to the house on the night of the murder?"

"He came back home a few minutes after taking supper."

"Was it before or after supper when you saw him coming from the back lane?"

"It was 'bout fifteen or twenty minutes before supper."

Mr. Moak then took out a map of the area immediately around the Billings home and hamlet of Fort Miller Bridge.

"Where was Mr. Billings going when you saw him last?"

"He was going towards the store."

"Where in the house were the family bedrooms?"

"Mr. Billings's room was off the sitting room on the first floor. My bedroom and Mrs. Billings's was off the sitting room toward the north "

"How were you sitting on the night of the shooting?"

"That night I was on the sofa in a reclining position when I saw the flash of the gun."

Maggie had gone too far. She had made a comment that Moak did not want in the room. He immediately tried to recoup. "Maggie, with the brilliance of the lamp on the table, how could you see the flash?"

"The light was burning in the room with its ordinary brilliancy."

Knowing he had a problem Moak changed direction before the hole got any deeper. "Where exactly was Mrs. Billings?"

"She was sitting in her rocking chair about two or three feet from the window."

"Maggie, you said your head was even with Mrs. Billings's how was that possible if you were reclining on the sofa?"

"The chair Mrs. Billings was in was a low one."

"How long did it take you to get to the piazza on the back of the house?"

"It took me 'bout a minute."

"Was it dark or twilight when you got outside?"

"It was quite dark."

"Did you look or listen for anybody?"

"I didn't think to look or listen for anybody. I just screamed 'Murder' two or three times."

Billings had testified before the Coroner's Jury, as to his activities on the night of the murder. The prosecution knew it was fundamental to establish Billings had sufficient time to accomplish all he said in that testimony. In contrast, the defense sought to condense the time making it impossible for Billings to have committed the murder.

Re-cross: Hughes was still on his best behavior as he questioned Maggie for the second time. For the first time, the jury was exposed to a perception held by both sides that there were clear camps in the community.

"Have you spoken to Mr. John Sherman since the murder?"

"I have only seen him once since the murder."

"When did the family eat the night of the murder?"

"Mr. Billings ate after 7 o'clock. The rest of us had supper about 6 o'clock."

"Maggie, what was the weather like the day of the murder?"

"There had been a severe rain that afternoon. It commenced between 4 and 5 o'clock. There were high winds and hail."

"Maggie, do you remember if Mr. Billings was home the day before the murder?"

"He was away."

"How does Mr. Billings earn his money?"

"He carries on a boat yard across from his home. He employs a number of men."

"What was Mr. Billings's behavior like when he was in the house?"

"Mr. Billings generally only came in around meal time. He never stayed around much. When he did sit, it was in the sitting room. He generally went to bed immediately after coming into the house."

"Maggie, do you know if he ever washed up in the Metcalf Office." The Metcalf Office was the name used to describe the locked storage room at the east end of the horse-shoe-shaped barns. The former owner of the Billings house was a doctor named Metcalf who had his office in this old building near the house. The room was no longer used as an office, but retained the name.

"I never knowed of him washing up there."

"No further questions at this time."

Re-dir: In closing with this witness, Moak was sure to take time to drive home the issue of Billings's knowledge of the families habits-knowledge which would provide him the best opportunity to commit the deed.

"Where did Mr. and Mrs. Billings sit when they were in the sitting room?"

"Mrs. Billings generally used the same chair, and always sat in front of the window. Mr. Billings sat in other parts of the room."

Re-cross: Hughes was not one to let another person have the last word. He asked Maggie one last question.

"Maggie why didn't you close the blinds that night?"

"Closing the curtains was not my duty." Justifying her behavior she continued, "The curtains were often left open."

"Do you remember if Mrs. Billings went anywhere that day?"

"She went to Schuylerville that morning."

The witness was excused.

Dr. Charles Grant

Dir.: Dr. Grant began his testimony by providing a summary of his resume in medicine. One of his claims was that he had served as the physician for Morrisey, the famous gambler from Saratoga Springs.

Dr. Grant had gone to Schuylerville on the morning of June fifth to assist Dr. Gow in a post-mortem examination of the body of Mrs. Mary Eliza Billings. He told the court he found a gun shot wound on the left temple, which made a hole about three-quarters of an inch in diameter.

The bullet had passed through the brain and lodged in the skull on the opposite side. The bones were splintered and the hole was irregular.

Dr. Grant told the jury that the thickest portion of the human skull is about half an inch; the thinner part is less than an eighth of an inch thick. He went on to say the bullet was flattened and battered when extracted, "it had an irregular form."

Holding up a black piece of metal, Ormsby asked as he handed the bullet to Dr. Grant, "Can you tell me if this is that bullet?"

Grant looked carefully at what was left of the bullet. "I recognize this as the bullet we extracted from the skull."

"Has its condition been altered since you first saw it?"

"It is substantially in the same shape and condition now as when taken from the skull."

"Based on your medical knowledge; how long would you say Mrs. Billings lived after she was shot?"

"The effect of the shot was instant death."

Cross: This early in the trial, it was not obvious to those in attendance that General Hughes had respect for this doctor. His questions were designed to get minimal information. After the first answer, there was a lengthy discussion of how the bullet was found and the damage it had done to the skull.

"Dr. Grant, were you assisted by anyone in the post-mortem?"

"Yes, I was assisted by Dr. Gow of Schuylerville."

"How much of the ball were you able to recover?"

"We extracted the whole of it."

"What angle did the bullet travel while in the skull?"

"The ball passed directly into and through the skull not at an angle."

"Did you notice an any discoloring around the hole in the window?"

"I did not notice any discoloration on the widow pane."

Dr. Frank Gow

Dir. The coroner from Schuylerville, 29 year old Dr. Frank Gow, stated that he had been summoned to go to the Billings house on the night of the murder by Clark Lockrow. According to Dr. Gow the summons was at exactly 10 minutes after 9 o'clock. He examined the remains and, at his request, George Washburn, the Justice of the Peace sent in twelve men to serve on a jury. Dr. Gow said he selected nine from this group to serve on the Coroner's Jury.

Dr. Gow told how after he impaneled the Coroner's Jury, he went into the room where Billings was laying down. The doctor asked Billings whether he had any suspicions as to who may have committed the murder. Billings responded, 'I think we had better all be arrested.'

About an hour and a half afterward the initial meeting the doctor suggested that a detective should be summoned. Billings had replied 'yes I think that would be a good thing to do.' The doctor added that he asked Billings if he would bear the expense? Billings had replied 'Yes, I will.'

The coroner went on to explain how he had sent Officer Pennock to Troy for a detective. Dr. Gow also explained that Jesse Billings was on the bed both times he saw him that night. According to Dr. Gow's description Billings was prostrated and broken in spirit. Dr. Gow testified that he had asked a magistrate for a search warrant to search the dwelling above the bank. The night of the murder Dr. Gow, Officers Pennock, Durkee and Donnelly examined the house, barns and lumber pile across the street. When Dr. Gow was asked by Hughes why the wood pile was examined, Moak objected. Judge Landon overruled, and Gow admitted it was because Jennie said she saw someone run there. In looking for tracks near the lumber pile, he could find no distinct ones, since so many people had already been over the area.

Dr. Gow testified at length about tracks that he found. There were tracks that led west on the lane. There were also tracks on the south side of the barn which he followed, with the light from two lamps, until they disappeared in the grass west of the barn. He found those tracks again by the northwest side of the barn. He followed these tracks until they disappeared in the grass between the store and the bank. The tracks were made by either a boot or shoe. Dr. Gow testified that he put a board over one track to be sure it would be preserved.

Cross: Dr. Gow admitted that he dismissed the first jury before it heard any evidence because the family of Mrs. Billings complained it was dominated by friends and family of Billings. Dr. Gow also admitted he had weighed the bullet the evening of the fifth, and it weighed 165 grams.

On redirect the prosecution tried to ascertain whether Billings's grief was real or merely an act.

54

Dr. Gow responded, "I did not notice particularly whether Billings's moaning was real or feigned. I did check his pulse. It was 90, which is quite rapid." Moak asked about finding any tracks in the garden on the evening of the murder. Dr. Gow answered. "We did not look in the garden for tracks."

On re-cross Hughes asked for a second time why Dr. Gow had searched near the lumber pile. An extremely heated exchange took place between the attorneys. Moak did not want it on the record or in the jury's mind that Jennie had claimed to have seen a man running in that direction. For a second time, the doctor had to admit that he was responding to Jennie's statement about what had occurred.

Edward C. Cochran

At the time of his testimony, Edward C. Cochran was a 24 year old magistrate from the town of Saratoga. In his official capacity, Cochran had recorded the testimony of Billings at his wife's inquest. The inquest, which was held in Fort Miller's Bridge, began the day after the shooting. The attorneys debated the admissibility of the previously sworn testimony. Since even in 1878 a person could not be forced to testify against themselves, the prosecution could not call Billings. Moak and Ormsby were reasonably sure that the defense would not put Billings on the stand. The prosecution desperately needed the jury to hear Billings's personal account of his activities that night; therefore, they wanted his testimony the previous June read into the record. The defense held the testimony was not voluntary. The judge ruled for the prosecution who then asked that Mr. Cochran read into the trial record Billings's testimony.

Jesse Billings's Testimony before the Coroner's Jury

On June 6, 1878, Jesse Billings was sworn for the People before the Coroner's jury. The Coroner's Jury was far less formal than the trial. It had been put together quickly and held in the Union store in Northumberland. So many people crowded into the store that, they sent men under the building with blocks, to shore up the floor. Even though this was not the grand jury or trial, the prosecution knew the proceedings were so important that Billings was examined by District Attorney Ormsby. Billings's testimony opened with his claim to be a merchant and farmer. After stating his age, and members of his family, and answering the usual formal questions, Billings testified as to his knowledge of the killing of his wife.

Billings stated that he had been told his wife's death was caused by a gunshot wound to the head causing instant death. He also attested that he had seen the bullet hole through the pane of glass.

"Have you not understood the family was sitting by the window?" Ormsby asked.

"Yes. I saw her dead body within a few minutes of the act."

"Where was her body when you saw it?"

"Her body was in a sitting position near the window, in the rocker."

"Was this the position she was in when she was shot?"

"I was told she was in the same position when the shooting occurred, except that her head had lapped over after having been shot." Jesse had maintained eye contact with Ormsby, now his eyes looked down for the first time.

"Did you inspect the wound?"

"I never examined to see where the bullet entered the head."

"Which side of your wife was toward the window?"

"In the sitting position her left side was toward the window."

"Where was the room where the shooting occurred?"

"The room was on the lower floor of my house."

"By what name did the family call this room?"

"It was known as the sitting room." [On the stand Billings's composure was remarkable, considering the death was only the day before.]

"Would you think that the ball fired through the window of this room would be even with her head?"

"A ball fired by a party from outside, hitting the glass where it did, would be about in line of her head."

"How long were you in the room with your wife last evening?"

"When I came there after the murder, I remained in the room where Mrs. Billings laid fifteen minutes."

"Was there anyone else in the room at the time?"

"Neighbors were there when I got there."

"Were they the only ones there last night?" Ormsby asked mundane questions, trying to see if Billings would yield incriminating information.

"More came after."

"What did you do during that fifteen minutes, while you were in the room?"

"I cannot tell of any particular thing I did during those fifteen minutes except to remain."

"Who was present in the room when you arrived?"

"I can't tell who was there when I arrived."

"Can you name anyone who was there?"

"I think Mrs. James Wilson, Tracy Washburn, my clerk, John Sherman, and my daughter, Jennie were there. I don't recollect who else."

"What did you do when you left the room your wife was in?"

"I went to the adjoining bedroom and laid down on the bed."

"Who took charge of the body?" [Through this line of questioning, Ormsby was trying to imply the Billings relationship had degenerated to such a level that he did not care enough about his wife to even prepare her funeral.]

"The body was left in charge of those there."

"When was the body moved?"

"The body was removed to the parlor in the middle of the night."

"Where were you until the body was moved?"

"Up to the time the body was removed, I was in the bedroom."

"When did you get ready for bed?"

"I think it was two hours after I went into the bedroom before I undressed."

"Why were your clothes wet?"

"My clothes were wet because I had handled soils and gone through some grass."

"Was there any mud on your clothes?"

"I had mud on my clothing."

"What time was it when you got undressed?"

"When I undressed and went to bed, I should think it was about 11 or 12 o'clock."

"Did you remain in bed all night?"

"Yes, I remained in bed all night."

"Was anyone with you in the bedroom?"

"John Sherman was on the same bed with me during the night."

"Did you go into the parlor to see your wife's remains this morning?"

"When I got up this morning, I did not go into the parlor to see the remains of my wife."

"Why not?"

"The door was locked."

"Did you tell anyone you wanted to enter the parlor?"

"I did not express any desire to see her."

"Have you seen her remains yet?"

"I have not seen her remains up to this hour." (2:30 June 5).

"Who have you asked to see her remains?"

"I don't think I have expressed any desire to see them since they were removed to the parlor."

"When have you seen your wife since the shooting?"

"The only time I saw her after the shooting was when I first came in the house and saw her remains in the rocker."

"Where have you been since the shooting?"

"I have been about my home all the time up to this hour."

"Do you know the particulars of the murder?"

"No, sir."

"You have been solicitous as of this time to know who the perpetrator was?"

"Yes, sir."

"It is about 18 hours since the crime was perpetrated is it not?"

"Yes, sir."

"What measures have you taken in these eighteen hours to ascertain the perpetrator, of this deed?"

"Talking with my neighbors and answering questions which my neighbors asked me. I suggested we should have several arrests made. I employed a detective from Troy."

"On whose suggestion did you employ the detective?"

"Upon the suggestion of coroner, Dr. Gow."

"How many people do you think were involved in the murder?"

"I could not tell how many were concerned in the murder."

"Do you suspect anyone of the murder?"

"I suspect some people in the murder."

· "Did you name these persons so the officers might make an arrest?"

"I did not name anybody to be arrested."

"Do you suspect any person?"

"I have no suspicions of any particular one."

"Then you have no ideas as to the perpetrator?"

"I have suspicions of an indefinite nature against certain persons."

"Name them." Ormsby was emphatic.

"I don't like to do that."

"Have you given the names of those you suspect to any officer?"

"I gave no name to the officers of any such person."

"Has any one asked you to name the person?"

"I was not asked to name such a person or parties."

"Why did you not give the names to the officers?"

"I deemed it my duty to keep such knowledge a secret from the nature of the case."

"When do you believe an arrest will be made?"

"I suppose the arrest could be made at any time."

"Are you aware that an arrest will be made?"

"I have no ideas about an arrest."

"Why do you feel there may be parties to the murder?"

"I thought there might be a conspiracy about it."

"Conspiracy against whom?"

"I would not like to name that person."

"Do you refuse to name them?"

"I do at the present time. It is, after all, a distant suspicion."

"On what grounds do you refuse to name these persons?"

"I think it is not prudent to do so."

"Not prudent to whom - yourself or the conspirators?"

"I mean the cause, and I should think that means myself."

"Did the proposition of a detective come first from you or the coroner?"

"From the coroner. I acquiesced in the coroner's suggestion."

"Have you made any suggestion on finding the perpetrator?"

"I have made suggestion in regard to ferreting out the perpetrators of this deed."

"And to whom did you make these suggestions?"

"I made them to Officer Alanson Chase."

"What do you mean by the term 'conspiracy'?"

"A conspiracy to commit the murder."

"When were you going to make your suggestions to an officer?"

"I concluded to keep still until after the examination."

"Was any one else involved in the decision?"

"Yes, my father."

"What did he suggest?"

"He suggested we wait till after the hearing, as we would then have a heading to go by."

"Where were you when this conversation took place?"

"We were sitting at the time of this talk in the bank building about ten o'clock this forenoon."

"Have you made suggestions to any officer of the law other than the one you mentioned?"

"I Have made no suggestion to any sheriff, deputy or officer in relations to the apprehension of the perpetrator of the crime, other than I have mentioned."

"Mr. Billings, have you consulted counsel?"

"I have not consulted counsel."

"Have you consulted with Mr. Foley or Mr. Ford?"

"I have not consulted with Mr. Foley, Mr. Ford or yourself."

"Has any one, since your wife was killed last night, accused you of being the perpetrator?"

"No, sir." At this point the record indicates that Jesse cried.

"When did you take dinner yesterday?"

"I took dinner yesterday at half-past twelve or one o'clock."

"Did you dine with your family?"

"I and my family did not dine together yesterday."

"Where did you take dinner yesterday?"

"I took dinner at Mrs. Harris's; my mother-in-law."

"Does she live with you?"

"She lives three and one-half miles north."

"Was her husband there?"

"She is a widow."

"How long were you at her house?"

"I was at Mrs. Harris's yesterday, probably for an hour or more."

"How long before that did you visit or call at Mrs. Harris's?"

"Several years."

"What was the purpose of this visit?"

"Yesterday, I went there to see Mrs. Harris. It was a passing call."

"A passing call. Where were you passing from?"

"I had been to Gansevoort, to see Samuel Thompson."

"And Mrs. Harris's is on your way?"

"I went a little out of the way to call at Mrs. Harris's and dined with her."

"Will you state the objective of your call on Mrs. Harris?"

"I stated to her my object was to get some dinner."

"When did you get to Mrs. Harris's?"

"I got there about 12 o'clock."

"When do you usually dine?"

"I usually dine at home at 12 o'clock. Often as late as half past twelve."

"So if you chose to go home for dinner you would have been late?"

"It would not have been too late for dinner if I kept right on without stopping at Mrs. Harris's."

"Did you give Mrs. Harris a different reason for your call?"

"I don't recollect that I stated any object to her for the call other than stated."

"Mr. Billings, why did you suddenly decide to visit Mrs. Harris?"

"I suggested to her the idea of a good visit."

"Was that your only purpose?"

"I thought we could exhaust our visit in an hour as to relating to a friendly intercourse."

"During your visit at Mrs. Harris's yesterday, did you suggest to her that you wished her to advise her daughter (your wife) to come home to her house to live-stating to her that you could not submit to live with her any longer or in substance that?"

"No, sir."

"Did you not state to Mrs. Harris, in substance, that you wished your wife to leave you?"

"No, sir."

61

"What request did you make of Mrs. Harris in regard to any family difficulties?"

"I made no request whatever. She suggested that she would take her oath that she had always been true in her family relations, but nothing was said about Mrs. Billings."

"Why did you discuss Mrs. Harris's fidelity?"

"Mrs. Harris had accused me of fashioning some assertions in regard to her in those respects."

"Did you not complain to Mrs. Harris yesterday that your wife had been making improper accusations against you in regard to your fidelity?"

"Yes, sir. I said those accusations were uncalled for and false in substance."

"Did you concede to Mrs. Harris yesterday the fact that, by reason of such accusations on the part of your wife, that you felt very unkindly toward your wife?"

"I conceded that it made a great deal of trouble and told Mrs. Harris that if she would give Mrs. Billings a little good advice, it would save a good deal of trouble on her part."

"So the only purpose for this visit was to have lunch and a little intercourse. It had nothing to do with her son, Mr. John Harris?"

"I think her son, John, has some feelings against me, and thought, after I found out John was not at home, I would have a little talk with Mrs. Harris."

"When did you leave Mrs. Harris's?"

"I left Mrs. Harris's possibly at 1:30."

"Where did you go when you departed Mrs. Harris's?"

"I came from there directly home."

"Did you make any other stops?"

"I made no other stops. I drove directly to my home."

"What did you do when you arrived home?"

"Put out my horse in the stable."

"What did you do after you stabled the horse?"

"I think I went in the house."

"Did you see your wife when you went into the house?"

"No, I did not see my wife."

"How long were you in the house?"

"I remained in the house but a few moments."

"Did you see your daughter while you were in the house?"

"I did not see my daughter while I was in the house."

"Where did you go when you left the house?"

"I then went to the store, a distance of about 15 rods."

"How long were you in the store?"

"I remained in the store long enough to get my mail."

Billings went on to testify that, he left the store to go to the bank, where he wrote four letters and did "some business". A little latter he harnessed the mustang and drove to Schuylerville where he stopped at the National Bank and the post office. Billings said he then went back to Fort Miller Bridge arriving after 5:00 p.m.

"Was that before or after the shower?"

"It was before the shower."

"Where was the horse?"

"I left the horse in the carriage house."

"What did you do after you put the horse away?"

"Then I went to the boatyard and looked over my boat-building operation."

"Why did you go there?"

"I had men to work in my yard. I wanted to see them at work."

Billings told the Coroner's Jury he remained at the Boat yard fifteen or twenty minutes, then went to his bank where he remained about the same amount of time.

"Where were you during the shower?"

"I was in the bank."

"What did you do after the shower?"

"After the shower, I went to the house."

"Was there anyone in the house when you got there?"

"When I went to the house, I found Mrs. Billings, Mrs. Gertrude Harris and Mrs. Harris, my mother-in-law, who had come to our house."

[Mrs. Billings's sister, Gertrude, had married a man named Harris so both her maiden name and married name were the same.]

"Did you speak to anyone when you were in the house?"

"I had a conversation with Mrs. Harris senior."

"Did you realize that your daughter and wife wanted to go to Schuylerville?"

"While I was there (in the house), I did not understand that my daughter or Mrs. Billings sought to go to Schuylerville."

"Which horse did you take to Schuylerville yesterday?"

"I drove was the mustang."

"And isn't this the horse your daughter drove?"

"The mustang is the one my wife and daughter sometimes drove."

"How long were you in the house after the storm?"

"I remained in the house long enough to take tea."

"Did you take tea with the ladies?"

"I understand the ladies took tea before."

"Then you took tea alone?"

"Mr. Terhune was there and took tea with me."

"Why did you not unharness the horse when you returned from Schuylerville?"

"I had the idea of going up on to my farm and for that reason I allowed the horse to remain in carriage house harnessed."

"Mr. Billings, how big is your farm?"

"The farm is 128 acres."

"Is the farm connected to your house?"

"It is connected with my house and premises."

"Then why would you need the horse to visit your farm?"

"The route that I take to the portion of the farm I sought to visit is to go through the village a little ways, then I go through a lane."

"There is no other way to that area through your own land?"

"There is a route directly from my back door to the corn-field on the hill."

"What is wrong with this lane?"

"I would describe it as a wagon way not a lane."

"But either way would bring you to your fields?"

"The route behind the house would lead directly to the east side of the cornfield. The route leading through the village would lead to the north side of the cornfield."

Billings explained that he owned several fields going west of his house. He told the jury that, it was his practice to visit his property two to three times a week. The fields were in order the cornfield, oatfield, a pasture, a meadow, then three pastures in a row. In the last three pastures were cattle, sheep and colts that did not "run together". Billings

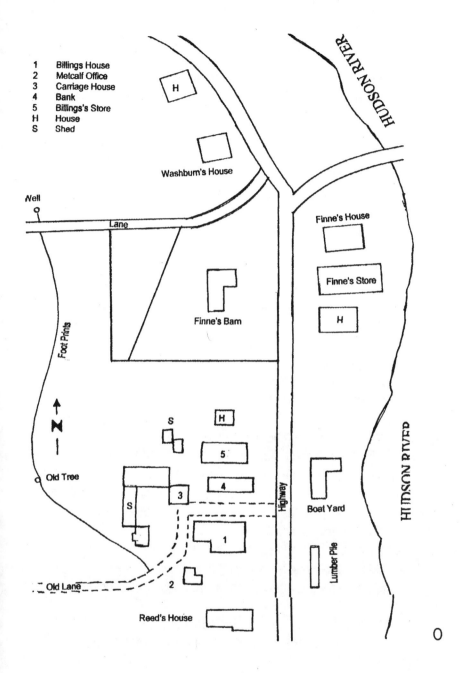

1	Billings House
2	Metcalf Office
3	Carriage House
4	Bank
5	Billings's Store
H	House
S	Shed

HUDSON RIVER

Well

Lane

Washburn's House

Finne's House

Finne's Store

H

Foot Prints

Finne's Bam

N

Old Tree

S

H

5

4

3

S

Highway

Boat Yard

HUDSON RIVER

1

Lumber Pile

Old Lane

2

Reed's House

O

65

estimated that, from the gate on the road to end of his property was about a mile.

"When did you go to check on the animals?"

"After the shower, I took the horse and wagon from the carriage house."

"When was that?"

"Shortly after I had tea. I went to the carriage house and found my horse had been unharnessed."

"Who unharnessed the horse?"

"I did not know by whom the horse was unharnessed."

"Who do you believe unharnessed the horse?"

"I concluded the women did it because the harness was thrown down carelessly."

"Did you know your daughter wanted to go to Schuylerville?" [Ormsby was trying to show Billings took the mustang to keep his family near the house.]

"I did not understand my daughter wanted to go to Schuylerville."

"What did you do when you found the horse was unharnessed?"

"I then thought I would go by foot. I made a start a foot. I went out and went back of the house and up into the field."

Billings explained that, although he had on rubber boots, the ground was too slippery, so he decided to return to his house. He walked across the field to the south fence which he followed until he came to the garden between his house and the Reed's. He climbed over the fence and carefully walked along the edge of the fence for about a third of the length of his garden. He then walked directly across the garden.

"Was the ground soft?"

"It was very soft. My feet sunk in."

"Did the boots pull off in the mud?"

"The boots were tight as I had my trouser legs tucked inside of the rubber boots.

"How large is your garden from south to north?"

"It is 3 to 4 rods [45 to 65 feet] across my garden from south to north."

"Did you leave the garden by the gate?"

"Having crossed the garden I got over the fence." [Jesse was 52 years old at the time and still climbing fences rather than walking through gates.]

"Did your boots leave dirt on the fence?"

"They would naturally leave dirt on the fence."

"Why did you go into the garden?"

"I took a notion to see my garden which is why I came there." [It was evident Billings's patience was beginning to run short with the seemingly meaningless detail of the questions. He had already said that he did not have a suspect.]

"Why did you not, in returning from the side hill, follow the side of the wagon road you went up on?"

"When I am out prospecting, I like to take different routes."

"Did you come through a hole in the south side of the line fence?"

"I did not pass along the south side of the south fence and come through a hole. I passed on the north side of the fence." [Billings was emphatic in his answer.]

"What did you do when you got out of the garden?"

"I then got back to my buildings. There is a little building in the yard called the Metcalf Office which I went to."

"Where is the door for entering this building?"

"There is a door on the north side and a door on the east side. We usually enter the building on the north door."

"Could the east door be opened from inside?"

"A person being in there could open the east door."

Knowing he was moving into the most important parts of the examination Ormsby asked, "From the Metcalf Office could a person see into your house?"

"A person in the Metcalf Office could see into the sitting room."

"And just how would a person be able to see into the house to where you wife was sitting?"

"From the east door one could see into the south window of the sitting room where my wife was shot. Of course the blinds would need to be open and curtains up."

"When you entered the Metcalf Office was there mud on the sill?"

"I did not notice that there was mud on the threshold of the door."

"Did you look for mud?"

67

"I did not look."

"Why did you get into the Metcalf Office?"

"I went in the office last night through the north door to get a measure to carry salt in."

"Was the east door open?"

"I think the east door was open."

"Who opened the east door?"

"I believe it was blown so by the wind."

"Isn't there salt in the barn?" [Ormsby was trying to show Billings did not need to go into the Metcalf Office.]

"There is one lot of salt in the barn where I got it yesterday afternoon."

"Don't you keep measures with the salt?"

"We keep measures in the stable, but I don't like to use them to carry salt." [Any farmer knew that once a measure was used for salt it would begin to deteriorate quickly.]

"How often do you salt the cattle?"

"We try to salt the cattle twice a week."

"If you salt the cattle so often, wouldn't it be natural to keep a measure with the cattle?"

"I would not think it natural."

"So you have to find a measure each time you go to salt the cattle?"

"To salt the cattle sometimes we take a measure, sometimes a box and sometimes a tin pan."

"So you keep the measures in the Metcalf Office?"

"I keep a little of everything like measures or of that nature in the office."

"So did you get a measure from the Metcalf Office?"

"I did not find anything in the office to carry salt in."

"So where did you find the measure?"

"I took a measure out of the carriage house and got the salt."

"How big was the measure?"

"I think it was a peck measure."

"What time did you harness the horse?"

Billings explained that, at about seven o'clock he harnessed the horse and headed north to go to the lane. At the entrance to the lane, he opened the gate and left it open as he pulled onto the clayey muddy surface. He went up the hill where he noticed the storm had knocked down rails from his fence and an old tree. He hitched the horse and walked over to examine the downed tree. After returning to the wagon, he drove to a spot near the red gate where he hitched the horse for a second time so he could fix the fences.

"I then went over Finne's lot to a place where I thought I could find hammer and nails."

Billings went to a spot where he thought the hammer and nails had been left. Finding them missing he returned to the horse. Billings continued on to the back lots where he herded the animals back into the appropriate pastures. He adjusted the rails of the fences enough to contain the animals for the night and walked back to the wagon. After driving the animals back to their pastures, Billings estimated for the jury he was a mile from the horse.

"When you got to the road, did you shut the gate?"

"No. I did not shut the gate."

"Why did you choose to leave the gate open last evening?"

"I almost always leave it open."

"So you did not close the gate. Where were you going?"

"I drove to Justice George Washburn's house, a distance of about twenty yards from the gate."

"How fast did you drive the horse down the lane?"

"I walked the horse down the lane. I did not trot him until I got on the level."

"How fast a trot were you going?"

"I had the horse travel at an ordinary trot on the flats."

"Who was at the Washburn's when you arrived?"

"When I got to the Washburn's, I found Mrs. Washburn, her son, Isaac, and her daughter, Phoebe."

"Were you there when Justice Washburn arrived?"

"Yes."

"How long were you there before Justice Washburn returned?"

"I can't tell you how long."

"How long would you estimate it was?"

"I guess it was ten to twenty minutes, perhaps longer, perhaps not so long."

69

"How far was it from the road to where you first hitched the horse?"

"It is about a quarter mile from the gate to where I first hitched the horse at the cornfield."

"Can you tell the jury what Mr. Washburn said when he entered the house?"

"When Mr. Washburn came in, the first thing he said was that Mrs. Billings was hurt."

"This is the first thing Mr. Washburn said?"

"The first thing Mr. Washburn did was to wind his watch."

"Didn't he tell you that your wife had been shot dead?"

"He did not tell me that my wife had been shot dead at all."

"Did you ask either of the Washburn women to help your wife?"

"While he was winding his watch and while I was asking how bad my wife was hurt, Mr. Washburn asked his wife if she would not come down."

"So how did you get to your house?"

"I got out of the house. I found myself stumbling along toward the wagon. Eventually I got down on the ground."

"Why did you fall?"

"I did not seem to have much strength."

"Did you drive to your house?"

"Mr. Isaac Washburn helped me up and into the wagon and drove my horse for me."

"Didn't you even ask if your wife was hurt?"

"I asked him in what way and how bad she was hurt."

"What did the Squire say?"

"He answered she was shot by pointing to his chin. I asked him how bad."

"How did the Justice answer?"

"He said he did not know how bad."

"Didn't he tell you she was dead?"

"He did not tell me she was dead."

"But you were weak walking to the wagon; you must have believed her dead?"

"I did not suppose she was dead."

"How came this to have such an effect on you if you did not know she was dead?"

"I feared the worst as I saw that Mr. Washburn was a great deal excited."

"How did you get out of the wagon?"

"I guess I got out of the wagon by myself."

"What happened when you first saw your wife."

"When I got in the room where my wife was, I got down on the floor.

Ormsby wanted to be assured that the rubber boots he had in his possession belonged to Billings.

"Are these the boots your wore the night of the homicide?"

"I should think they are the boots."

"Where and when did you put them on and take them off on the night of the homicide?"

"I got them on at the foot of the bed in the afternoon. I took them off in the bedroom after my wife's death."

"How often had you worn the boots?"

"I never wore them before."

With these lines Jesse Billings's testimony was over.

Since all he did was read the Coroner's Jury testimony into the record, the defense did not cross examine Edward Cochran.

Mr. Lewis Cramer

Dir. A civil engineer from Saratoga Springs, Lewis Cramer had been retained by the prosecution to make a map of the area around the Billings property. He testified to the validity of the measurements. He also testified that there was a distance of 4,279 feet from the point where the prosecution contended the shot was fired to Washburn's by way of the well. He testified that he had replicated the trip Billings was believed to have taken driving the same mustang from the red gate. The time of the trip was 8 minutes 50 seconds. Mr. Cramer then listed a variety of distances on the map.

Cross Hughes conducted a cross examination which was characterized as thorough and ingenious. Through careful questioning, Hughes made Cramer admit that it had not rained nor had it been muddy when he had completed his timed trip. Hughes was able to have Lewis admit his timing was completed in day time, not in the dark of night. There was also significance in the fact that Cramer had driven the horse at a rapid rate the entire way. The only weakness was that Hughes could not get Cramer to admit that he could see where the sheep had been salted.

By the time the testimony of Cramer ended for the day, the temperature next to the open window was recorded at 85 degrees; it was suspected to be over 95 degrees in the center of the room where the attorneys and jury were placed.

Day 4

After just one full day of testimony, commentary regarding Billings's chances for acquittal began to materialize in various newspapers. These analyses usually appeared in conjunction with articles on the events of the trial. It was evident that, like major trials today, journalists felt that the case rested in the hands of the attorneys not in the facts or in a prevailing value of justice. On September 14th, the Troy Daily Times carried this speculation as to Billings's chances:

General Hughes is acting as the principal counsel to attempt the rescue of the man (Billings) from the impending danger that now impends over him. Hughes is one of the most successful criminal lawyers in this section of the state. A glance at his experience would indicate this. He has previously defended four murderers, some of whom were confronted with proof a hundredfold more positive than that in the present case, and whose crimes were a vast deal more revolting and had none of the mitigating circumstances to offset them that may be called forth in the Billings conflict. Yet Hughes succeeded, through dint of legal tact and shrewdness, in saving the necks of every one of the men whom he defended, even though one was sentenced to the gallows. And each of these clients was a poor man, so that all he had for an incentive was the pride that every practitioner takes in winning his case. His client now is wealthy; is willing to spend thousands in the conflict; can readily instruct his attorney to carry the case to the highest courts, and will use every expedient to bring the result to the final victory that has marked his career so far. On this score the friends of Billings place great faith - and justly they may. The criminals defended so far by Mr. Hughes, and to whom I referred, were Secor, Gregory,

Smith and Shaw. The last named trial will be recalled as a most notorious one, that took place three years ago. The accused was proven guilty of having poisoned his wife and five children, was convicted and sentenced; yet Hughes saved him through a new trial and acquittal. Will not his efforts be equally as potent in the case of Billings, where the proof thus far adduced is purely circumstantial.

Lewis Cramer re-called

Re-dir. Overnight the prosecution had time to regroup. All who had been present the day before knew that Hughes, through his crafty examination, had virtually converted a prosecution witness into one for the defense. Moak now sought to have the record clarified. "What type of boots were you wearing when you timed yourself?"

"They were heavy top boots."

"And at what speed did you have the mustang travel down the lane?"

"I trotted the horse."

Re-cross Hughes smiled at the jury as he approached the witness. He was sure the members were all aware what had happened overnight. He elected not to dignify the new story with questions. He looked disdainfully at Cramer and asked an inane question. "Are all the buildings on this map made to the same scale?"

"Yes, 50 feet to the inch."

Cramer looked confused as he was excused from the witness stand.

John Hodgeman

Dir. Cramer's assistant, John Hodgeman, had also run the course that the prosecution alleged Billings had taken. On direct examination, Ormsby was able to get into the record that the ground was soft when Hodgeman had made his timed run in nine minutes. Hodgeman also stated that he walked the horse thirty feet before he climbed into the wagon. Hodgeman added he was wearing heavy top boots.

Cross Under cross examination, Hodgeman stated that he had followed Cramer. Since he was only 25, he wanted to get a better time than his boss. Unfortunately, he had to stop running because he "ran out of breath." Hodgeman also stated that he had to cross one deep ravine before he got to the well. Hughes knew that, as farmers, the jurors would know that if the prosecutors' theory was plausible any ravine would be even more difficult to cross at a run by a fifty-two year old man carrying a gun in the dark.

Jennie Billings

The room was thick with anticipation when Miss Jennie Billings walked to the witness stand. The members of the audience were immediately taken by her decision to wear the attire of deep mourning. All those present were especially responsive to the way she had draped her heavy black veil. The veil was 'deftly' swept to one side so that the jury and judge could see her face, but the view from the reporters' table and gallery was obstructed by the nearly opaque material. The extent of the reporters' venom for this slight was apparent in their reports. The narration of a reporter from the Troy <u>Daily Times</u> perhaps best exemplifies this animosity. He described Jennie as having; `a rather masculine cast of features, and a decided Roman nose – not large enough to be conspicuous, but sufficient to indicate a firmness of character and pertinacity of purpose, should her abilities become adequately cultivated or developed. She is quite tall, but has a dowdish or affected manner that is strikingly apparent in every gesticulation or intonation.' As if these attacks were not enough, he went on to say, `Miss Billings is a peculiar person in disposition.'

Even in 1878, it was good advice not to get into a disagreement with someone who buys his "ink by the gallon and paper by the ton".

As Jennie began her direct testimony, her father turned his chair away from her and buried his head in his hands as though he could stifle her words by not listening. As she began to speak, Jesse's father, the Revered Dr. Jesse Billings, leaned forward and placed his hand on his son's shoulder. Those present were stuck by his gentle voice as he said, "Forgive her; she is under the influence of others." Jesse Billings Jr. let his hands down and turned his chair to face his daughter. Throughout the remainder of her testimony that day, his face demonstrated no emotion. As she left the stand, that was to change.

As a witness, Jennie's words did not fare any better with the press than had her attire. The reporters characterized her as having the less appealing traits from each parent. The combination was put in the darkest of lights. Jennie was perceived as having inherited from her mother the 'predominating vindictiveness'. Her father was credited with contributing 'shrewdness' and 'ingenuity' to her personality. Overall, she was described as 'cunning' and 'foxy'. She was even described as exhibiting more relish than grief for her tragedy.

In the article characterizing Jennie's testimony in her father's trial, The Troy Daily Times reminded its readers of her behavior the previous July. While awaiting a summons to testify before the grand jury, she was sitting on the porch of one of the hotels in Ballston Spa. Knowing she was about to speak against her only surviving parent, she was engaged in 'undue levity' until reminded by her relatives of her position and of the occasion.

To those who may have been regarded as neutral, Jennie was considered to be easily influenced. To most of those present, she was considered to be a puppet of her mother's family.

The examination of Jennie was conducted by Foley. This was his crowning moment. He had been involved in the case even before the coroner's jury had convened. As a young and promising attorney, he knew that this was his chance.

Dir.   "I am eighteen years old." [Jennie sat poised, ready to strike the blow that would convict her father.]

"Jennie where were you when your mother was injured?" [After two days of watching Hughes artistry, Foley was using his most restrained demeanor.]

"I was in the sitting room with my mother when she was injured."

"Exactly where in the sitting room were you?"

"When my mother was shot, I was sitting at one window, she at the other."

"Were the curtains raised or down?"

"The curtain to her window was raised. The curtain at the other window, where I sat, was down."

"Jennie, do you recall if the blinds were open or closed?"

"The blinds were open where I sat, but not open at the other window."

"What did you do after you heard the shot?"

"I ran out the side door and screamed 'murder'."

"What was your state of mind?"

"I was very much afraid after passing mother."

[It was imperative that Foley dissuade the idea that Jennie had seen a man running across the highway. If her father had committed the crime, he had to have made his escape through the back fields.]

"Jennie how is your vision?"

"I am very nearsighted."

"Can you remember how you felt when you reached the front yard?

"When at the front door, I was very faint."

"What, if anything, did you see as you reached the front door?"

"I thought I saw a man's hat just above the lumber pile."

"Do you remember seeing anything else?"

"No sir. I was so excited."

"You say you were excited?"

"Yes, sir; I was very much excited."

"Jennie, were you aware of any difficulties between your mother and father?"

"Yes, sir. There were difficulties between them all through my life."

"Did your parents share the same bed chamber?"

"No; for the last eight years my mother and father slept separately."

"Jennie, how are you certain they slept separately?"

"My mother always occupied a room with me until of late."

"Which room was this?"

"In the summer, the room downstairs, off the sitting room. In the winter, we usually used one of the chambers upstairs."

"Where did your father sleep?"

"Father usually occupied another room off the sitting room."

"When did you first leave your home for school?"

"I went away for the first time in 1873."

"Jennie do you ever remember a conversation between your father and mother about kerosene?"

"About three years ago there was a conversation between the two of them over kerosene."

"To the best of your recollection, what was said?"

"My mother said that father had placed bed clothes against her room door." [There was a long dramatic pause.] "She said he set them on fire."

"Did your mother tell you what she did?"

"She said she called several times to father."

"What did your father say?"

"He said there must be someone in the house." [Again a pause.] "She said she wanted to scream, but he wouldn't let her. He told her to keep still, and he took hold of her."

"Did he ever explain why there was a fire?"

"Mother told me he set the house on fire to get the insurance money."

"Did she ever say how much money?"

"Yes. $1,000."

"Did your mother believe him?"

"No. She said he was trying to burn her up."

"Did she ever accuse your father of this act?"

"She said to him, 'What would Jennie have said if she had come home and found her mother burned to death'?" [Her voice was trembling as she spoke this last sentence. After the words had been emitted Jennie burst out crying on the stand. It took several minutes before she was able to resume her testimony. When she was ready, Jennie resumed her testimony without a question being asked.] "Father asked her for some money."

"Did she give your father any money?"

"She gave it and said 'You now have got my $900'."

"Did your mother ever talk about a smell that night?"

"She said her hands smelt as if she had been filling a kerosene lamp when she woke up."

"Was your father there when your mother told you this story?"

"Yes, Father was present."

"Did your mother ever tell the story in your father's presence other than the one time."

"Yes, I have heard her repeat all of this to my father."

"Jennie, did your mother ever, in your presence, talk to you about chloroform?"

"I heard her talk about chloroform in my presence."

"How many times did she talk about the chloroform?"

"Many times. I am not certain how many."

"Can you tell the court the last time she talked about the chloroform?"

"The last time was this year."

"Where was your father when she brought it up this year?"

"He was present in the room at the time."

"What was it that your mother said?"

"Mother told father that he had put something on her bedclothes and on her hands."

"What was it that your mother did?"

"She got up and went to the door where she caught her breath."

"What did she tell you she did then?"

"Mother said she had to go to the door two or three times before she fathomed it was the bedclothes that was bothering her."

"What did your mother do when she finally realized what it was the bedclothes that were making her ill?"

"She told me she went to go to my room. She saw my father's shadow in the hallway."

"Did she say anything to your father?"

"She said she told him he was trying to take her life."

"How did your father respond to her accusations?"

"He said he had a toothache and was trying to get some cotton."

"Jennie, do you remember when it was that this chloroform incident happened?"

"Not exactly, I was quite young."

"If you were young, how do you remember it so well?"

"I remember her telling me of it many times after." [As an afterthought, Jennie added:] "She had come to my room and stayed there the balance of the night."

"Were your parents sharing the chamber at the time of the chloroform incident?"

"They were not rooming together at the time."

"Where was your father sleeping that night?"

"He had removed himself to upstairs that night and gave up his room to her."

"The room where she was sleeping, was it partitioned off from his room?"

"Yes, sir."

"Did your mother every speak to you of the chloroforming?"

"Yes sir. She reminded me often of the circumstances."

"Since you went away to school, how much have you been home?"

"During the past four years, I have generally been home only summers."

"When exactly did you get home and leave each year?"

"For the first two years, I got home in June and left in September or October."

"So you were only home in the summer?'

"I was home one fall."

"When did you return home to live?"

"I returned home permanently in the last of April of 1877."

"Have you been home since then or visiting?"

"Since last April I have been home most of the time."

"Jennie, do you remember what your father said when your mother accused him of trying to kill her with the kerosene?'

"No, sir; I don't remember."

"Do your remember what your father said when she charged him with trying to kill her with the chloroform?"

"No, sir; I don't recollect."

"Do your remember any other problems between your mother and your father?"

"I remember when he tried to kick her."

"When was that?"

"That was in the daytime last spring."

"What was the cause of the problems?"

"That trouble started over an allusion to Mrs. Curtis, the woman who lived in rooms over the bank that were fitted up for her occupation."

"Were you there when the trouble started?'

"No, I was in the next room."

"What did you see?"

"My mother ran from the dining room into the sitting room where I was."

"What was your mother's condition at the time?"

"My mother was running. She was very excited."

"And your father?"

"My father was after her. He was very angry."

"You said he kicked her?"

"Before she could get the door closed, he kicked her."

"Was it a hard blow?"

"Yes, it was very hard."

"What was your father's state?"

"He was very angry."

"What occurred next?"

"She locked the door and yelled at him to leave her alone. She told him there was 'law for the case'."

"What did you do, Jennie?"

"I told him to leave her alone."

"What did your father say to you?"

"He told me to stop my noise."

"What did he do next?"

"He went out."

"Do you recall when the Curtises moved into the bank?"

"Mrs. Curtis moved over the bank last fall."

"Do you remember conversations between your mother and father regarding Mrs. Curtis?"

"Yes, sir; there were many discussions these last months."

"What was the nature of these conversations?"

"My mother objected to her living there."

"Did your father say anything when your mother complained that she was uncomfortable with Mrs. Curtis?"

"Yes. He replied in an angry manner that Mrs. Curtis was a decent woman and that mother should stand by her."

"How did your mother respond?"

"My mother said, Mrs. Curtis was not a respectable woman."

"Was this the only conversation your parents had about Mrs. Curtis?"

"They yelled about her many times."

"Do you remember how many times they had these conversations?"

"I don't recollect, but they occurred quite often."

"Have you ever heard your parents talk about Mrs. Curtis's suit against your mother for slander?"

"Yes."

"Did they talk about that very often?"

"I don't remember how often the subject was talked about."

"Were you home when the kerosene fire occurred?"

"No, I was away at school."

"But you believe it to be true?"

"There was evidence of it upon the boards beside my mother's door."

"What was the evidence?"

"There was quite a place burned and blackened."

"So you saw the burned board?"

"No, it had been planed off before I saw it."

"Did your father ever talk to you about sending your mother to an insane asylum?"

"Yes, he did."

"When was this conversation?"

"In the spring."

"Were you alone when he spoke to you?"

"No. I was in the sitting room with a little girl named Mary Lynch. She was living in the house."

"What occurred?"

"My father came into the room. He said that, if I had any influence over my mother, he wished I would talk to her."

"Did your father say why he came to you at that time?"

"He said mother had been to the Reverend Mr. Ford and had said to him that she would ruin his business."

"How did you respond?"

"I told him to get rid of Mrs. Curtis."

"Did your father agree?"

"He said Mrs. Curtis would sue for slander and would recover $1,000."

"Did your father say anything else?"

"Father said that if I would swear that she was crazy, he would not have to pay the suit." [Jennie paused just long enough to catch her

81

breath, then continued her diatribe.] "Then he said that, if I did not swear against mother, he would send the clerks away to board and send me to school and close the house."

"Was that the end of his threats?"

"He said she ought to be drowned."

"What did you say?"

"I said, if anything happened to my mother, I would spend the last dollar to bring him to justice."

"Did either of you say anything more?"

"Not that I remember."

"When did this conversation occur?"

"It was February last."

"Were there any other problems between your mother and father?"

"I remember hearing of difficulties in the spring."

"What do you remember of these difficulties?"

"Mother showed me her arms. They were black and blue."

"Where, on her arms, were they discolored?"

"The marks were on her upper arms."

"Do you remember your father coming home on the night of the murder?"

"Yes, sir. I accused him of the murder. I said to him 'three times and out'."

"What was your condition when you said this?"

"I was considerably excited."

"Do you remember saying anything else to him?"

"No."

"Have you heard from your father."

"I have received these letters."

[The letters were received by the court as evidence.]

"When did you receive the letters?"

"Yesterday."

"Jennie, please try to think back to last spring. Was there an incident when you and your mother were in the wagon?"

"I remember an occurrence last spring when my mother and I were going to Saratoga Springs. We met my father between Grangerville and the River. He was driving a team and the lumber wagon."

82

"Was he going to Saratoga Springs also?

"We were going in opposite directions. As we passed, he struck my mother across the back with a whip and said, 'Where are you delfers going now'?"

"Did he hit her hard?"

"He struck her very hard."

"What kind of whip was it?'

"It was a whale bone whip."

Foley continued to try show the extent of the ill feelings between the parents when he changed directions again, asking, "Do you remember an occurrence with a pocketbook?"

"Some years ago my father took my mother's pocketbook and paid the men in the boat yard from her money."

"How did your mother respond?"

"Some time afterwards when he was away she sold some coal and kept the money. She told me she did it because he had kept hers."

"What did your father do when he found out about the coal money?"

"He chased her into the bedroom and took her by the arm."

"Did you have occasion to see her afterwards?"

"Mother showed me the arm that night. It was all black and blue."

"Were there any other incidents?"

"One day last spring, mother was working about the house. Father came in and said, 'Work away Beckie. That's all you are good for.' Then, as he left the room, he called out 'You are one of those damned Harrises.'"

"Did he ever talk about your mother's qualities?"

"He would always say 'So and so was a splendid woman, but you are nothing'."

"Did they quarrel much?"

"They was always quarreling whenever they met."

"How did your mother handle the disputes?"

"Mother always tried to avoid meeting him by going into another room when he came into the house."

"Was this always the case?"

"Some, but mostly since January last."

"Did your father ever compare her to other women?"

83

"Father once said he would spend thousands of dollars on other women, while she should work in his kitchen."

"Where were you the day before the murder?

"Mother and I had attended the wedding of my uncle, John C. Harris, at Saratoga Springs."

"When did you leave for the wedding?"

"We left the house about noon. Then we went up to my grandmother's in the morning."

"What horse were you driving?"

"The mustang pony my father gave me."

"When did you get home after the wedding?'

"We reached home about 9 or 10 in the evening."

"Did you see your father that day?"

"No, sir. Not as I remember."

"What did you do the day after the wedding?"

"Mother and I stayed home all day." [This is in direct opposition to the testimony of Billings and Maggie, both of whom said they went to Schuylerville.]

"Was your father about?"

"He went away early."

"Did you see him when he returned?"

"I did not see him to speak to him."

"But you did see him?"

"I saw him coming up the road from Schuylerville. He was driving the mustang pony."

"What did he do with the horse when he got home?"

"He put it in the barn."

"What time was it when he came home?"

"It was between 4 and 5 o'clock.

"Did he put your horse away?"

"No, I went out and unharnessed it."

"Was this before or after the shower?"

"Before."

"What did you do with the horse after you unharnessed him?"

"I put him in his stall."

"Were you alone when you unharnessed the horse?"

"No, my mother assisted me."

84

"Where was your father when you were in the barn?"

"I don't know where he was."

"Did you have occasion to see your father again that evening?"

"Yes; I saw him drive the mustang out of the yard that evening after the shower."

"Where was he going?"

"He drove the three quarter buggy up the river road."

"Did you see him again that evening?"

"Not before my mother was shot."

"Did your mother and father eat at the same table."

"The same table, but at different times. Since January, my mother has been avoiding my father."

"Who ate first?"

"Mother usually ate first. If father came in, she would leave the table."

"How did your father speak of your mother?"

"He would say she was 'a nobody'. He was always saying she 'was one of those damned Harrises'."

"Where did your mother sit when she was in the sitting room?"

"My mother usually sat in the chair she was in when she was struck by the bullet."

"Did your family have a dog?"

"At the time of the murder, we had a dog."

"Where would the dog have been that night?"

"The dog usually stayed around the house unless it was at the store or about with father."

"Can you describe the dog?"

"We had it about two years. It was a medium size dog. It was brown and black, a brindle dog."

[Jennie had missed his message, so Foley found himself asking a more confining question.] "What was the dog like at night?"

"It was very savage at night. Especially when strangers came around."

"Did you see the dog after your mother was shot?"

"I saw the dog that night. I don't know for sure if it was before or after the shooting."

"Do you have any recollection of the dog that night?"

"I do remember that, after the shooting, the dog came in the side door and ran up to mother."

"Do you remember if the dog barked that night or not?"

"I don't recall. If it did I didn't hear it."

Graciously, Foley walked away. He turned to Judge Landon, saying, "No further questions."

Cross   Senator Hughes knew that this was a time to use kid gloves. To be perceived as assaulting this delicate victim would not serve his cause. He began his comments, "When did you turn 18?"

"I turned 18 in October 1877."

"Are you aware your father is on trial for the murder of your mother?"

"I am aware he is on trial for the murder of my mother." [The spite was evident in her voice.]

"Are you aware there was a coroner's jury held after the murder?"

"Yes." [Jennie had dropped the use of "sir" with respect to Hughes.]

"Why were you aware of the coroner's jury?"

"I was anxious at that time to find out the perpetrator of the crime."

"How long were you at your father's house after the murder?"

"I stayed at my father's until the Sunday following the murder."

"Where did you go when you left your father's home?"

"I went to my aunt's. Mrs. Harris."

"And where have you spent your time since you left your father's house?"

"I have been with the Harrises."

"When did you arrive in Ballston Spa?"

"I arrived on Wednesday to attend this court."

"When did you arrive on Wednesday?"

"It was about three o'clock."

"Have you visited your father since coming here?"

"No."

"Have you called upon or made any suggestions to his counsel?"

"No."

"Have you done anything that would throw any light in his favor in this case?"

"No."

86

"Have you done anything that would benefit him in this case?"

"No."

"Have you made any effort for that purpose?"

"No."

"Were you in Ballston Spa at any time since the murder?"

"I was here to attend the grand jury."

"Did you see your father at that time?"

"He sent for me after I testified."

"Did you visit your father?"

"I had an interview with him in the cell downstairs."

"How long were you with him?

"I stayed about two hours."

"Have you written to your father?"

"I have written to him once since he was in prison."

"Why did you write to him?"

"It was in answer to a letter he had written to me."

"Was your letter long or short?"

"It was very brief."

"Are you aware your father wanted you to remain in his home?"

"Yes. My father desired me to remain at home and attend to his affairs."

"Did you do as your father requested?"

"No."

"When you left home, what family was there to attend to his business?"

"There was no one." [Thinking quickly, Jennie added,] "His father was there."

"Isn't his father an elderly man?"

"Yes."

"When did you go away to school?"

"In 1873."

"How old were you then?"

"I was a young girl, only 14 years of age." [At this point in her testimony the record shows that Jennie again broke down. Her weeping lasted several minutes.]

"Where did you go to school when you were 14?"

Through a series of questions Jennie told of the various schools she attended first a boarding school at Mechanicville then switching to Fort Edward where she went until January 1875. She then went a select school in Hudson returning in April 1877.

"Who was the hired man at the time of the murder?"

"Sam Philo."

"Who was the servant girl at the time of the chloroform?"

"Mary Chase."

"Who worked in the house at the time of the kerosene affair?"

"There were two foreigners about the house at that time."

"Was Tim Madigan working there at any time?"

"Yes."

"Where were you seated at the time of the murder?"

"I was sitting west of the window."

"How long had you been there when you heard the shot?"

"About twenty minutes."

"Who was in the sitting room when you arrived?"

"I was first in the room. Mother came soon after."

"How long were you alone?"

"But a few minutes."

"What were you doing at the time of the shot?"

"After a few minutes, we were engaged in conversation. I think my mother was speaking to me when the shot was fired."

"Where were you when you saw the man's hat?"

"I was on the front piazza when I saw it. The hat was visible behind the lumber pile across the highway."

"What do you remember about the hat?"

"I thought it had a stiff brim."

"Jennie, do you remember telling John Terhune you saw a man run out the front yard and across the road?"

"No."

"Do you remember telling Mr. Terhune the man had on gray clothes and a stiff hat?"

"No."

"Do you remember telling Mr. Durkee of such an incident in the presence of O. C. Lockrow?"

"No."

"Do you remember telling of the incident in the presence of Mrs. Mary Pasnow or Coroner Gow?"

"No."

"Do you remember telling Mrs. Howard Thompson or Mrs. Wilson?"

"No."

"Do you remember having been called on by Mrs. Pasnow since the murder?"

"Yes. It was in August."

"Do you remember talking to her about the evidence?'

"No."

"When do you remember the first difficulty between your mother and father?"

"There were problems my entire life."

"You said that you saw evidence of the kerosene fire. What was that evidence?"

"It was grease spots on the carpet beside my mother's room."

"Do you recall exactly what your mother said about the spots?"

"Mother said to father, 'You have tried to take my life twice'."

"How did your father respond?"

"Father responded that he had accidentally tipped over a lamp in the sitting room."

"Did your mother say anything further?"

"Mother replied, 'What was the fire doing at my bedroom door'?"

Jennie then requested of Judge Landon if she could please be excused. The judge released her. As John Foley escorted her from the stand, she collapsed as if in a faint. Her father was heard to say, "It is all an act." She was taken upstairs where she was allowed to lie down. Jennie remained in the building for several hours. Before she left, she spoke about comments made in the courtroom as she was being carried out. Her comments were considered by the press as proof that she had not actually fainted.

Daniel S. Gilbert

Dir. It was Wednesday morning when Daniel Gilbert, a deputy sheriff from Saratoga Springs, arrived upon the scene of the murder. He had checked the garden and fields for tracks. He noticed that the tracks in the garden led to the Metcalf Office. When he looked inside he found the rubber boots. The tracks seemed to make a good match to the boots. Gilbert measured the distance between tracks and found it to be four feet suggesting that the person was running. It was his impression that, when the murderer was fleeing the garden, he was so close to the fence that he must have held it to avoid falling.

Gilbert had received the gun from Chase and had taken it to the grand jury. Gilbert identified the gun and shell for the jury. Ormsby almost hesitated as he turned the witness over to Hughes.

Cross   Those gathered knew of Hughes's success the day before with Cramer, the map maker. What the audience did not know was that they were about to watch a master at work. To suck Gilbert into a sense of security, Hughes began with easy questions. Daniel reviewed his impression of the tracks. He admitted that after he found the boots, he did not look for others. The ground on the night of the fourth had been so wet that it would not "hold a shape firm". By Thursday the fifth the ground had begun to dry, but even so he had not tried on the boots to see if there was a match. Gilbert admitted that he was not certain the tracks were made by the boots.

Under Hughes's guidance, Gilbert went on to support Billings's testimony before the Coroner's Jury. On Wednesday he had examined the wagon tracks and was certain the wagon had gone to the end of the lane.

Although Gilbert arrived at the scene on Wednesday, it was Thursday before he spoke to Billings. Gilbert stated that when he confronted Billings, he had said, 'It is a terrible thing that has happened'." Gilbert said Billings had gone further saying, "If you are an officer, I would like to find out who did it." Billings went on to say he would pay the expenses.

When Gilbert talked to Billings, he ultimately acknowledged, "Egad, it looks like they suspect me. There is a conspiracy." Under this veiled, tight cross Gilbert said "I said, why don't you square yourself."

Billings answered. "What do you mean?"

Gilbert responded. "I mean you are suspect." Gilbert added that Jennie had told of seeing a man run toward the river. If there is a gun to be found it will be in there. "A diver should be got to search the river. Will you pay the expense?" Gilbert said Billings agreed to pay, but later suggested that they wait a day or two. Gilbert testified that he added, "It should be done at once." Billings said he would defray the cost. "Yes, he did seem earnest in his desire to find the murderer." In confidence, Billings had given him the name of the person whom he felt had committed the crime. Gilbert refused to provide the name unless compelled by the court. Billings had said at the time that he was surprised because "He could not believe the man was bad enough to do such a thing." Billings had told Gilbert later that he was assured the man had not committed the deed.

There was a series of questions asked to determine if a person running out the back could have been seen from the Billings's back porch as he ran the route claimed by the prosecution. It was obvious that Hughes was trying to show that the maid, Maggie Mahoney, should have seen someone. Gilbert admitted there were spots where a person might be seen, but noted that he had not looked when it was dark.

Moak was disappointed. One of the themes of the prosecution was that Billings had been an obstructionist to the investigation. Minutes before, their witness had painted an entirely different picture of the man. His only point made on re-direct was that if the murderer had stayed close to the barn, he would not be visible to anyone, either from the house or the bank.

Senator Hughes asked the court if Miss Billings was well enough to continue her testimony. Mr. Pike informed the judges that he had been in contact with Jennie's physician, and she would be unable to return that day.

Ira Parker

Officer Parker's testimony was virtually the same as that of Gilbert. The only difference were Parker's statement concerning another set of tracks different from those shown on the map, and that there were numerous tracks around the garden. The tracks he followed were closer to the Reed property line than to the trail on the map. The unmarked trail went up and over the hill. The "Parker tracks" were three feet apart, except at the top of the hill where they were sometimes four feet apart. Ira could not swear, "but the tracks were made by another boot."

William Wolf

Wolf was a deputy sheriff who resided in Waterford. He was with Parker when he followed the trail. In his opinion, prints from the boots found in the Metcalf Office reasonably matched the ones found in the garden. "The Wolf," as he was referred to by now, testified that the Billings gun weighed six pounds nine ounces.

John C. Sherman

Dir. Jennie's fiancee had turned 27 the preceding August. He had resided with the family since April, 1876. At the time that he heard the shot, Sherman testified that he was in Billings's store dealing out eggs. He then walked out to the desk and heard Jennie screaming. Under Ormsby's questions, Sherman assured those present that from the time of the shot until he was out of the store was about half of a minute. He ran into the Billings's house where he found Mrs. Billings in a chair, apparently lifeless. He remained in the house until Mr. Billings returned, a period of about twenty minutes. Referring to Billings's behavior, Sherman testified, "He asked, 'what is the matter?' or something like that. Then he went up to where Mrs. Billings was and threw himself at her feet. He made some endearing expression, using the word 'wife'. Then he fell over on his side and lay there for ten or twelve minutes."

"Did he move during the period he was on his side?" Ormsby asked.

"No, sir. Nor did he speak."

"Did you hear Jennie say anything to her father when he was in the sitting room?"

"I don't recall her exact words, but when he first got there, she said something about him being responsible for shooting her mother."

"How did Billings reply to her recrimination?"

"He didn't."

Sherman's answers then went back to earlier in the evening when he had seen Billings, first at the Bank and earlier at the store. While Sherman had dinner, Billings had passed through the room wearing rubber boots.

The questioning then went to the issue of the gun. On the Sunday before the murder, Sherman had been in the wagon house with Billings, talking about the failure of the Greenwich Bank. They had heard a shot, and Billings asked about the gun. Sherman, who had seen and handled the gun at least twenty-five times since his arrival, said that the last time he saw the gun it was in the small room over the store.

According to Sherman, the gun in question was a breech loading carbine. Sherman then identified the gun in evidence as the Billings gun. After the murder, there was talk about the gun, so Sherman had searched the store, but was unable to find the gun anywhere. The next time he saw the gun was when it was shown to him by Officer Chase on Friday, the seventh.

John told the story of Mrs. Billings stoning the bank in April. He was in the store when Mrs. Billings ran in with Jesse right behind her. He caught up to her at the desk; grabbed her by the arms and said, 'Now for the river." Sherman said she replied, 'Jesse Billings, take your hands off me; there is law in the case.' He then asked her if she would stone the bank any more. During the time he held her, which was less than a minute, Billings had pushed her ten or twelve feet. He let her go, and she left the store. Sherman had seen her arms later, and they were black and blue.

Sherman went on to testify that, after the murder, Billings had accused him of not being around when he needed him. Billings had gone on to say that Sherman was not in the store at the time of the murder. Sherman did not reply to Billings's accusations. Billings told Sherman that a reliable source had told him that John had conspired to get Mrs. Billings out of the way because he was secretly engaged to Jennie, and that Mrs. Billings opposed the marriage. Billings had told Sherman, "you will be arrested before nightfall."

Ormsby asked Sherman how he had responded. "I said, 'If you wish to bring me into this scrape, you can go right ahead.'"

The direct examination closed with Sherman answering a series of unrelated questions. He stated that there had never been 'ill feelings' between Billings and himself. Mrs. Billings had not opposed the marriage because she never knew of their plans. "Yes, I have heard of Mr. and Mrs. Billings dispute over Mrs. Curtis."

Cross Under Hughes's guidance, Sherman assured the jury that Billings was a very successful business man. He owned boats and built boats for others. He was a farmer, owned the store and the bank. According to Sherman, Billings also bought potatoes for the markets in New York. Billings had very little to do with the store, allowing the two clerks to manage the operation. The bank was not really for business, but it was the site where Billings managed his various businesses.

In discussing the Billings family's relations, Sherman said he tried to avoid any rifts. Sherman said, Billings was frequently required to be away on business. On several of his trips to New York, Billings had taken Jennie along. The entire family had gone together to the Centennial (The National Celebration in Philadelphia).

Sherman went on to tell how Mrs. Curtis had a husband who lived with her in the rooms over the bank. There was a door with a latch handle that lead from the bank to the private rooms. On one occasion, Mrs. Billings had told him that Billings was alone with Mrs. Curtis when he (Sherman) was looking for him on business. Sherman had never seen Billings in the private rooms, but had seen him in the bank when Mr. Curtis was not there. On three occasions Sherman had been in Mrs. Curtis's apartment. One was a social evening; on other occasions, he had gone alone "on business." Sherman had been told by Mrs. Billings not to go to Mrs. Curtis's rooms so he never went there in search of Billings.

Sherman went on to testify that he had returned to North Hebron after the funeral. He had visited Jennie at least once or twice a week since she had gone to reside at her uncle's William Harris. He had stopped his wagon in front of the home where Maggie Mahoney lived, when he heard her call out. He had not visited Mrs. Passnow, but had seen her at William Harris's.

On the night of the murder, Sherman met the screaming Jennie next to the elm tree in front of the house. Sherman went on to say that he ran into the house followed by Jennie. He also told the court that on the evening of the murder, there were many other people present at the Billings's house including Mrs. Finne. Sherman explained that when Billings came in after the murder, Sherman did not pay him much attention. Sherman told the court it was Isaac Washburn had helped Billings up and into his bedroom. Sherman had spent the night upstairs at the request of the ladies.

Day 5

Mrs. Ella Reed, who was to testify this day, was a tragic witness. Mrs. Reed was the daughter of Peter Ray of Pittstown, New York. Peter Ray had been shot down in his own dooryard five years previously. No one had ever been arrested in the case. Her sister, Sarah, was the domestic servant in the home of Mr. and Mrs. Alvinza Finne.

All those gathered could not believe how well Jesse Billings Jr. had been able to handle his denunciation by the prosecution over the preceding days. Through the constant barrage of insults, he remained indifferent to Moak and Ormsby. He may have been aided by the bouquets of flowers that were daily arriving in his cell. The women attending the court found him forgivable.

John C. Sherman recalled

When he arose this Saturday morning, Sherman knew that this was going to be a very unpleasant day. As it turned out, he was right.

Cross After the court crier had called the session to order, Hughes rose up to address the witness. This was one person whom Hughes intended to roast. The defense attorney began by returning to the Curtises situation. Sherman responded to the first question, "Mr. and Mrs. Curtis lived in the Reed house from April until October." During that interval, Sherman testified, he had not visited the Curtises. "The trouble between Mr. and Mrs. Billings began before the return of Mr. Billings from New York in January." Sherman answered a later question.

He went on to explain that, while Billings was away, Mrs. Billings told the young clerks that they should stay away from Mrs. Curtis. The other clerk affected was Brumagim, who had boarded with the Curtises for a period. When confronted by Mrs. Billings, Sherman told her that he, "would not call upon Mrs. Curtis again."

The line of questioning turned to Billings access to the gun. Sherman assured the court that, on the Sunday before the murder, when Billings and he had heard a shot, Billings had asked, "Where is my gun?" Not, "Where are the guns." The reference to a second gun was that of Percival Hunter. Sherman stated that, when he first saw the gun, he had searched the entire store for shells but was unable to find any that would fit. He told Billings the gun was upstairs but did not know who had placed it there. In answer to one of the more interesting questions Sherman stated, "I never saw that gun or any gun in Mr. Billings's hands."

Sherman testified that Billings had lost his set of keys to the store at the Centennial in 1876. Since that time, Billings had always called on him to open the store.

Sherman went on to testify that Brumagim had left the store in March. He was replaced by Charles Cramer, Billings's nephew. Cramer was boarding in the Billings's house on June fourth. Sherman and Cramer had covered the store for each other as they went separately to the house for evening tea.

The stoning of the bank was revisited. Sherman conceded to Hughes that Billings had released his wife after only a few moments. "Yes", he had seen marks.

Sherman went on to explain that when he was confronted by Billings regarding his engagement to Jennie, he had not replied. Sherman admitted that he was engaged to her without the knowledge of her parents. "Yes, Mr. Billings did point out to me the difficulty of my position if I could not show where I was the night of the murder."

Sherman testified that, "It was about a year ago when I first heard about Billings trying to take Mrs. Billings's life. She said at the table, 'You have tried twice to take my life'." Sherman answered the next question, "I suppose he did respond 'Oh wife, what folly'." Sequencing the story, Sherman stated, "It was nine or ten months afterward that I heard Mrs. Billings tell the means that Billings had used to try to take her life." She said it was by kerosene and chloroform. Sherman told the court that Billings appeared to take these charges pleasantly. Billings had laughed off the charges of murder as he had laughed off his wife's allegation concerning Mrs. Curtis. In the spring, when Billings was going out, Mrs. Billings would call after him, 'You'd better not be going to visit your posy-pot.' "Yes, she was referring to Mrs. Curtis."

When Sherman saw the gun at Chase's house on Friday, he had said, "You are going to arrest me, I suppose."

Re-dir. Under Moak's leading questions, Sherman testified that the room, where the gun was kept, was never locked. He also related that he had never had a conversation with Billings about taking his wife to an insane asylum. The conversation, which was in February, was the one in which Billings told him at the dinner table that, "He would give him $1,000 to take his wife off his hands. That she was a fit subject for a lunatic asylum." Sherman told the court that he was present on the Thursday after the murder when Billings had stood on the steps of the bank and read the account from the Albany Press. "He didn't appear to be affected much by it."

Re-Cross The questions asked by Hughes changed the perspective on the reading of the paper. Sherman admitted that there was only one paper in town that day and that was the reason Billings read it to the throng that had gathered. Sherman also admitted that when Billings had offered the thousand dollars it was done in a joking manner. What Billings had said was, "John, you want a wife. I'll give a thousand dollars and the best horse I have, if you'll take mine."

Greatly relieved that it was finally over, John Sherman returned to his seat in the gallery.

Mrs. Ella (Addie) Reed

Dir.   "I remember the night of the murder," began the testimony of the woman who lived in the first house south of Billings. Her property was adjacent to the garden where the murderer had stood when he shot Mrs. Billings. By now it was obvious to everyone involved in the case that the exact time of the murder was an essential element.

"I had lit a lamp at 8:30. I heard the shot about five minutes after, and then screams about a minute after that." If they are on their side, attorneys dream about witnesses such as Mrs. Reed. If witnesses such as Mrs. Reed represent the opposition, attorneys have nightmares about the way they appear to a jury. She was a humble, sincere, simple, person who was believable based simply on her presence. Mrs. Reed had turned the lamp down and raised the curtain. She told the court that the blinds were shut, but the window was open. After the shot, she looked through the gap in the slats of the blinds. "I saw a lady run out into the Billings's yard. I couldn't distinguish plainly, but it appeared to be Jennie." [Mrs. Reed was nervous fearing the wrath of Hughes who had just dissected Sherman.] "I supposed it was Jennie I heard scream 'My mother is shot'." Mrs. Reed told the court that   there were two windows on the first floor of the Billings's house that face her home.

"About five minutes later my husband came into the room. I put on a shawl and changed my slippers for button shoes before I went outside. My husband and I joined quite a few other people at Finne's store. One of the people in the group at Finne's was George Washburn. When he left he started for home at a normal walk." [Whether Washburn and the Reeds were together at the Finne's horse block was one of the issues that both sides were trying to resolve, since this fact would impact the time schedule.]

Cross   On cross examination, Mrs. Reed stated that her house had only one window that looked at the Billings's house. She also noted that she really had no accurate knowledge of the time as she had nothing important to note that would make her care about the time after lighting the lamp. She was, however, certain that it was 8:30 when she lit the lamp, as she had taken the opportunity to look at the clock. She also stated "My husband stopped at the Billings's gate, but did not go in." She went on to say, "My husband has a pair of rubber boots that he runs about the premises in."

Charles Teft Jr.
Dir.   Mr. Teft, a police justice from Saratoga Springs, testified that on June 6, he had been in Billings's cornfield. He cut a stick the same length as the boot prints. Later he had measured the stick against the boots owned by Billings noting they were the same length. He also testified that there was an impression in the heel print. Teft told the court that boot prints were found at the junction of the oat and corn field and on the south side of the cornfield.
Cross   Mr. Teft was forced to admit that, although he was a justice, he was really at the scene out of personal curiosity "same as other people." He admitted that while in the fields walking with Leake, he saw many other people there.

Alanson Welch
Dir.   Mr. Welch, of Schuylerville, was at the Billings's farm on Thursday after the murder. He, Edward Hammond and Alanson Chase had all gone up to the red gate. They could clearly see where a wagon had been hitched, turned around and driven down the hill. "Where the horse had been hitched the grass was trodden down and made muddy."
Cross   Alanson assured Hughes that there were tracks made beyond the gate going out to the outer fields. These tracks were made by a different wagon. Alanson was sure because the width of the tire tracks were different. Welch was the only witness to testify that there were two sets of wagon tracks on the lane.

James H. Lloyd
Mr. Lloyd was a photographer from Waterford. He had been employed by the prosecution to take pictures of the Billings house and

property. Under direct examination he explained how he took and developed eight pictures which were placed into evidence.

Lewis Cramer recalled

Dir. Mr. Cramer was recalled by the prosecution for the purpose of placing into evidence a map of the interior of the Billings's house. Cramer stated that he had called on Jennie two days previous to this testimony to point out the location of the tables and chairs.

The defense asked no questions of Cramer. Hughes felt he had won a major point just by the admission that Jennie had helped make the map but was unable to attend the court.

Day five was a Saturday. Before closing for the day the judge asked both sides how long they thought they would need to present their case. Judge Landon was scheduled to preside over another murder trial beginning September 23. Both sides predicted their case would take several days. The judge asked if they should continue for the afternoon or dismiss. Both sets of attorneys claimed that they had business in other courts that required their attentions so, at 12:30, the judge dismissed the court until 9:30 Monday morning.

The Jury

The jury was sequestered in the American Hotel in Ballston Spa. The judge told the jurors that if they wished to visit their homes they would need to make a formal application to the court. Burr, Wiswall, Abbott, and Corp all were given permission to visit their homes; each would be accompanied by a deputy sheriff.

Day 6

Hosting the *case celebre* of 1878 placed Ballston Spa at the center of the universe of American trial sites. Through an incredibly active telegraph, reporters from New York City, Albany and Troy were able to have their articles reprinted in papers throughout the country. Capitalizing on their temporary notoriety, the local citizens were out delighting in the night life. The restaurants, taverns and hotel lounges were alive with opinions, solicited or not, on these warm, early fall evenings.

The cross examination for the defense was led by Hughes. Pike or Ormsby had asked the direct questions for the prosecution; however, as was usually the case, Moak asked the re-direct.

99

Edward Hammond

Dir. Edward Hammond, a farmer, resided about a mile west of Billings. His testimony was desired by the prosecution to resolve the issue of Sam Philo's possible complicity. On the day of the murder, Sam Philo worked for Hammond. As a day laborer, he also lived in the Hammond's house. According to Hammond, Philo had been living with his family since May. Hammond created an alibi for Sam Philo when he testified that Philo was sitting on his piazza on the night of the murder when he went to bed at 8:30 p.m.. He added that Philo had complained of not feeling well the day of the murder and had "gone off" but was home around 5:00 p.m.. Hammond stated that he had wakened Philo in his bed under the stairs on the day after the murder.

On the day after the murder, at about 9:00 a.m., Welch, Chase and Hammond had all gone up the lane behind Billings's house. Near the red gate they noticed that a horse had been hitched heading west. Hammond testified that the horse had been turned around at the gate. The prosecution wanted to show Billings was not in his back fields but rather close to the house.

On cross Hammond admitted he could not swear the horse was turned around at the gate. This point was essential, as the defense was trying to show that Billings was telling the truth to the Coroner's Jury when he said he drove the wagon further down the lane before he turned it around.

Hammond also testified about seeing the tracks in the garden. Hammond testified that he had measured the tracks in the cornfield with a stick, and they were the exact same length as those in the garden.

Daniel S. Gilbert recalled

Re-dir. A critical issue in Gilbert's initial testimony was how close to the fence Billings had walked. Daniel related that a horse with a plow could get fairly close to a fence, but a hard border near the fence was inevitable. He went on to explain to the jury of farmers that this hard border would not show foot prints like the soft dirt in the center of the garden.

Gilbert had interviewed Billings the night of the murder. Billings told him that he had not walked on the Reed's side of the fence but had walked near the fence in order to wipe the mud off his boots. Gilbert challenged Billings testimony that he (Billings) could walk that close to the

100

fence. [Before the Coroner's Jury, Billings had already countered, saying he had walked close by holding on to the top board of the fence.]

Gilbert further stated that he went into the Metcalf Office, "which seemed to be a general store room," the day after the murder because he saw muddy footprints on the threshold. Inside, he picked up the rubber boots, which looked as if they had been "cast there". The boots had a frog imprint in the sole near the heel. This imprint exactly matched the tracks in the cornfield. On cross examination he could not swear that the tracks in the garden were deeper than elsewhere.

In a classic example of how the evidence was mishandled, Gilbert talked about his examination of the window, which he had checked for powder marks. He did not feel there were any present, but had wiped about an inch of the window with his handkerchief. It was blackened, but he did not think it was gunpowder. He did not examine the other pane in the window to see if it would also yield a black mark. He did not keep the handkerchief because he did not think it was important.

Gilbert tried the east door in the Metcalf Office. It was very tight on the bottom and could not be closed without making some noise. The door needed to be lifted to close tightly and could not be closed hastily.

Re-cross Gilbert had received the rifle in question from Officer Chase. The gun was in his possession until the grand jury. He had seen no rust on the gun either at the time he was given the gun or when he turned it over to the grand jury.

Alanson Chase

Dir. Chase, a constable residing in Schuylerville, was the man who found the gun in the well. Chase had been assigned to watch the Billings house the night after the murder. Chase testified that Billings had answered all of his questions fully. Chase added that Billings had told him to do all he could to ferret out the murderer. He testified Billings told him to follow any tracks that were not where he (Billings) claimed to have walked.

When Chase and Marcus Cary went to the well on Friday morning, they found a set of tracks in the grass, which indicated that someone had been their previously. According to Chase, the well was covered by three boards. Two were coverings and the third was a batten to hold the other two in place. In Chase's opinion, the boards covering the well had not been disturbed. Chase testified the gun would not fit through the small hole between the two boards.

Chase told how marks had been made in the gun as a result of removing it from the well with the grappling hooks. He also told there was a shell in the gun when it was found.

While Chase had the gun, he overtook John Sherman, who was walking on the road. Shown the gun, Sherman asked "Are you going to arrest me?" Chase responded, "No." and took Sherman to his (Chase's) home. Chase brought the gun out and Sherman failed to identify it because it did not have a spring. Chase showed him the spring. Sherman burst out crying saying, "This is the gun." Sherman then asked Mrs. Chase for some brandy and wiped his eyes with a handkerchief. Chase described Sherman as "looking as if he felt baldly."

Chase went on to say that neither he nor Billings had spoken about compensation.

Marcus Cary

Dir.   Cary, a neighbor of Billings, substantiated Chase's testimony. He said that he had known of the well and the house that used to stand near it. On Thursday morning Cary had walked up to the old well with David Prosser. The two of them examined the well and, in his opinion, the center board covering the well had been disturbed. That afternoon he went back to Billings's house where he told Detective Chase about the well. Cary was with Chase when he grappled the gun out of the well. Based on the marks created by the grappling hook, Cary positively identified the gun in evidence as the one found in the well.

Cross   Cary testified that the well was twenty-five to forty feet from the lane. He stated that Officer Chase had opened the wet gun to see if there were a shell inside.

Based on the gnaw marks in the fence, Cary thought that a horse had been tied near the red gate.

Charles Reed

Dir.   Reed was the husband of Mrs. Ella Reed who had testified the previous day. Reed was important to the prosecution for his testimony was to be used to establish a time frame or at the very least a sequence of events.

Under direct examination Reed stated that, at the time of the shooting, he was on the piazza of the Union Store [owned by Finne] where he was employed as clerk. According to Reed, at the time he heard the shot it was not very dark. After the shot, he talked briefly to Finne then went back and closed up the four doors to the store, leaving by the front door. Reed then talked to Finne a second time as he was standing near his horse block. Reed then ran his own house. He rapped twice before his wife would come to the door. After he was inside, he lit a lamp then went into the dining room and sat down. Then he went into several other rooms to be sure they were secure. Finally Reed helped his wife get ready to go outside and back to Finne's. As he passed Billings's house, he stopped at the gate. At the moment he was in front of Billings's gate, Charles Cramer drove by, but did not return his wave. When he got to Finne's horse block, there were several ladies present along with Finne and George Washburn. Three to five minutes after Reed's arrival at Finne's, Washburn moved off at "a good walk for him in the direction of his house." Reed then went back into the store and put the books in the safe. While Reed was in the store, James Nichols, came in and they "passed words." They both left the store where Reed talked to Finne yet another time. As he was talking to Finne the final time, Isaac Washburn stopped as he was driving by in Billings's wagon. Minutes later, Isaac Washburn returned with his sister in the wagon. Reed and Finne walked down to Billings's where they found Billings on the floor.

Cross   Under a rigorous cross examination, Reed admitted that he was nervous after hearing the shot, but was absolutely clear on what he had done on the night of the shooting.

William Durkee

Dir.   At the time of the murder, William Durkee was a constable for the town of Northumberland where he had resided for the past five years. Under direct examination, Durkee testified that he had wound his watch at 8:25 just before getting ready for bed. Durkee said, he heard the shot and "hollering" about five minutes later. Almost immediately William Carey knocked on his door. He dressed and went down to talk to Carey who told him of the murder. He then went to the Billings's house. In all it was three to five minutes after the shot before he got to the Billings's house. Billings arrived fifteen to twenty minutes after Durkee.

Mrs. Vandenburg

Dir.   Mary Chase Vandenberg had worked in the Billings's house for two to three years. She was only thirteen when she went to work for the Billingses. Mary was able to recollect that she slept on a lounge in the dining room the first summer. At the time, Mrs. Billings's bedroom was on the first floor off the dining room. Jesse Billings's room was upstairs. Mary testified that Billings could get to his wife's room without passing by her bed. One night Mary awoke to Mrs. Billings standing over her asking for a glass of water. Young Mary helped Mrs. Billings to an open window. When Mrs. Billings was 'restored', she asked Mary to get Jennie. Mary found Jennie sleeping in her mother's bed with her head covered. Mary put Mrs. Billings in another bed in the same room. She went on to testify that when she got out into the hall where she saw Mr. Billings going upstairs, she called after him, but he did not respond. Mary said that when she returned to the room with the Billings women, she closed the door and they all slept through the night. In the morning, at breakfast, Mrs. Billings accused Mr. Billings of sneaking into her room and holding something under her nose. Billings denied the accusation, threw water in Mrs. Billings's face, and said, 'That's the Harris of it." Jennie threw water at her father and told him to 'leave my mother alone.' According to Mary, Billings left the table, storming out the door. [Jennie had testified she was not at home when the incident occurred.]

Cross   Mary remembered that Billings had a toothache at the time, but she did not remember him saying that he was up the night before putting chloroform on the tooth. She was certain the incident occurred in the summer but was unsure of the date and would not even suggest which month. Mary admitted this was the only night she slept downstairs. She was only "pretty sure" that she had called to Billings that night. She also said she could not remember any strange smells in Mrs. Billings's room. Mary stated that she had only been subpoenaed that day. [The implication of waiting until the last day was that the defense would not have time to develop questions.]

Re-dir.   When Moak entered the arena under re-direct, Mary added that she was reminded of the incident by Baucus on August 20 when he had called at her house. She also remembered that Mrs. Billings had said she received money on the day of the incident.

Percival Hunter

Dir.   Mr. Hunter, of Wilton, was a patron of Billings's store. He testified that, about two years earlier he had placed his gun at Billings's "for purpose of sale." At the time, he had seen Billings's own gun which he thought was the same as the one in evidence, but he could not swear to the fact.

Mr. Walter Curtis

Dir.   Those in attendance waited with baited breath as Mr. Curtis was called as a prosecution witness. They were sure that at last they would learn the truth about the relationship between Billings and Mrs. Curtis.

In July, following the murder, the Curtises had moved back to Sandy Hill [Hudson Falls]. Walter testified under direct examination that at the time of the shooting he was on the front porch of Billings's store with Clark Lockrow and others. To dispel him as a suspect, Ormsby had Walter swear he did not have a gun in his hand that night. Walter said that he had never seen the Ballard .44 before.

Cross   Under Hughes's examination, Curtis stated he was 33 and had married his wife in 1876. He was a saw filer at the mill. (In large saw mills it was necessary to have someone sharpen the circular saws. This was usually done by a person not capable of hard labor.). Curtis testified that he and his wife had boarders living with them most of the time. He said he heard charges made by Mrs. Billings against his wife. He testified that on one occasion Mrs. Billings had come to her window and yelled, "That's right Jesse go and see your whore." She also said, "That's nice to stick a whore house under my nose." Curtis had seen Mrs. Billings running up and down her stoop, hugging the post and calling to Billings, "How's your posy-pot."

Re-dir.   Moak asked how Billings behaved in the presence of Mrs. Curtis. "Billings behaved himself like a gentleman in the presence of myself and my wife." When pressed for more information, Curtis said, "He never took any improper intimacies with my wife in my presence." Curtis did admit that Billings would call on them two or three times a week.

Frederick Leggett

Dir.   Leggett testified that he had worked as clerk for Billings in 1877. When handed the rifle in evidence, he stated that while employed by

Billings he saw the gun in the store. Leggett told the court, the rifle was kept not in the window but in a room upstairs.

Cross   The correctness of Leggett's direct examination was apparent when he said he did not know if the gun was a rifle or a smooth bore or when the gun was out of sight he could not tell how many bands there were holding the barrel to the stock.

Day 7

The number of women attending the trial increased each day. By the first Monday, the number of women in the gallery exceeded the males. Each day there was a group of women who moved to seats closer to the accused. By the seventh day, many of the women had assumed seats that were only two rows behind Billings. Ever the diplomat, Billings took the opportunity to shake several of the ladies' hands before he sat down.

In the fall of 1878, the place to be seen in the Capital Region was in the audience of the Billings trial in Ballston Spa. This was clearly evidenced by how stylishly the women were dressed as they entered the court each day.

By day seven, the press were beginning to complain about their accommodations within the court room. They were provided the usual press table, but because of the large numbers of reporters covering the trial, including those from New York and other cities, the writers were literally bumping elbows.

Sam Philo

Dir.   Philo was a fifty-year-old day worker who, on numerous occasions, had worked for Billings. He testified that on the day of the murder he spent the afternoon and evening at Hammond's where he was employed. Philo had his dinner at 6:00 p.m. Sam went to bed in a space under the stairs some time later, but was not sure of the time.

Cross   The defense chose not to cross examine at the time.

Mrs. Mary Passnow

Dir.   Two women named Mrs. Passnow testified at the trial. Mary Passnow was with Maggie Mahoney the day after the murder at the time Billings made his comment about the bullet hitting its intended victim. According to Mary Passnow, the conversation had been opened by Maggie who said that she was afraid the bullet had been meant for her.

Mary's recollection was that Billings responded "you need not be afraid; whoever fired that bullet hit the one it was intended for." She also heard Billings direct Maggie to tell Jennie he wanted to see her. Mary was present when Jennie refused to see her father. Mary had told Billings that she thought, it was "cruel death". Billings had answered he thought it "Was an easy one."

Cross Mrs. Passnow said that when the comment about the "cruel death" was made, Charlie Cramer and Jennie were in the room with Billings and her. Mary reiterated for the court that, when Billings made the remark about the bullet hitting its intended victim, he was responding to Maggie's persistent comments that she was sure the bullet was intended for her. She also said that in the same conversation, Maggie had told Billings he "did a bad job going over to the Harris's." Mrs. Passnow said Billings responded to the Harris comment: "That it was. I didn't know this would happen." Billings had gone on to say, "What was done can't be undone."

Mrs. Passnow told Hughes that, when she arrived at the Billings's house on the night of the murder, Jennie was still in the road running back toward the house. Jennie screamed she saw a man run across the yard and around the lumber pile. On the night of the murder, Jennie said nothing to her with respect the man's dress but on the following morning she spoke of the slouch hat. She said that Jennie had added the fact that the man ran so fast she could not tell what kind of clothes he wore. Mrs. Passnow went on to explain that on or about August 25, at the request of Jennie, she had gone to the Harris's home. At the August 25 meeting, Jennie asked if she had ever said anything about the man in the soft hat. Finding the answer was affirmative, Mrs. Passnow said, "Jennie asked me not to say so." Mrs. Passnow responded, "I will not lie for you or your father." While Mrs. Passnow was at the Harris's, the elder, Mrs. Mary Harris and Mrs. William Harris, were both present.

Re-dir. Mrs. Passnow said that Jennie was very excited when she remarked about the hat. She said that the comment was not directed to her or anyone else in particular, but rather was made to all assembled. She also said that she saw Jennie talking to the Curtises on the morning after the murder. Mrs. Passnow particularly noted Jennie talking to the Curtises because she believed that they were the cause of the problems.

107

Re-cross Mary Passnow admitted that, while she was at the Harris's in August, she heard Mrs. Mary Harris tell Jennie that "she (Jennie) was near sighted and that she must not say that she saw a man as she could not see."

Mrs. Mary Harris

Dir. "I am the mother of Mrs. Billings." With these simple words the testimony of one of the prosecution's most important witnesses began. The widow, Mrs. Mary Harris, was the mother of Eliza Billings, the murdered woman. Of equal importance, Mrs. Billings had spent a portion of the day of the murder with both Jesse Billings, Jr. and Eliza.. Angry, bitter and hostile, sixty-eight year old Mrs. Harris's appearance would be interrupted for the testimony of her girl, Lizzie Hill.

The direct examination of Mrs. Harris focused on several areas. The prosecution wanted to demonstrate that one possible motive for the murder was money. Ormsby and Moak wanted the jury to hear of the amount of property that Mrs. Billings brought to the marriage. The implication was that Mrs. Billings might get the money back if there were a divorce. They wanted to imply that the burden of repaying the funds could have been a sufficient motive for Billings to commit the crime of murder.

Dir. Mrs. Harris testified that when her husband died in 1862, he left an estate to be shared among his four children. Mrs. Harris had also lost a son in 1868. Her deceased son had no heirs, so he left his estate to his brother and sisters. Although Mrs. Harris was not certain, she believed that her daughter had received a total of two or three thousand dollars from the various estates. When cross examined on the same point, she was able to list approximately $2,800.

"I remember the night my daughter was shot," Mrs. Harris returned to the testimony that she wanted so desperately to provide.

"Billings was at my house that day." She continued her hostile testimony.

"Did your daughter have any distinguishing marks?" [Ormsby was not fishing; he knew the answer before he ever asked the question.]

"My daughter, while she was living, had a mark on her forehead."

"What kind of a mark was it?"

"It was quite a scar over the eyebrow near the hair."

"How big was the scar?"

"It was about an inch long."

"When did you first see the scar?"

"I saw it when it was fresh."

"And when was that?"

"When she first had that mark, she had lived with Billings three or four years."

"And how long have they been married?"

"They were married about 22 years."

"When did you first see Billings on the day of the murder?"

"On the day of the murder he got to my house in the forenoon."

"How long had it been since he last visited you?"

"He had not been there in about two years."

"Did he live a great distance from you?"

"We lived about three miles from him."

"Did Mr. Billings ever pass your house during those two years?"

"He frequently passed the house." [If Mrs. Harris's testimony were true, Billings was going out of his way. Mrs. Harris lived in a beautiful old house that still exists. The house is at the center of a long loop on an unpaved road named Harris Road. To go by this house, one needs a reason; no one would ever just pass by.]

"Who was at your house when Billings arrived?"

"When he came there, Lizzie Hill, Millie Nelson, and John Nelson were there."

"Were they the only ones there while Billings was present?"

"Another boy came by."

"Was your daughter, Gertrude Harris, there?"

"Gertrude was not there."

"Did Billings say why he happened by your house that day?"

"He said he had been to Gansevoort to see Mr. Thompson."

"So for the first time in two years he came from Gansevoort to your house?"

"He said he had let his horse take its own way, and it had come here."

"How did Billings start the conversation?"

"He asked if my son, John Harris, was there. I told him John had gone on his wedding tour."

"What did he say next?"

"He asked me if I run the establishment by myself. I told him, I always run it, even when John was home."

"Did you invite him to dinner?"

"No. He asked for some dinner, saying he was feeling faint."

"Did you oblige?"

"Yes, and I asked him how Eliza and Jennie were."

"How did he respond?"

"He said they were out to all hours of the night."

"When was the last time you had seen your daughter and Jennie before his visit?"

"Eliza and Jennie had been with me to Saratoga the day before."

"Was his only comment about his wife and daughter that they were out late?"

"He complained that Eliza would not work and help the girl, who was very slender." [Staring directly at Billings, Mrs. Harris continued her developed speech.] "Billings said he wished I would take Eliza away so she would not hurt his business."

"Is that all he said?" [Ormsby was sure this was playing well with the jury.]

"He said he should kill Eliza and Jennie with trouble."   "Did he say how your daughter would be killed?"

"He said my daughter would die in an insane asylum."

"And what did he say about his own daughter?"

"He said that, if Jennie went against him, he would not leave her a dollar of his money."

[Ormsby became concerned that Mrs. Harris was getting too angry and her persona might turn the jurors against the case. He tried changing direction.] "Did you ask Billings how he spent his money?"

"I asked him if he gave Mrs. Curtis $50 to commence her slander suit."

"What did Mr. Billings say to this charge?"

"He said Mrs. Curtis would come on to him in court and would probably take $1,000 or $2,000 out of him."

"Were there any other words between the two of you?"

"I asked him why he put chloroform under my Eliza's noise and tried to strangulate her while she was asleep."

"How did he respond to these allegations?"

"He said, 'why aunty, what sharp darts; they go through me like an arrow'."

"How ever did you respond?"

"I told him I was not his aunty."

"Were any other charges made?"

"I accused him of the kerosene affair. I told him about the marks on her arm and face." [The anger and hostility of the older woman was piercing the courtroom.]

"Did you say anything about your daughter leaving him?"

"I told him that, after the slander suit, she would not live with him any longer."

"How did he answer this threat?"

"He said no one would swear against him as he controlled more than any other four families in town." [It is not clear what circumstances would cause anyone to swear against Billings, so it would seem Mrs. Harris was trying to offset the witnesses for Billings who were to follow. The prosecution always tried to put forth that Billings bought some of the witnesses.]

"Did Billings make any explanation of how the marks came to be on Mrs. Billings?"

"He said she 'stunned' (stoned) the bank. Then he also remarked that she had no business to interfere with him. He said it was 'cause she stunned the building that the marks came to be on her arms."

"What did he say when you were making those charges?"

"He kept saying; 'No more of them sharp darts. They go through me like arrows'."

"He made no defense for his behavior?"

"He said Eliza had no business coming to me with her complaints."

"Are you aware of any other problems between your daughter and Mr. Billings?"

"Billings caught Eliza one time up in the chamber. Billings said to my daughter, 'Now I've got you up stairs and diseased you. It is all I care for you'." [The reference was to a charge that Billings deliberately infected his wife with venereal disease.]

"Surely Billings responded to these charges."

"Billings said, 'You've got me where the hair is short'."

111

"He only said, 'you've got me'?"

"His face was red, and I told him that showed guilt."

"What did he do then?"

"He covered his face."

"He didn't defend his reputation?'

"All he said was Eliza had no business to come here with her talk."

Ormsby had pursued that issue far enough; he wanted to get to the relations between the mother-in-law and Billings, "Did he make any accusations against you?"

"Mr. Nelson was there when he arrived. He asked why such men came here."

"And what did you tell him?"

"I said to get money or pay interest."

"Is that all he said about you and men?'

"I asked if he had been calling his wife's mother names, and he said he had."

"What did you do when he accused you of illicit behavior?"

"I took a Bible and put it on his knee." [Sitting up proudly Mrs. Harris continued.] "Then I put my hand on it and told him, 'So help me God, I never knew any other man but my husband either before or after his death.' Then I asked him to do the same." [The smirk on Billings's face was obvious to the entire jury.]

"Did he so swear?"

"He said, 'You can't catch me in such a trap'."

"Did he say what would happen to your daughter?"

"He said Eliza would die in an insane asylum."

"What did you say when he said this?"

"I told him I thought he would die in a State Prison."

[Ormsby knew it was time to calm things down.] "How long was Mr. Billings's visit that day?"

"I think he was there an hour and a half."

"Did he talk about the note he had signed for your daughter?"

"He said that there was not a dollar that belonged to her."

"Did you agree that, all that the family had was his?"

"No. I asked him about the horse her brother had left her. He said he had sold her horse and traveled with the money."

As Mrs. Harris concluded her direct testimony, it was apparent that both she and the prosecution team felt that they had covered the points they wanted to make. It was now in evidence that there were serious differences between Billings and the entire Harris family. The root of the problems was Billings's "god," money. The difficulties had apparently become so intense that Billings did not want his wife to seek the counsel of her mother. Ormsby also believed that he had shown Billings was involved in illicit relations, since he would not swear, on a Bible, to his innocence.

Cross   Hughes appeared elated as he stood to begin his cross examination. Hughes knew that such hostile witnesses were easy to question. He had a series of traps in mind, so he began with easy questions. After all, he did not want to be perceived as some kind of demon attacking a grieving mother.

"I am the widow of John Harris."

Hughes continued the pretense of being solicitous. "When did your daughter and Mr. Billings marry?"

"The year my daughter married Billings was twenty two years ago last January."

"Was there any litigation between any of your children?"

"There was some litigation between Eliza and her brother, John."

"I see." Hughes observed, knowing he had demonstrated that there were also problems within the Harris clan.

"When did you first see the mark on your daughter's forehead?"

"I saw the mark on her forehead about three years after her marriage."

"Where were your daughter and Mr. Jesse Billings married?"

[During the summer, the newspapers had carried articles which implied that the two had run off and that the marriage was not condoned by Mrs. Harris.]

"My daughter married at our house."

"And where did the two of them reside after the marriage?"

"Billings and my daughter stayed with me about two months after they were married."

"When did they move out of your house?"

"They went to keeping house in June or July." [six months not two]

113

"Mrs. Harris, isn't it true that your daughter often stayed away from your house for long periods, sometimes even more than a year?"

"After her marriage, there was never a time that she left my house and stayed away for a year."

"After her marriage, did your daughter ever travel out of the area?"

"She went up to her grandfather's, near Syracuse"

"Wasn't her stay there for months?"

"I will swear she was not away a month."

"If she didn't stay away a year, how often did Mrs. Billings visit you?"

"She usually came to my house two or three times a year." [The families only lived three miles apart.]

"When did Mr. Billings buy his home for your daughter to live in?"

"I think Billings bought his place the year after he was married."

"Did your daughter ever work at keeping house before her marriage?"

"She had not kept house before they went into that house."

"Did you see your daughter on the day she died?"

"I was at my daughter's house about 4 o'clock on June 4."

"Had your daughter been about her place that day?"

"She reported to me she was at Schuylerville that day."

"Did you see Mr. Billings at his house?"

"I saw Billings when he came for tea."

"Did you join him for tea?"

"It was after I had had my tea."

"Did Jesse ask you to join him?"

"When Billings sat down at 6, he asked me, 'Aunty won't you sit down and take supper with me'?"

"And did you accept his offer?"

"I told him I had already taken mine."

"What did you do after you left the Billings house?"

"I left for Schuylerville about 6."

"Did you stop at the Billings place again that day?"

"I returned to the door of Billings's house about 7."

"How long were you inside on your second visit?"

"I didn't go in. I talked with my daughter at the gate for about five minutes."

"Did you see Mr. Billings when you came the second time?"

"No, I did not see Billings there."

"After you left the Billings's, where did you go?"

"I went from there directly home."

"When did you reach your house?"

"I reached my place about half past eight." [The jurors all knew there was no way it would take an hour and a half (7 till 8:30) to go three miles.]

"How long after you got home did you hear the news about your daughter?"

"I was home about ten minutes when I heard what had happened to my daughter."

"How did you hear?"

"Charles Cramer told me." [Cramer was seen by Reed leaving the murder scene after the shot, somewhere around 8:40. If Mrs. Harris was to be believed with respect to all aspects of her testimony, then Cramer covered in ten minutes, the same distance she covered in an hour and a half.]

"What did you do when you heard?"

"I immediately returned to the Billings house."

"What time was it when you got back to the Billings place?"

"Don't know exactly what time I got there."

"Don't you carry a watch?"

"I carry a watch."

"Why didn't you check your watch?"

"I was much excited and paralyzed with fear."

"Did you see Billings when you got back?"

"I did not see Billings there that night."

"What did you do when you got to the house?"

"I went upstairs."

[Hughes had made his point that Mrs. Harris picked when she would be exact about time and when she would only estimate. He changed direction going after her direct testimony.]

"Mrs. Harris, when was the last time you saw Mr. Billings drive by your house without calling?"

"Can't remember the last time I saw Billings drive past my house without calling."

"How many times in the past five years has he passed without stopping?"

"Within the past five years, I don't recall that he passed without calling."

"But did you testified that he passed without calling?"

"I said that because I have heard of his passing."

"You recalled the litigation between your children, Eliza and John; who did Mr. Billings support?"

"At the time of the litigation between Eliza and John, Billings acted on behalf of his wife and against John."

"How did the family react to the litigation?"

"Some feelings grew between Billings and John."

"What was the nature of their feelings?"

"The feelings grew out of the law matters."

"Didn't Mr. Billings speak well when he came to your home that day?"

"When calling on June 4, he spoke well enough, but he showed anger in his voice."

"What was it that he called you at his visit?'

"He called me aunty'." [At this time 'aunty' was an informal term used as an endearment.]

"Was that the first time he ever called you that?"

"He often called me that."

"Did Mr. Billings remark about your house?"

"He spoke about my place looking so nice."

"Didn't you show him around your house?"

"He asked to look around my place."

"Did you show him around?"

"I showed him around and told him who was in the pictures."

"Was this tour before or after dinner?"

"This was after dinner."

[Having established that the words between them at dinner did not result in a total discord, Hughes pushed home the point that the situation was not evil.] "Out of respect for Mr. Billings, didn't you move your table setting for dinner?"

Reluctantly, Mrs. Harris admitted that she had set her table over in another room after Billings arrived.

"In your conversation with Billings, who brought up Eliza and Jennie?"

"I asked Billings how Eliza and Jennie were. He said they were out late last night. He said they did not get home until 11 o'clock the night before."

"Did you respond to his comment?"

"Think I told him it might not have been so late."

"At dinner, did you talk to him about a man having concubines?"

"I might have told him about a man in Oneida County who had concubines in the house, and that man had cut his own throat."

"How did that story deal with Mr. Billings"

"I said that Billings would yet cut his own throat."

"Did Mr. Billings respond to this charge?"

"Billings said he would not cut his own throat, but he thought Eliza would die in an insane asylum."

"After this discussion, what did you say?"

"I told him next about the chloroform."

"How many times previous to this visit had you brought up your daughter's claim that he had used chloroform?"

"I had never spoke to him of the chloroform until that day."

"How long before that day had this chloroform incident happened?" [The contempt in Hughes voice was obvious.]

"It was eight years after it happened."

"So you brought it up because you had just heard about it?"

"I heard about it four or five years before I told it to him."

"Remind me; how did Mr. Billings respond to the charge?"

"At the time, Billings spoke about things going through him like darts."

"Mrs. Harris, isn't it not the case that Mr. Billings was laughing as he answered?"

"I will swear he was not laughing."

"Did you bring up Mrs. Curtis, or just other women in general?"

"I mentioned Mrs. Curtis to him by name."

"What exactly did you say about Mrs. Curtis?"

"I asked him why he kept her over the bank."

117

"What did he say?"

"He said she was a decent woman."

"Mrs. Harris, of what religion are you?"

"I was a member of the Presbyterian church."

"How much do you provide to that fine church?"

"I do not now support the church."

"What did Mr. Billings say about Mrs. Curtis going to church?"

"He said Mrs. Curtis was a member of the church."

"What did Mr. Billings suggest you should do with Eliza?"

"I think he said I might give Eliza some good advice."

"Then all he asked was that you give her advice?"

"He wanted me to take her away as she was injuring his business."

[Hughes was enjoying his ability to get Mrs. Harris to reflect hostility in her voice.] "What did you ask Mr. Billings about the kerosene incident?"

"I told him he had tried to burn up my daughter and his house."

"How many times did you bring up the kerosene incident before?"

"I had not spoken to him about it before."

"So this was the first time you ever brought up the incident?"

"I might have alluded to it before."

"How had he acted when it was spoken of before?"

"There was something said, and he rather denied it."

"Mrs. Harris, when you talked of the incident, didn't Mr. Billings explain that it was an accident?"

"He never said it was an accident, or that he accidentally tipped over the lamp."

"In what papers was the incident reported?"

"There was not much said about it. It was kept rather quiet."

"Knowing of all these incidents, surely you entered a complaint with some magistrate?"

"I did not enter a complaint against him before any magistrate."

"How did the marks on Eliza's arm enter the conversation?"

"I asked him about the marks on her arms."

"Did he admit the marks?"

"He said he did it to scare her and get her to stop stunning the bank."

"When did you tell him you heard about the marks on her arm?"

"I never told Billings I had heard of the marks. I said, that I had *seen* the marks."

"When did you hear the story about Billings and your daughter in the chamber?"

"Heard about him taking her upstairs in January last."

"At dinner, what remarks did you make about that incident?"

"I told him that I knowed he told her he had diseased her and that was all he cared for her."

"What did he say to that charge?"

"He said, 'You have me where the hairs are short'."

"Mrs. Harris, didn't Mr. Billings deny the whole story?"

"He did not deny the imputation for himself or his wife." [Mrs. Harris continued quickly.] "His face turned scarlet and I told him it showed guilt."

"Mrs. Harris, if you knew of these incidents, why didn't you address them sooner?"

"This was a delicate matter for me to talk about then or now."

"Mrs. Harris, have you ever seen a man blush before?"

"I have seen a man blush before."

"At dinner, did you accuse Mr. Billings of calling you names?"

"I asked him why he called me bad names. I wanted to know if it was to irritate Eliza."

"Mrs. Harris, where were you able to find the Bible?"

"My Bible was where I can handle it every day."

"Remind the court what you did with the Bible."

"I laid it upon his lap. I laid my hand on the Bible and declared my innocence."

"What did he say about you that caused you to want to swear on a Bible?"

"I won't say the word he said; it ain't decent."

"So you swore your innocence?"

"I swore my innocence; I'm a good woman."

"What did you do next?"

"I asked him to swear the same."

"And what did he say?"

"He said, 'You won't get me to swear to this'."

To show that they talked about topics other than each others flaws, Hughes asked, "Did he ask you about your paper mill?"

"He may have said something that day about the paper mill business. I don't recall either way."

"Why would he want to know about the mill business?'

"There is water power on my farm." [Her pride was obvious.]

"Didn't Mr. Billings come back in after he had gotten to his horse?'

"He did not come after he got his horse," Mrs. Harris said defiantly.

"What were his last words that day?"

"The last thing he said before going away was that Eliza would die in an insane asylum."

"And how did you reply?"

"I replied that he would die in a State Prison."

"At dinner did you and Mr. Billings talk about anything else?"

"The selling of her horse and spending the money was talked about."

"Mrs. Harris, did you testify before the Coroner's Jury?"

"Yes, I testified before the Coroner's Jury."

"When was the Coroner's Jury?"

"That was in the same week that I had my talk with him."

"Mrs. Harris, did you tell the Coroner's Jury of your conversations?"

"I repeated the conversation there."

"Did you testify that Billings said he would kill Jennie and Eliza with trouble?"

"I think I testified there that Billings would kill Jennie and Eliza with trouble."

"At the Coroner's Jury did you speak about the chloroform?"

"I testified before about the chloroform."

"Did you speak of the kerosene affair."

"Yes."

"Did you tell the Coroner's Jury about the chamber affair?"

"No."

"Did you tell the Coroner's Jury about the insane asylum?"

"No."

"Did you tell the Coroner's Jury about saying that Mr. Billings would die in a State Prison."

"No. I weren't asked." [Her animosity was building.]

"Mrs. Harris, where has Jennie been since June fourth?"

"Since the murder, Jennie has been most of the time with her aunt."

"How has Jennie been faring since she has been with her aunt?"

"She has not been well since her mother's death."

"Did you report about the darts to the Coroner's Jury?"

"Not as I recall."

"Have you seen newspaper reports about your daughter being worth a lot of money?"

"I have seen newspaper statements that my daughter was worth $40,000."

"Did you make any effort to deny the report?"

"We did not deny it."

As he returned to his seat, Hughes felt he had made the point on her credibility. He was able to show the blind that she had manipulated the media to make her points, that her recollections were in the manner that suited her. Sitting down, he thought that the humble Mrs. Harris was not someone from whom he would want to borrow money.

Re-dir.   Moak was in charge of the redirect examination. With Mrs. Harris painted in dark colors, it was essential that he, at the very least paint Billings the in same color.

"What was Billings like when, at dinner in your home, he accused you of being mean?"

"On June 4 when he accused me of being mean, he showed anger."

"What were the signs that he was angry?"

"His eyes were bloodshot, and his face was red as blood."

"Did he tell you he was a wealthy man or that he didn't need Eliza's money?"

"No. He said his business was not paying him."

"Mrs. Harris, was Billings good natured?"

"He was not good natured."

"What was he like at dinner?"

"He was cross."

121

"How could you tell he was cross?"

"His looks were against him."

"Were his eyes usually bloodshot?"

"I never saw his eyes look as bloodshot so much as that time."

Re-Cross Although Hughes always enjoyed examining the oppositions witnesses, he found Mrs. Harris provided a special pleasure.

"Mrs. Harris, when did you first notice Mr. Billings's eyes?"

"I noticed his eyes when he came in."

"It was a hot sunny day; didn't that usually cause his face to be red?"

"His face was uncommonly red."

"Did his face change during dinner?"

"His face changed at times."

"Wasn't Jesse good natured when you took him into the parlor to look at the pictures?"

"His manner was not exactly good-natured while in the parlor."

"Did Billings ever tell you to cut off the tap to his wife?"

"When Billings took Eliza away (after six months of marriage), he told me to give her all I was going to and then cut off the tap, for she shouldn't come back, and he would not have any of those damned Harrises about him."

Re-Dir. Moak needed to be sure that one possible motive was wealth, so he returned to Mrs. Billings's inheritances.

"How was your son, William's property divided?"

"The property got divided up among my children."

"How much did your daughter get?"

"Eliza got about $1,200 to $1,400."

Lizzie Hill

Lizzie Hill was eleven years old when she testified. There was a lengthy debate as to whether, based on her age, she was competent to testify in a murder trial. Judge Landon, in words he would later lament, said that he enjoyed hearing the testimony of children since they were usually the most truthful.

Lizzie Hill, Mrs. Harris's ward, was at the house when Jesse Billings came to visit on the day of the murder. Her testimony, regarding what had transpired during that lunch was virtually the same as that of Mrs. Harris.

There are a few noteworthy points in Lizzie's testimony. The defense pushed the young girl to admit that she had been taken from the poor house in Washington County by Mrs. Harris. As was common at the time, Mrs. Harris provided room, board and clothing for her ward, but received the services of a young servant. In her testimony, Lizzie acknowledged that she was responsible for doing the laundry, and dishes, setting the table, and making lunch. The intention was to make Mrs. Mary Harris appear to be a user.

When asked the exact language which had been used at the lunch between Mrs. Harris and Billings, Lizzie refused to answer in court. She agreed to whisper the words to the judge who rephrased them for the record.

Lizzie assured the court that she had not been coached as to what to say in court. To challenge her statement, the defense repeatedly asked Lizzie to repeat portions of her testimony. She reacted like a tape recorder giving verbatim answers as if from a script.

Mary Ann Lynch

Dir. Mary, like Lizzie Hill, was a young housekeeper. Mary, although only 14 at the time she testified, had worked and lived in the Billings household on two occasions totaling eleven weeks. The second time she worked for the Billingses was during the period of February-March, 1878. Mary testified that she had heard Mrs. Billings ask Billings "not to visit Mrs. Curtis so much." She also testified that she had heard Billings say to his wife, "Mrs. Curtis was as far ahead of her as God is above an Injin."

Cross Mary testified that she had heard Mrs. Billings refer to Mrs. Curtis as Billings's "posy-pot", "dolly varden", "rosebush" and "rosebud". Mary also said that she had heard Billings tell Jennie to visit Mrs. Curtis and to apologize for her mother. According to Miss Lynch, Jennie responded that, "she would not call on Mrs. Curtis if she was the last woman in town." Miss Lynch also admitted that Mrs. Billings did not want Sam Philo around, since as he did nothing and was intoxicated a lot. As Miss Lynch put it there were "troubles" between Philo and Mrs. Billings.

She had heard Jennie tell her father that if anything happened to her mother, she would spend every dollar on revenge. According to

123

Miss Lynch, she never saw Billings chase Mrs. Billings. Miss Lynch said that if Billings entered a room, Mrs. Billings would leave the room and if it was dinner time, Mrs. Billings would take food on a tray in another room. Miss Lynch never saw Billings lay a hand on his wife in anger.

Day 8

Each day as Billings entered the court, he was met by a general stare from a curious audience. He met their gazes, not with bravado, but with the appearance of a man consumed by a set of circumstances which were beyond his control. Billings's behavior was in strict contrast to that of the lawyers from both sides who were always in the room early trying their best to impress the consistently large crowd. Although Billings seemed a little nervous, as if overly sensitive to the surroundings imposed upon him, he was generally solemn. To those present, Billings seemed neither defiant nor despondent before the tribunal.

The Ballston Spa <u>Journal</u> described him in the true style of 1878 in their first set of court notes September 18, 1878. Nothing is put on for effect, and those who look upon him begin to doubt whether a monster, equal to the dark crime of murder, can dwell in such a human form. His countenance is open and attractive, indicating intelligence, ability, and general good qualities. Out of court he would be viewed as a gentleman of prepossessing appearance and manners. It remains to be seen by the developments in court whether a fair exterior covers a fiendish nature.

Cornelius Markum

Dir. The chief detective on the police force of the city of Troy, Cornelius Markum, was the thirtieth witness called in the trial. He came to the murder scene at the request of the coroner, who paid the city of Troy $10 for his services. Markum arrived at the Billings's home on Wednesday afternoon, the day after the murder. He spent that afternoon following the tracks. On direct, Markum testified that Thursday was spent examining tracks with Wolf and Pennock. He found scattered tracks leading toward the hill (away from Billings's house), along the Reed's side of the fence. Markum stated that these tracks were very far apart. When the tracks reached Billings's cornfield they were both in the first row away from the fence and two feet apart indicating that the person was walking.

The tracks stopped several times, as if the person had stopped to look back or to listen. He said the tracks in the Billings's flower bed were three feet apart. When they tried to fit the boot to the track, it was a perfect fit; however, they were not able to find a single track where there was an imprint of the frog or the tap that was on the bottom of Billings's boot. Markum went on to say that they were not able to make a frog when they tried to make an imprint with Billings's boot. The tracks in the garden that Billings admitted to making, in his testimony before the Coroner's Jury, were a perfect fit, and the heel tap could be seen.

Cross   Markum testified that he visited the well alone on Thursday evening after hearing from Chase and Carey about its discovery. Markum had crossed the fence to the west of the well and said that there were tracks in the grass leading to the well, as if someone had been there, but he did not look closely enough to swear that the person had actually gone to the well. He noted that the person who had been there previously had approached from the west. (the opposite direction of the Billings house). He noted that the well was covered by three boards but did not notice that any had been disturbed. There was a gap between two of the boards about 2 1/2 inches in width.

The feeling of the reporters was that Markum's testimony swung both ways. He did follow tracks that matched the size of Billings's boots; however, the tracks in the cornfield could have been made by Officer Durkee, who testified previously that he had walked the exact same path.

Charles Leet

Dir.   The first expert witness, who had never been to the scene was called by the prosecution. He was Charles Leet, a 55-year-old manufacturer of metallic cartridges from Springfield, Massachusetts. Leet's testimony revolved around four areas: the distance from a gun that the residue of powder can be found, the shape of the hole in the window, the bullet found in Mrs. Billings, and the power of a bullet fired from a .44 caliber carbine.

Leet testified, based on marks on the ball that the bullet was a .44 caliber cast ball cartridge. He also stated that the bullets made for a .44 caliber weighed 220 grams. Leet said that there were specially-made cartridges in which the lead weighs 165 grams, although nearly all available cartridges weighed 220 grams. Upon firing the gun found in the well into pine boards or logs the average wastage was 10 to 12 percent. [Following Leet's example a 220 gram ball would then weigh between 193 and 198 grams, while a 165 gram ball would weigh between 146 and 149 grams.] The defense was able to show that he had made his test on wood, not on flesh and bone, so the wastage could be different.

The hole in the window was keyholed, according to Leet. Keyholing could occur in two ways. Either the bullet was fired at an angle to the window (a bullet shot directly at a window will create a circular hole), or if the bullet canted. Canting occurs when a bullet turns in flight. He testified that, at the request of the district attorney, he had tested the gun found in the well, and, because it was dirty, at 50 to 100 feet, the bullets always canted.

There had a debate about if powder residue was present on the window sill or glass. Existence of powder would imply the weapon was a pistol. According to Leet, residue of powder can be found up to 40 or 50 feet away from where a shot is fired. He stated that none of the powder found at that distance would still burn. He had made this observation by spreading paper along the trail a bullet would follow.

Cross Under cross examination, Leet pointed out that a .44 caliber carbine fired at 500 yards could put a ball through eight to eleven pine boards. At 50 feet it would go through thirteen boards.

Hughes was able to manipulate the witness into stating that all the lead from the bullet should be found in Mrs. Billings's head. When Leet talked of finding the lead in Mrs. Billings's head, Mrs. Harris covered her eyes and cried. Billings leaned forward intent on Leet's words.

Thomas McConakey

Dir. Another out-of-town officer who came to Fort Miller Bridge to take part in the investigation was Thomas McConakey. McConakey, an officer in Waterford, arrived on Wednesday, but did not take part in the investigation until Thursday. McConakey's contribution was threefold. He testified like so many previous witnesses that he also had observed the tracks. He also indicated the number of people who were walking around the crime scene. Among those he named who were looking for tracks on Thursday were: Reed, Baucus, Ward, Wolf, Markum, and Parker. He further said that, although it was Thursday before he took part in the investigation, he was the first to notice the imprint of a frog that appeared in two of the footprints.

Cross McConakey's testimony basically follows Markum's with respect to the tracks near the Billings garden. He concurred that there was only one pair of tracks that ran on Reed's side of the fence. McConakey added that he tried on one of Billings's boots and then stepped into the soft earth. He testified that the imprint he made contained the frog in sole of the boot.

Thomas Ward

On Wednesday, before eight in the morning, Ward, whose term as an officer had expired, joined Durkee and Woodward in looking for tracks. They "discovered tracks leading to the swale near Reed's property and the mud on the fence. Under cross examination, he denied that Durkee had told him at the time that the footprint on the fence was his. Ward and Woodworth then went up to the Finne Lane (the one Billings claimed to use). There he noted the horse track coming down the lane. The distance between tracks was 5 feet 10 inches, which he interpreted as an "ordinary gait".

Ward told the court that he had served a summons on Mr. Curtis in November of the previous year. When he got to the door, Mrs. Curtis answered. Mr. Curtis was across the river, but Billings was there. He said the door was open but he did not go in.

Mrs. Amanda Palmer

Dir. Amanda, the wife of William Palmer, a lock keeper on the canal, testified on both the eighth and ninth days of the trial. Mrs. Palmer was 28 at the time and perceived by both sides as a neutral witness. She and her husband resided in the fifth house north of Billings. She did not hear the shot, but she did hear the screaming. Amanda was present when Billings came into the sitting room and said, "Oh! my wife." She added that he "then got down at her feet."

Amanda testified that Jennie came over and said to her father, "This is a pretty time for you to fall at momma's feet, when you have done this cruel deed." Amanda told Moak that Billings asked to have Jennie taken from the room.

Cross Amanda added that Jennie had been moaning and grieving for some time before Billings asked that she be taken from the room. His request for her removal was not a result of Jennie's comment to him. Under cross and redirect she was asked if the words which she claimed that Jennie had said were correct, since they differed from those in other reports. Amanda held that these words were the ones used by Jennie that night.

Amanda also testified that Jennie had said that she saw a man in slouch hat run out of the yard and across the street.

Re-dir. Moak had Amanda repeat the statement that Jennie had made her remarks about the running man while she was "very much excited."

John Hammond

Dir. Hammond resided near Bacon Hill with his father, Edward. John stated that he was with Sam Philo the night of the murder. Hammond assured the court that Sam went to bed some time between 8 and 10 o'clock. He thought it was closer to 8. John saw Sam the next morning before he (Sam) arose.

Cross Hughes was mild in his examination. Hammond admitted that, the shortest way from his home to Billings's was across the fields by way of the same lane, that Billings said he used to get to his back fields.

Day 9

This day was a treat for the spectators. It had been rumored that the prosecution was approaching the close of its case and needed to put Jennie back on the stand. Anticipating Jennie's return, spectators packed the room to its limits. In the middle of the room, sitting in a plain, light brown dress trimmed in red and a stylish hat was Mrs. Emma Curtis. When her identity was discovered, a general murmur arose in the room. Noticing the nudging and murmurs at her side, Mrs. Curtis turned and directly faced one of her detractors. Emma's eyes did not flinch from those of the other woman until she had compelled her to look down. Mrs. Curtis confused her critics even more when she helped to calm the small baby of a woman sitting next to her.

As a result of her presence, everyone admired the delicate woman who had been implicated throughout the testimony. Emma's small features, bright blue eyes and clear complexion were the envy of every woman in the room. When compared to her husband, Mrs. Curtis was considered to be the "better man of the two."

Sam Philo was a stark contrast to the beautiful Mrs. Curtis. Overall, Sam was considered as harmless as a child. Philo was a wiry man, strong as a mule, who had spent his life as a farm hand. Even in the court, his hair and beard were uncombed. It was understood that he spent more time with tanglefoot than with women. Strong drink was the company of his life. He was blessed with a gift for retaining the memories and stories of a small town. For a bottle of strong whiskey, Sam would supply the reporters with the complete background of each witness. Unfortunately, as the evening wore on, and for no additional charge, Sam included the history of each witness's horse, dog and marriage.

Mrs. Amanda Palmer recalled
Re-cross Hughes asked that the handsome Mrs. Palmer be recalled. The defense wanted to be sure that the jury heard again the recollections of one of the few witnesses who might be perceived as neutral. Amanda again stated that on the night of the murder she had hurried to the Billings house where she had seen Jennie almost immediately. Jennie told her that she had seen, "A man run from the yard across the road and around the lumber pile." Amanda was certain that Jennie said she thought, "the man had a slouch hat on." Mrs. Palmer insisted that what she had testified were the words actually used by Jennie on the night of the murder.
Re-dir. Moak understood the danger that existed with Mrs. Palmer's testimony. On re-direct he brought out the fact that Jennie was, "Very much hysterical at the time." Amanda assured the court that the words used by Jennie were also not directed at anyone, but rather spoken in a loud voice to all who were gathered in the room. Although Moak pressed several times, Amanda would not say that Jennie only said that she saw a shadow.

Miss Ella (Eliza) Ward
Dir. Miss Ward had moved to a house in Schuylerville from a house on the river south of Finnes' store. The house she had occupied in Fort Miller Bridge was across the street and a little north of Billings's businesses. She said that one morning in March, at about 8:30, she watched Mrs. Curtis go into the Billings Bank building. According to Miss Ward, "a little while later I watched as Billings entered the bank." Referring to Billings and Mrs. Curtis she said, "They stayed some time."

Mrs. Ward went on to say that, while the two were in the bank, he had watched two men go to the bank, "turn the knob and try to get in, and then go away." One half hour later, Billings left, followed shortly afterward by Mrs. Curtis. Ormsby had finally put on a witness who supported his contention that Billings was involved with Mrs. Curtis.

Cross   Hughes was inexplicably confident as he approached the witness. In his most nurturing tones, he got Ella to admit that she lived in a home owned by Finne. She also said that she had seen Mrs. Curtis enter the building on other occasions. Reluctantly, Ella acknowledged that she was aware of the fact that Mrs. Curtis was in charge of keeping the bank. The hint of a smile was present in the corners of Hughes's lips as Miss Ward told of standing at the window watching the events of the morning. The trap snapped when Miss Ward said that Mrs. Billings was in the sitting room with her at the time of the incident. Miss Ward was not neutral, but obviously imbedded in one of the camps. [The prosecution was nearly complete and Miss Ward was the only witness placed on the stand who could be considered a friend of Mrs. Billings]

David Prosser

Dir.   Prosser of Schuylerville was one of the numerous curiosity seekers who had wandered around the Billings property in the days following the murder. Prosser was with Marcus Cary when he went to the well on the Thursday following the murder. They had picked up one of the boards covering the opening of the well and looked inside. The water was within 4 to 5 feet of the ground. The two men talked about the advisability of placing a board across those already in place.

Cross   Utilizing the skills he had shown previously, Hughes turned this prosecution witness into one for the defense. Prosser said that at the time he was at the well, on Thursday afternoon, there were no tracks other than the ones made by Cary and himself. Prosser also said that the boards covering the well had not been disturbed prior to his arrival. Prosser added that he had examined the fence and saw no marks indicating that someone had climbed over.

Re-dir.   The only recovery possible for Ormsby occurred when Prosser assured the court that there was grass near the fence that could have wiped the mud from the shoes of anyone who might have climbed the fence.

Andrew Ball

Dir.   Ball told the jury that he was in Billings's store for a "big hour" prior to hearing the screams. During that entire time John Sherman was within his sight. As Andrew remembered it, John Sherman preceded him out the door when they heard the screams.

Miss Jennie Billings returns to the stand

Jennie had been sequestered in a room on the second floor prior to her testimony. As happened the first time, she was led by Mr. Foley and her grandmother. Every eye in the court was fixed on the procession as they entered.

Cross   Undaunted, General Hughes resumed the cross examination. "I have learned you have been ill since you were here before?"

"Yes." [Her voice weak.]

"Do you feel able to be examined this morning, Miss Billings?"

"I will try."

Jennie then went on to explain her conversation with her mother regarding the fire: "At the time my mother accused him about the kerosene, she said he was trying to burn her up. After that, she said, 'how came the fire to be at my bedroom door'?"

"Did you hear your father say that he had tipped over the lamp and that the oil splattered on the board and set in on fire?"

"I did not. All I heard him say was he tipped over a lamp." [Jennie was obviously sullen and stubborn.]

"State for the court the first difficulty you can remember between your father and mother; can you please state the circumstances."

"That would be about the chloroform."

"And what was the next incident?"

"The kerosene fire."

"Where there any others?"

"The next was about Mrs. Curtis."

"When was it that the difficulties between your parents shifted to Mrs. Curtis?"

"That would have been in January last."

"How is the date fixed in your mind?"

"I went with father to New York in January."

"Do you know when in January?"

131

"Around the 18th."

"How long were the two of you in New York?"

"We were there about a week."

"Do you recall if the problems over Mrs. Curtis first grew out of the clerks' calling there?"

"I don't recall."

"Was the bank finished when Mr. and Mrs. Curtis moved into the building?"

"I think it had not yet been completed."

"Can you tell the court when Mrs. Curtis first began doing work around the bank?"

"I am not certain as to the day."

"When did the trouble over Mrs. Curtis begin between your mother and father?"

"Not until after we returned from New York."

"How are you certain it was after you returned and not before?"

"Father had found fault with a girl mother was keeping. She let her go while we were away. When we got home, father said to mother, 'Becky, how are you getting along?' Mother was angry and said, 'What kind of place are you keeping over the bank'?"

"How did your father answer?"

"I don't know what he said."

"If you were there, how could you not recall?"

"I was not present when they had the conversation." [Hughes caught Jennie testifying to facts to which she was not a witness.]

"Were you away much of February and March?"

"I don't know if I was away much of the time."

"Do you recall any conversations between your mother and father about the clerks spending time with Mrs. Curtis?"

"I remember something about mother complaining to father when we got back from New York."

"After you got home from New York, did you hear your mother apply any names to Mrs. Curtis?"

"I don't understand you."

"Did you ever hear your mother speak from the house to your father when he was out of doors, something perhaps about Mrs. Curtis?"

"Yes."

132

"Would Mrs. Curtis have been able to hear?"

"Yes, quite probably."

"Did your father ever ask you to apologize to Mrs. Curtis for what your mother said?"

"I don't remember."

"Have you ever heard your father's name used lightly with other women except Mrs. Curtis in all your life?"

"I have. I heard about it when I was in New York."

[Sensing that Jennie was being less than truthful, Hughes pressed on:] "Where were you in New York when you heard it?"

"I don't recall."

"How many years ago were you told of your father being with a woman?"

"I have no recollection of the year."

Was it a man or woman that told you that your father had been intimate with women in New York?"

"I don't recall."

"If it was a gentleman, was it a young man?"

"I don't think I would converse with a young gentleman about such subjects." [Jennie knew the rules of Victorian society.]

"Did you ever hear anything about your father in the region?"

"Except for the Curtis woman, I have only heard what I told you about, in New York."

"Have you ever been out in society with your father?"

"Yes, I have."

"What was his manner when out?"

"My father's manner was pleasant and social. When he was with others, he was disposed to make merriment."

"Do you remember that when you were a little girl, he would repeat certain nursery rhymes?"

"Yes."

"Were some of these melodies of Mother Goose?"

"Yes, sir."

"Did one of them have a line like 'Dickey, Dickey, Dilver'?"

"Yes, he used to say that to me." [Jennie voice was bitter and cold. Her glare at Hughes was even more cutting than her tone.]

"Did you speak to your father on the day of the murder?"

133

"I recall that I said a word or two to father that day."

"Do you recall if he spoke pleasantly to you?"

"I don't remember now how he spoke."

"Did you generally speak to your father when you saw him prior to that day?"

"I believe I spoke to him every time I saw him."

"When you spoke pleasantly to your father, did he not respond the same?"

"He would not always respond pleasantly to me."

"Can you give the court a time when your father did not speak pleasantly to you?"

"I can't tell any particular time."

"Did your father and mother talk often?"

"Not in the period before the murder."

"How long before the murder was it that your mother and father stopped talking?"

"I don't recall."

"Did they have any conversation within the month before the murder?"

"I believe they did."

"Did you see them have any conversation within the week before the murder?"

"Yes, I believe they did."

"Jennie, on the day you and your mother passed your father on the Grangerville road, did he have a load in the wagon?"

"I don't think my father was driving a load at the time."

"Do you recall if Van Tassel was with him?"

"I don't recall as Van Tassel was there."

"Who was driving your wagon?"

"I was driving our horse."

"Was your father sitting or standing in his wagon?"

"Father was sitting down." [When this testimony was given, those in the court understood how difficult it would be for someone sitting down in a wagon to swing a whip so as to hit a person on the far side of a wagon going in the other direction.]

"What words were exchanged as you passed?"

"Nothing was said, only what I have told."

134

"Would you repeat what was said?"

"Father said, 'Where are you dilfers going'?"

"That is all that happened?"

"No, I told you; he hit mother across the back with a whip."

"What did you say to his behavior?"

"I did not say anything, nor did mother."

"What did you do?"

"I drove right along at a good clip."

"When did this incident occur?

"Some time last spring after we had gotten back from New York."

"Didn't your buggy have a top?" [The implication was that the sides supporting the top would have prevented Mrs. Billings from being struck by a vehicle moving in the other direction.]

"No, as I recall it was the side bar wagon."

"Jennie, when did your father give you a horse?"

"As I recall, it was in 1876."

"Did he give you a carriage at the same time?"

"Yes.'

"Did he give you your own harness?"

"Yes, harness, robes, a complete outfit."

"Miss Billings, do you have a set of seal skins?"

"Yes."

"And how long have you had these seal skins?"

"About three or four years."

"Didn't your father drive the mustang regularly?"

"Father did not drive my horse, the mustang, much of late."

"On the night of the murder, did you see your father drive the mustang into the yard?"

"Yes, I saw him."

"Did you unharness the horse?"

"Yes, I wanted the barn cleared so I could drive my aunt's horse into the barn."

"Jennie, how many carriages could be put in the carriage house at a time?"

"Three or four, if you put them side by side."

"When you saw the mop board after the kerosene affair, was it blackened?"

135

"No. I supposed it was planed."

"Where in the room was the mop board located?"

"It was on the west side of the west bedroom door, off the sitting room."

"Was the board painted or varnished?"

"At the time, the boards were varnished, but they were painted some years ago."

"Was your father's house very well furnished?"

"Yes."

"What happened to the carpet on which the kerosene was spilled?"

"I believe it is still on the floor."

"Earlier you testified that your mother said to your father, 'What would Jennie do if you had burned me up?' How did your father respond to your mother?"

"I don't remember what he said."

"Did your mother ever say why your father set the fire?"

"Mother told me father said, he 'wanted to get the insurance money'."

"If your father desired money, why did he stop the fire?"

"He made her promise to give him some money."

"Your mother gave money to your father?"

"Yes, she told me 'that is how he got my $900'."

"Miss Billings, would you look at the mop board. Would you indicate where it was planed." [In response to Hughes, Jennie passed her hand over a small section of the board that was depressed from the rest. The entire area was less than a foot in length. Pointing to the short area, Hughes then sprang his previously concealed trap.] "Then these are the only marks about the house that imply your father tried to burn the house?"

Jennie did her best to recover. "I saw the spreads that were also damaged."

"Jennie, how did your mother recover from the chloroform?"

"Mother said that, on the night of the chloroform, she went to the door and gasped for breath."

"Jennie, didn't your mother have trouble with her breathing?"

"I never knew that my mother had any difficulties that affected her breathing at any time."

"On what occasions would your mother talk about the kerosene or chloroform?"

"It was when some difficulty sprang up between father and mother that she would allude to the chloroform and the fire."

"Did she bring up the chloroform and fire at other times?"

"Not to my knowledge."

"Where these two events the extent of the accusations made by your mother?"

"No; she said he tried to kick her."

"Where was she when he tried to kick her?"

"Mother was at the threshold of the hall door when father kicked at her."

"How did your mother respond?"

"She tried to get the door closed."

"What did your mother and father say to each other about the incident?"

"I don't remember that they said anything to each other."

"Miss Jennie, what month was it when the kicking incident occurred?"

"I have no memory of the month."

"Did your mother show you any marks?"

"No."

"Did you know Mr. Curtis?"

"Yes, when I saw him."

"Did you visit Mr. Curtis when he lived in the Reed's house?"

[Jennie was defiant as she informed Hughes:] "I was never in Curtis's house in my life, when he lived in Reed's house or elsewhere."

"Jennie, in what year did the difficulty with the pocketbook occur?"

"I do not remember the year."

"About how long ago was it?"

"It may have been ten years before mother's death. I don't know for sure."

"Jennie can you state positively that the pocketbook was the first difficulty that you remember between your mother and father?"

"Not positively."

"What happened with the pocketbook?"

"Father took mother's pocketbook and went out to the boat yard and paid some of the men from her money."

"Were you at home at the time?"

"I was on the grounds."

"How did your mother respond to your father having her pocketbook?"

"I think she insisted on having it back."

"Didn't your father return it to her?"

"He would not give it to her."

"Jennie, didn't your father say to your mother, 'You'll get your money back. I don't want to go to the bank.'?"

"Not that I recall."

"How long after the incident with the pocketbook was it when your mother sold some of your father's coal and didn't give the money to your father?"

"I can't say how long it was between."

"Was your father dealing in coal at the time?"

"Yes, he was."

"Did your mother keep some of the money from coal she had sold?"

"Yes."

"What happened when your father asked for his money from the coal?"

"Mother and father had a struggle for the money. Father took mother by the arm."

"Did your mother give him his money?"

"No, but after I saw marks on her arm." [Quickly Jennie added,] "They were black and blue."

"Miss Billings, did you ever see your father assault your mother before the time that she would not give him his money?"

"No, never before."

"Do you know the fact that the flesh of ladies will turn black and blue on slight pressure?"

[Arrogance showing, Jennie responded.] "There must be some pressure."

Moak interrupted, claiming that there was a great deal of difference in women regarding how fast they will get black and blue.

General Hughes, in his eminent style, replied in his loud voice, "That may be, and you, Mr. Moak, may know, but I stay about the house and have no experience in that kind of behavior."

Returning to Jennie's testimony, Hughes asked, "When was the first time your father ever said to your mother that she was one of those 'Damned Harrises'?"

"I have heard father say those words ever since I can remember. Whenever he was upset, he would say that mother was one of those 'damned Harrises.'"

"When your father said that phrase weren't there always difficulties between he and your mother first?"

"No, sometimes he would say it when mother had not said anything first."

"Did your father ever come home from a neighbors and say of the woman, 'She is a damned splendid woman'?"

"Sometimes father would say that."

In an attempt to demonstrate Billings was not pursuing young women Hughes asked, "Did your father ever say that of Mrs. George Washburn?"

"Yes, he said it of her."

"Does Mrs. Washburn have sons and daughters who are grown?"

"Yes, she does."

"Did your mother ever call for Mr. Washburn?"

"Yes, last winter."

"Why did your mother send for Mr. Washburn?"

"He is the Justice of the Peace and mother had trouble that night with Sam Philo."

"Did your father wish for your mother to work in the kitchen?"

"I don't know how he felt about her kitchen work."

"What did your mother say when your father claimed to be spending thousands of dollars on women while she worked in the kitchen?"

"I don't recall how mother responded."

"Do you remember if he said that the reason was because he was paying money to have work done out of the house that could have been done in the house?"

"I don't recall, but I don't think so."

"Were they talking about Mrs. Curtis at the time?"

"They may have been."

"How much work did you do in the kitchen?"

"I don't work about the kitchen."

"Last year, where did you travel with your father?"

"In 1877 we went to Canada, ...Ottawa."

"How long were you gone?"

"About a week or ten days."

"That same year did you go to New York?"

"Yes, in July."

"Did your father take you to the 'Centennial' in Philadelphia?"

"Yes, I went with him."

"Do you know a Mr. Durkee from Fort Edward?"

"Not that I can recall." [There was a story circulating throughout the community that Jennie had to leave the school at Fort Edward after she and a friend went for a ride with her cousin Cramer. The story was that they were drinking wine bought by Durkee.]

"Did you speak to your father when you returned from your uncle's wedding, when he came out to put the horse up?"

"I don't recall if I did or not."

"Did your mother speak to him?"

"I don't think mother spoke to him."

"What time was it when you got home from Saratoga Springs?"

"I am not sure, as to the time."

"What time was it when you saw your father drive out of the yard on the night of the murder?"

"I am not sure, some time after tea."

"Were there times when there were fun and pleasantry at the table?"

"Sometimes."

"Was your father fond of talking and joking at the table about any subject?"

"He would berate mother."

"Miss Billings, I asked was your father fond of talking and joking at the table about any subject?"

"Yes, he was fond of joking."

"Did your father ever say anything to your mother about drinking strong tea?"

"Yes, he would say it was another nail in her coffin."

"Who made your mother's tea?"

"Mother made teas expressly for herself."

"Did your father say her tea was making her nervous?"

"I never heard him say that."

Hughes was about to begin a series of questions about the night of the murder. He was only able to say, "On the night of the murder..." before Jennie broke down and cried in court. Hughes went over to L'Amoreaux and Billings for a brief consultation. They agreed they had made their points. Nobly, Hughes remarked that he did not wish to disturb the witness any further.

Re-dir. On redirect, Foley asked only one question., "Did you see a burn hole in the bedspread?"

"Yes when I returned from school."

Re-cross After only moments, the handling of this delicate witness was placed back in the hands of Hughes. During the intervening time Hughes had consulted with his client. "How long after the fire did you see the bed clothes?"

"I am not sure."

"Jennie, did you not understand that, when the call, "Fire!" went out, your father rushed into the vacant bedroom next to your mother's and pulled off the bedclothes to put out the fire?"

"I never heard him say so."

"Did you hear him say that he put it out?"

"Not that I recall."

"What kind of bedspread was used to extinguish the fire?"

"I am not an expert in bedspreads." [Jennie's tone expressed her belligerence.]

"Would you be able to tell if was wool or cotton?"

"Yes"

"Could you tell if a bedspread was quilted or not?".

"Yes." Hughes had made his point, Jennie, like her grandmother, had a very selective memory. He moved back to his chair and sat down. He was careful not to appear smug.

Unlike the first time that Jennie testified, Billings did not turn his chair. Rather, he leaned forward, placed his elbows on the table and rested his chin on his hands. He looked directly at Jennie. No emotion was evident neither anger, love nor frustration.

After seven days of testimony and thirty nine witnesses, Moak announced to the court that the prosecution rested. Before he turned the case over to the defense, Ormsby took the opportunity to remind the court that Jennie Billings was not a voluntary witness. She had not appeared before the grand jury until she was subpoenaed. It was only in obedience to a similar subpoena that she had testified before this court. Each person in the room judged for himself the credibility of this statement.

The reporters talked during a five minute break. They were trying to determine the exact word used by Billings toward Jennie and her mother. Some heard the word "dilfers"; other heard the word as "delfers"; still others believed that she said "duffers". An older man in the crowd was listening to the dialog. He approached the group and said that a delfer was a loose or bad kind of woman. After the morning's testimony, there was still no agreement but many felt that the word used by Billings was "dilvers"; referring to the nursery rhyme Billings had repeated to his daughter many years before.

Summary of the Prosecution

Through the People's testimony, the prosecution was able to establish some solid facts. They demonstrated that Billings owned a rifle that was found mysteriously in an abandoned well. The empty cartridge indicated the rifle had been fired. The family was in constant dispute. These points anyone in the court would have agreed were true.

The prosecution had failed to be conclusive on some other key areas. Billings may have been unaccounted for at the time of the shooting; but that didn't prove he was at the scene. Ormsby and Moak had not called Mrs. Curtis. They left the issue of an indiscreet relationship open to speculation. These gaps troubled the reporters covering the trial.

Other points had almost gone for the defense. It was clear Billings did not like his wife, but that is far short of feelings serious enough to pull the trigger and end her life. No witnesses were put on the stand that indicated Billings had ever used the rifle. The presence on the stand of Mrs. Harris and Jennie made many people feel sympathy for Billings. Events following the murder and before the trial such as the attempt, by Mrs. Harris to conscript Mrs. Passnow had gone badly for the prosecution. They had totally failed to find a single witness to testify that Billings hindered the investigation.

It was learned later that some of the defense attorneys wanted to end the trial without putting on a defense, holding that the prosecution had proven nothing. Billings insisted that they put on a strong defense.

The Defense Opens

The defense opened by re-calling some of the witnesses for further cross examination.

Walter Curtis recalled

Walter testified that he had not received any money, and definitely not $50, from Billings to commence the suit against Mrs. Billings. When asked the source of the money for his attorney, he told the court that he had gotten the money in two payments, one for $5 and one for $10 from his father-in-law.

John Hammond recalled

Hammond was a witness to the issue of time. Hammond was with Bemis when they saw Dr. Gow on his porch. A man drove up and spoke to the Doctor. The Doctor rode off with the man. When Hammond got home he looked at his clock it was five minutes to nine.

Under Moak's examination Hammond countered the prosecutors allegation with "I keep as good a clock as any man has got."

George Bemis recalled

Bemis testified that like Hammond it was 8:55 when he "got home."

It was 2:15 when Messieur L'Amoreaux commenced the opening statement for the defense. His words were deliberate and thoughtful. His style, if not his content, impressed everyone in the room.

"It is obvious, when I look upon your faces, that this jury fully understands the painful duty that must ere long be discharged by you as fair, honorable and high-minded men. When this dark crime first occurred last June, it was almost instantly given out that Mr. Billings was the guilty person. That tone, with the wisdom of time, has changed. The rights of the public, the prisoner, and all should be protected by you, our peers. You have seen to it that he has what the law presumes to give him-that he is innocent until he is proven guilty. You must judge and render your verdict on the evidence. With a fair and impartial investigation, we will show to you his innocence of the terrible crime that has been committed."

"We will not say to you that his house was a paradise. You must regard the wife in the grave and the daughter on the witness stand. The defense against family has always a singular and unpleasant nature. There was unrelenting hostility exhibited by the whole Harris family; there was even litigation. This hostility led to the vow made by the defendant's daughter that she would spend every last dollar to have him punished. She made no distinction in her remark as to guilt or innocence, right or wrong. Despite all of this, her father had uttered no word but of kindness and affection for her, but, when his life was in peril, she never did the first thing to relieve his melancholy and wretched condition. However this case turns, she has laid up many sorrows for herself, unless she is utterly devoid of sensibility, or any instincts of natural affection. Can she, in years, palliate all this? She says that she will not forget the night of June 4th for many years. Yes, during the balance of her life the skeleton of when she testified to on the witness stand will stare her in the face."

"In this trial, too, the People have had the confidential clerk of Mr. Billings and others he employed working against him. We have heard these accusations and have had to remain with our mouths closed-now it our time to speak."

"They speak of wealth and the object intended." [L'Amoreaux pointed to Billings.] "This man came into this court with the prejudice that he was a rich man who could buy his discharge for the accusation laid at his door. Have any of the jury been approached or tempted? If so, disclose it now, at this time!" [Not one juror moved or make even the slightest gesture.]

"We are further embarrassed by the fact that another family has been traduced with this case. That family is the Curtises. The evidence thus far has not disclosed anything against Mrs. Curtis. She was a tenant of one of Billings's buildings. That was all. Her name was dragged in to show a motive. Mrs. Curtis was subpoenaed by the People, but not brought to the stand, where she could vindicate herself from the imputations of unchastity, and making illicit commerce of her person with Mr. Billings. Mr. Billings was bickering with his wife; but is he singular in this? The prosecution would have you believe that the Billings home was the only one that was less than perfect. Haven't these conducts occurred with other families?"

"The very charge that this man would burn his beautiful home, all its memories and treasures, is so unreasonable to even put forward as a discussion. To believe that this man, who the People say is so wealthy that he could buy the jury, would destroy his home for $1,000 defies all reason. Even if you could stretch your imagination far enough to presume that he could burn his home, they want you to believe this single act, committed years ago, was motive to kill his wife in June last."

"Another motive for the defendant doing this horrible murder is sought to be deduced from the fact that his wife had a large fortune. This was published all abroad as a very large sum. But how much would he get if he were set at liberty today? Not a dollar. His wife held a note for $900, the payment of which he could not evade by putting his wife out of the way. And Jennie today, if she succeeds to her mother's estate, will get it out of her father's estate no matter what becomes of him. His wealth is argued against him; but how paltry compared with the rich county of Saratoga, which commands large resources."

"Mr. Billings's light talk to his clerk about taking his wife off his hands was commented upon. These remarks were pleasantries, and not serious words. He is a man of jovial disposition, and was so regarded by all the circles where he visited. Billings's conduct when he came in and found his wife dead, and his prostration under it, were just what might have been expected. Did he act like an assassin the next day, when approaching his wife's form, cold in death? How natural that he should say, 'To bad, too bad; would that I could die.' These words were not in public. It was in the privacy of the death chamber. Do these acts look as if, a few hours before, he had fired the fatal bullet through her head?"

"They said that with his immense wealth, he would control everything that came his way. The district attorney has employed his extensive resources fully, and in doing so he has done right. We don't complain of this; we are glad of it, but we ought not be prejudiced by the fact that we have used what means we could. What the prosecution, with its army of witnesses and talent have done, we have seen. But we come here to repel these accusations and to obtain what we claim as our rights."

"The People say that the prisoner ought to be convicted because he had a gun which was found back on the hill in a well. If he had the gun and fired it, why take it so far, when he could have thrown it in a pond nearby or in the river, where it never would have been found. And if it had not been found, the People would have used that fact as going to show the accused was guilty of murder. Is it not probable that a person who had the only keys to the store, the habitat of the gun, would have the time and motive and interest in having the gun found. Were Billings out of the way, Sherman could then marry who he wanted and have access to the wealth which he said was from $200,000 to $300,000."

"The tracks, the tracks; they are worthy of little attention. There were so many people walking around that tracks were made by throngs. Reed himself testified to making the three in his flower bed." [L'Amoreaux then used the map to show the route Billings had used on the night of the murder. The route showed all of Billings's actions from 7 p.m. until he reached the Washburn's house,] "Several minutes before the shot was heard." The defense attorney went on: "We will have witnesses that will support Billings testimony before the Coroner's Jury. We will show that a man rowing a boat on the river saw Billings hitch his horse to the Washburn's post and go into Washburn's house five minutes before he heard the shot. There was also a woman nearby who will testify that she saw a man run around the lumber pile."

"The prosecution want to convict Mr. Billings because he went to Mrs. Harris's. They would have you to believe that if Billings wanted to kill his wife, he would advertise his intentions from the housetop."

"Jesse Billings is not a tyrant. Jesse Billings is not a murderer. If we could but see his heart, we would be convinced of these simple truths."

"We will try to show you that Mrs. Billings never came to her death by a bullet fired from that gun. You should not place much weight in the testimony of the expert, Leet. You are farmers with eyes of your own. You can see for yourselves."

"It will further be shown that a stranger had been seen on the fatal afternoon prowling around. A hat like that sworn to by Jennie Billings was found behind the lumber pile nearly opposite the house. The hat, when it was found, was so dry it could not possibly have lain there during the rain of the previous day. And so all of the circumstances which have been arrayed, an effort will be made to explain them to the satisfaction of the jury. It will be shown that the bullet produced in court never came from the gun of Billings. A ball from his gun would have gone through eight or ten boards of an inch thickness at a distance of 500 yards. But the ball that killed Mrs. Billings did not go through her head. If it is shown that the gun found did not shoot the fatal ball, the prosecution fails. There is no mystery in this case which developments of this trial may not explain: Mystery shrouds the perpetrator of the crime, but the defense is not called upon to show who did the dark deed. We, under the laws of our Empire State, need only to show that all the circumstances, when properly viewed, relieve the defendant from the accusation under which he now stands in court."

L'Amoreaux walked confidently back to his seat. In his heart he believed he had convinced the jurors that every point in the prosecution's case was, at best, weak.

Isaac Potter

Not to be outdone by the prosecution, the defense hired a surveyor from Troy to produce a map of the area around Fort Miller Bridge. Isaac Potter had developed a map far superior to Cramer's. In his testimony, he listed the distances between all the points that Billings claimed to have been on the night of the murder. In all, Billings walked 12,275 feet or 2 and 3/10 miles.

Day 10

Those who had viewed the prosecution's closing the day before talked on the steps of the court about what happened to two of the key witnesses who had been reported as subpoenaed. The infamous and spicy Mrs. Durkee was never called. Mr. Curtis had been called to the stand, but Mrs. Curtis, who was even in court, was never been presented to the jury. Many wondered why the prosecution had made such a production of these notorious women, yet failed to put them on the stand.

Isaac Potter recalled

Cross   Potter's primary contribution to the trial was an excellent map. The morning began with Moak seeking to provide the jury with insight into the rise in altitude on the property. The lane that Billings had taken crossed property on which there was only a slight grade, except for one portion where there was a steep hill. The steep grade caused the view of the Billings house to be blocked at several points. Moak also focused Potter's testimony on the places indicated on the map from which you could not see the Billings house.

Moak wanted a clear understanding among the jury that the road north out of the hamlet had virtually no incline. This meant that even an older man, such as George Washburn, could walk home fairly rapidly.

On re-direct Hughes was able to get into the testimony that it was possible to hide a boat in the culvert near the front of the Billings's house without its being observed from almost any point in the hamlet.

John Terhune

Dir.   Terhune had been employed by Billings as a painter approximately half of the time since the spring of 1871. His duties consisted of painting buildings, boats and carriages. Terhune appeared to be extremely tense on the stand as his part in the drama unfolded before a crowded audience. The degree to which his nervousness was a result of a lack of a history in public appearances and how much was attributable to other reasons is unclear. In June last, Terhune was employed by Billings; as part of his employment, he took his meals with the family and slept in the house. On the evening of the murder, Terhune had taken tea with Billings.

After tea, Terhune was in the outbuildings selecting paint cans to be used the next day. Terhune's statements about observing Billings's movements in the neighborhood of the house corresponded with Billings's testimony before the Coroner's Jury.

When the shot was fired, Terhune was at the Union store. Almost immediately upon hearing the screams, he ran down to the front of the Billings house where he saw Jennie near the elm tree. The elm was outside the fenced yard near the highway. Along with others, John followed her into the house where he heard her remark about seeing someone run out the front gate and across the highway. According to

Terhune, she told everyone present that the person had on light clothes and a black slouch hat. Noting that there were plenty of people in the house to help, he went back outside and crossed the street to see if he could apprehend the person. When he got to the lumber pile, he decided it was not wise to be looking for an armed person without having a weapon himself, and he returned to the Billings house.

That night he examined the bullet hole in the window from the inside and outside. Carrying a lantern while he was outside, he observed smut stains around the hole. He testified that he never went to sleep that night, instead he spent the night in Billings's room. According to Terhune, Billings only slept in short intervals. When Billings did slip into a restless sleep, Terhune heard the accused keep calling out, "poor Jennie, poor Jennie." This was alternated with, "Poor father, my poor old father." At some time during the night, at the request of the neighbors, Terhune had helped move the body of Mrs. Billings.

Cross   Terhune testified that he didn't really remember the way Billings was dressed when he left the house the night of the murder. Terhune told Moak that he was usually done with his work at dinner but on this evening he decided to prepare for the next day. In preparation he had gone into the Metcalf Office and taken out cans to use the next day. He had placed the cans in the long shed behind Billings's house. In answer to Moak's questions, Terhune said that he was nowhere near the east door of the Metcalf Office and, yes, the door was usually held closed with a nail. Terhune's testimony was complicated because he was asked to cover the same ground twice. His observations were important because his movements allowed him to witness Billings as he walked through the garden and around the barns.

As if to show that Terhune's actions were foolish, Moak pressed and pressed that an animal could easily have gotten into the shed. He apparently wanted to show the lack of wisdom of using the shed over the enclosed Metcalf Office for storage. Terhune countered with the proximity of the shed to the house that he was painting and his supplies.

Terhune related how he was in the house when Billings got there after the murder. He had no knowledge of who was in the wagon, since he was inside. Terhune did not have any rubber boots, nor could he say for certain that any other person gathered at the house that evening had on rubber boots. Terhune told the jury that he had spent the night in Billings's room at the suggestion of Isaac Washburn.

Terhune had read Billings's testimony in the various papers. He was aware of Billings's claim that, it was daylight when he had made the tracks in the garden. Terhune testified that he had seen Billings make the tracks, but was not asked about the time when he testified before the Coroner's Jury. In reference to seeing Billings in the garden during the daylight hours, Terhune said it would "be a hard matter to tell why I did not tell about it" to the district attorney. The best that he could say was, "They didn't ask." Terhune admitted to telling the defense counsel about the tracks and the time, but had not discussed the same with Billings in any of his four visits to the cell. He had been to see Billings "as to work."

Terhune said that, in his presence, Jennie twice told the story of the suspected assailant. The first time she gave more details as to the color of the clothes than the second time. Present the first time were: Nichols, Clark Lockrow, Charles Cramer and Sherman. Terhune was uncertain who was present the second time, but he was sure that Cramer was not there.

Re-dir. Terhune told Hughes that he had been mixing the paints in the shed for weeks without any problem with animals. When asked why he left the lumber pile, he answered, "I concluded, if there was a man there who had committed the murder, that it weren't a very safe place for me." He also stated that when he arose the morning after the murder at 4:30, he had seen the east door to the Metcalf Office open.

As Terhune walked to his seat in the audience, the case took a twist that excited the crowd. L'Amoreaux asked that the defense have the bullet so that they could have an expert perform a test on it. Moak indicated that this would be fine as long as an officer of the court were present to "overlook the examination." General Hughes was livid. He pointed out to the court that the prosecution had sent the bullet all over the country and now expected the jury to believe that they had lost a piece of it (reference to the decrease in weight from 220 grams to 165). Hughes continued, "Your honor, the defense should be allowed the privilege of examining it without being under the eyes of the spies for the prosecution."

Judge Landon suggested that a deposition be signed by General Hughes on his professional word of honor that he would not lose sight of the lead. Further, it should be returned as the defense received it.

Moak objected to the judge's offer on the grounds that he did not want to have to put Hughes on the stand to prove that it was the same bullet.

Now that he could play with the opposition's argument, Hughes was in his favorite position. The General stated, "If I desired to convict my client, I would tamper with the bullet. It is of vital importance that the bullet be returned as received." L'Amoreaux the constant mediator suggested that Judge Crane and the county clerk oversee the examination. Hughes countered his own team member suggesting that the Sheriff appoint an officer to observe.

"No, sir. No, sir! We will never consent to that under any circumstances," Moak bellowed out.

Judge Landon told Ormsby to select a deputy sheriff to be present during the examination by the defense team. Ormsby selected his witness Officer Gilbert of Saratoga. Hughes knew that he had scored big, both with the sheriff's office and with the jury, showing the paranoia of the prosecution. Naturally he assented to Ormsby's selection. The gun and bullet were handed to Gilbert in the presence of the clerk, and the attorneys went to lunch.

Five Witnesses

The last five witnesses of the day were called to testify that they saw the tracks of the horse in the lane. Each testified that the horse had gone to the end of the lane before being turned around. Their names and what else they added follows.

Reuben P. Woodworth

Dir.   At fifty Woodworth was one of the local grocers in Fort Miller. At seven in the morning on the day after the murder, Rueben, along with James Wilson and others, were on Billings's property looking for tracks. His group had started investigating from the back of Billings's house. The tracks in the garden were deep and proceeded in an eastward direction (toward the Billings house). He told the court that they found no tracks on the Reed side of the fence.

Woodworth saw foot prints that climbed over the fence leading to the tree and back. He witnessed no tracks across the lane in the direction of the well. He had seen tracks in the cornfield that led to the oatfield. Woodworth saw tracks going back along the south fence, that was the path Durkee had taken. Woodworth said that the hoof prints implied that the horse had trotted.

Cross   Woodworth's memory fluctuated under cross examination. Since conversations with Moak were to be part of the testimony, Ormsby lead the prosecution's questioning. At first, Woodworth did not remember going to Moak's room at the San Souci; then he did recall meeting in the room. He was adamant that he did not tell Nelson Morey that the horse "went down the hill at a break-neck speed." Upon seeing the tracks with Ward, he did not agree that the tracks went south, but he did not say so at the time. He was not with Gilbert when tracks were measured; as Woodworth put it, "Don't remember no such thing". He was at the Coroner's Jury but did not recall anything being said about the boots fitting the tracks. In what would become a trademark of the prosecution, they would testify through their questions, as Woodworth testified that he never told Moak that he knew about the tracks in the lane. Woodworth also denied ever making a financial offer to Susan Durkee "if she would leave town".

Louis Gorham

Dir.   On the night of the murder, Gorham heard the shot at his grocery business. A few minutes later, Norton came to the store and told him that Mrs. Billings had been shot. He told his wife what had happened and left for Billings's. Gorham stopped along the way at Wilson's. Before he arrived at the Billings house, Louis saw Billings driving into the yard. His estimate was that it was fifteen minutes between the time of the shot and Billings's arrival.

Cross   A shot was not a special sound and initially had little effect on Gorham. It was not until Norton's arrival that he took special interest. Moak was on the attack. After hearing the news Gorham had told his wife; then he went into his saloon where he found Passnow, Yott and William Palmer. Gorham left for the scene with Yott and Passnow. He stopped at the Wilson's for just a few moments and caught up with the other two just before the juncture of the tow-path and the highway. At no time did Gorham see a man running south on the tow-path.

J. Howard Thompson

Dir.   Thompson a prominent resident of Northumberland, explained that, although he had not measured the distance, the strides of the horse were not far apart, indicating that it was not running. Thompson, as a farmer, "was accustomed to driving on all kinds of ground," and paid particular attention to the tracks. He noted that the lane had deep ruts from hauling heavy loads over the ground. [Thus it would be difficult if not impossible to have a horse run over the lane.]

Cross   Moak asked just how far apart the strides were. Thompson testified that at no point was he unable to step from one print to the next. Thus, it was surely less than three feet between strides. Moak was able to continue spinning his web of intrigue by connecting the families of Thompson and Billings; Billings's mother was Thompson's cousin.

James Wilson

Dir.   Wilson had learned of the murder on the same night that it occurred. Along with Louis Gamash, he had seen large tracks leading from Billings's gate to the river. They had measured the distance between the tracks and found it to be four feet, four inches from toe to heel.   That night they had also looked for tracks near the east fence and the cloverfield; they did not find any signs of tracks.

Cross   Moak immediately accused the witness of being the source of the article in the Republican that explained the Billings's defense. Whoever was the source, there was a strong indication that the person knew the strategy to be used. Wilson strongly objected to the implication. To Moak's questions, he answered; "Yes," he was on the Coroner's Jury and "No," he did not know others had claimed to see other tracks prior to his arrival. "Yes", he did have an interest in the case; he had been employed by Billings to drag the river for a weapon. The tracks he followed from the gate leading to the grass were distinct; but then they could not be followed.

Re-dir.   Wilson assured Hughes that, when the guard gate was open, the current was very swift in front of Billings's.

Jonathan R. Deyoe

Dir. A deputy sheriff from Northumberland, Deyoe was one of the few people who had a legitimate reason to be walking over the scene of the murder and the vicinity of the alibi following the murder. He examined the window and saw where the dirt had been smeared. He told the court that there was nothing much on the glass after Gilbert wiped it with a handkerchief. He had seen Gilbert's handkerchief and observed that it was "quite black".

Cross It was disclosed in the cross examination that Jonathan's brother had married one of Jesse's sisters. Jonathan also said that the soil had different consistencies at varying points around the property. He was with Gilbert when they found one print near the south fence where the stick that they were using as a measure "nearly fitted."

Day 11

The Billings's trial was before newspapers ran photographs. With only sketches, it is not surprising that on several occasions Justice of the Session William C. Tallmadge was mistaken for Billings. On this day a couple of ladies who came to the courtroom slipped up next to Constable Dater and asked him to point out Billings. Out of boredom, or as a joke, Dater pointed to Deputy Sheriff Griffen who happened to be sitting near the bench. The ladies expressed their feeling, "Oh, what a fine looking man - now we'll go." They left never realizing that, as they told their grandchildren about seeing the most notorious man in the county at the time, they had only seen an honest hard-working chap.

The eleventh day of the trial was a Saturday. Perhaps the fact that it was a weekend explains Judge Landon's decision to hear testimony only until the noon meal.

Orson Garnsey

Dir. Garnsey's testimony was the longest of the abbreviated day. He worked around the town as a day laborer on various farms. In April preceding the murder, Garnsey began to work for Billings. About May 25 or 26, Garnsey was in the fields turning out a cow for Billings. He had been told that, while he was in the field, he should fix any rails that were down. To the best of his memory, it was Billings who told him where, in the field, to find a pail of nails to fix a fence. When he finished mending the fence,. at his own discretion, he returned the nails and hammer to Billings's barns. [This was the hammer Billings told the Coroner's Jury he was not able to find].

Garnsey lived in the first house south of the Union store, in a home owned by Finne. On the night of the murder, he was sitting on his back porch, washing his feet, when he heard the shot and the screaming that followed. He walked through his house, out onto the front piazza where he saw people running toward the Billings house. He went back inside, put on his boots, then "took to a run down to Billings's place." Along the way, he met George Washburn coming north. When he was in front of Billings's wagon house, he saw Cramer and Gamash "putting up a horse." Garnsey went briefly into the Billing's house where he saw Mrs. Billings's body and the hole in the window. When he came back outside, he saw Cramer get in the wagon and drive north.

At the time of the shooting, Garnsey's wife was "quite sick." He decided to leave the Billings's and head for home to be with her. When he got near home, Finne and his hired man were in the barn, unharnessing a horse. He went over to talk to Finne. In going to Finne's shed, he passed near the horse block. There was no one else at the horse block at the time. When he was back in his house and changing for bed, he heard a wagon "passing toward Billings's." In Garnsey's judgment, the wagon passed about twenty minutes after he heard the shot.

Cross It was essential to the prosecution to discredit Garnsey's testimony. If what he said was true, then everyone else's statements would fall into place, if not with respect to time, at least in sequence. He provided a time frame that allowed Washburn to get home while Billings was there. Garnsey also provided the timing for Billings's ride home. Most important, Garnsey provided a delay in the prosecution's trump card, Thomas Virtue's ride.

Under Moak's extensive questioning, the old farmer showed almost no variation. Garnsey had chosen to enter the Billings's house through the back door because he was following Van Tassel who had a lantern and entered through the back. He didn't have any idea if the front door was open; he didn't look at or go near it. He went into the sitting room. There was a great deal of excitement there, so after three or four minutes he left. He didn't recollect seeing anyone at the front gate when he went in to Billings's but Curtis was at the front gate when he came out.

He had gone to within thirty or forty feet of the wagon house. By the light of the lantern, he could see that two men were trying to harness Billings's gray horse. Moak tried to emulate Hughes's ability to discredit a witness by an inability to recall detail. Garnsey appeared just too honest for this type of questioning, yet Moak persisted. Garnsey had no idea what type of lantern it was; the lantern was lit and he could see. He had no idea what part of the harness they were putting on when he first saw them, but the horse was facing south. The boy (Cramer) got in the left side of the wagon and pulled out.

With all the detail he sought on the most minor points, Moak avoided most questions on the time or events that occurred while Garnsey was at Finne's barn. It was obvious that Garnsey had a total recall of the sequence of events that fateful evening. Garnsey admitted that people in the hamlet had gathered "in knots", but held that there were no people at the horse block when he went home.

Garnsey would not budge on the time he heard the wagon going by in the direction of Billings's. Moak thought he won when Garnsey could not tell how many people were in the wagon or the type of wagon Everyone else in the court room thought the old farmer won the exchange when he said he just couldn't tell, by the sound alone, how many people were in the wagon or its type.

Frank Coffinger
Coffinger was one of those people who attorneys naturally learn to hate as witnesses because it is impossible to be sure what they are going to say. Coffinger's domination of the court room began when the court clerk called out his name. At first he didn't answer. He was called a second time. Still no answer. On the third call, he rose, strolled to the witness's chair, crossed his boney arms and said for all to hear, "Here I be."
Dir.   Coffinger resided with his brother on the first road west of Billings's fields. He had not heard of Mrs. Billings's death until the morning after. On the stand, he told the defense attorneys that he remembered seeing Billings in his fields after the storm. He had shown Potter place where Billings was seen to note on the map. Although Billings was one field away, Coffinger judged he was salting sheep, since he had a measure in his hand.

156

Cross It didn't take anyone, except Moak, long to realize that the prosecution's "pitbull" had met his match in Coffinger. When asked details about the size of the measure, Coffinger told all in a loud voice, "I couldn't tell the size; I was 60 rods (500 feet) away from 'im." When Moak tried to capitalize on the distance effecting his ability to recognize Billings, Coffinger said, "Could tell it was him by his appearance." When pressed to contradict himself, Coffinger added, "Nothing particular to call my attention to him that evening 'cept it was him."

Coffinger did not flinch as he told the court that he had been arrested for shooting a man. He didn't recall the details, but believed the man's name was Smith. "I forgot all 'bout it till you brought it up," he told Moak.

In the signature example of "he said or he said before," Moak asked if Coffinger had ever told John Hammond that he had not seen Billings salting his sheep. Coffinger would not admit saying it, then again he wouldn't swear he didn't say so.

On redirect he told the court he was arrested shortly after July 4th taken before a magistrate and released.

William Brumagim
Dir. A clerk in Billings's store from November 1877 until April 1878, Brumagim had returned from his new home in South Amboy, New Jersey to testify. About one month to six weeks after coming to work at the store, he discovered a gun in the "wool room". Brumagim brought the gun downstairs. He assured L'Amoreaux that he and Sherman had measured the gun to see what size cartridges it required. The two young clerks then went on a search of the store for the right cartridges. Finding none, he placed the gun on the shelf behind the eggs, where it remained until he left. He told the court that, coincidentally, Sherman had picked up the gun on the day he left work.

During his employment in the store, Brumagim had lived in the Billings's house and eaten at their table. There were no problems about Mrs. Curtis until after Billings went to New York in January. While Billings was away, Sherman attended to the business in the bank. It was during this period that Mrs. Billings told Sherman and Brumagim that they should avoid Mrs. Curtis. Although, Brumagim had been in the bank to see

Sherman about prices while Mrs. Curtis was there, he had never seen any "improprieties."

He described Billings's behavior as, "Fond of joking, jocose and merry." According to Brumagim, Billings was always pleasant to his wife.

Cross Moak was bent on detail. Even so, Brumagim barely modified his perceptions. He did say that Mrs. Billings almost always started the joking, but Billings was quicker and inevitably it would get "quite thick." The joking often ended when Mrs. Billings "invariably got mad" and left the table. Pressed and pressed by Moak, Brumagim continually held that Billings always held his temper.

The remainder of the cross examination focused on the gun and boots. Brumagim said that he remembered Palmer and Dominie Ford seeing the gun while it was on the shelf. The boots in evidence were like some of the old stock in the store when he was there. To his recollection, some had still been in stock when he left two months before the murder.

George Norton

Dir. On the night of the murder young Norton, who lived in Thompson Mills, had walked across the bridge and stopped at the Union store and Billings's store. While he was at the Union store, he saw Billings go by in the side bar wagon, driving the mustang horse. When he arrived back at the boarding house, he noticed the clock the time was 8:30. About ten or fifteen minutes later, he heard the shot and screaming from across the river. He grabbed a boat and along with Frost, Hitchcock, Bates and Crandall, crossed the river, landing in front of the lumber pile. The time from the shot to the conclusion of the crossing took about three to five minutes. When Norton got to the house he saw Sherman and then left to get Officer Donnelly. It was fifteen minutes from the time of the shot until he was back in the house, after alerting Donnelly. Norton was able to provide very exact times because on the fifth of September he had someone, (he did not recall who,) time him as he reenacted the events.

Cross Moak was surprised when Norton said he chose Sept. 5 since it had stormed that day, and the current would be the same as on the fourth of June. He had re-enacted at the suggestion of Patsey Mack and Baucus. Moak was able to get young George to add that he did not notice anyone between Durkee's and Gorham's but then he "weren't looking for nobody but Donnelly." He was in Billings's house two times: when he first

158

crossed, and after he went for Donnelly. He described the mood inside the house as, "Things were pretty generally stirred up." Norton had seen Billings come in from the dining room on his second visit. He concluded with, "No, I weren't at the Coroner's Jury."

Day 12

Over the weekend, members of the jury were allowed to attend church in Ballston Spa. As they sat in the care of the deputy sheriffs, seeking spiritual guidance, they found themselves being pointed out by the members of the congregation. No matter where they looked among those assembled, someone was staring back at them.

Sunday afternoon, Messr. L'Amoreaux entertained the reporters at his elegant home in Ballston. Always the congenial host, he talked with the reporters about what had occurred, but would not venture into the defense's plans for the remainder of the trial.

On Monday morning, the reporters were greeted by a box of button hole flowers. They had been provided by Mrs. Middler whose husband had been at Billings's side since the beginning of the trial. Mrs. Middler was the sister of Mrs. Mary Harris, Jesse Billings Jr.'s mother-in-law. In a typical ploy associated with the trial, the reporters felt that, "she did not intend to subsidize the press representatives in the interest of the defendant." Instead, they rationalized that the gift was, "merely sent them as tokens of her keen appreciation of their handsome appearance and talent." Thus satisfied, that acceptance would not interfere with their presentation of the trial they, "adorned the lapels of the their coats with the fragrant flowers."

By Monday, at least one newspaper had time to discuss (perhaps with L'Amoreaux) the prosecution's tactic of asking witnesses about conversations they had supposedly held between the time of the murder and of the trial. The prosecution was alleging conflicts between their testimony in the trial and comments made outside. The press was already noting that the witnesses seemed puzzled by the questions and statements allegedly made by them. The Daily Saratogian claimed, "Exactly how and in what manner the prosecution obtained such information is still a mystery." Even more important was how this tactic was playing with the jury.

The time the shot was fired was one of the most important points in the testimony. It was known Billings was not at home until after the murder. It was also already understood from his Coroner's Jury testimony that he was at the Washburn's for some period of time. The prosecution needed to show the time of the shot was early as early as possible to provide for the time necessary for Billings to establish his alibi. Conversely, the defense was trying to establish that the time of the shot to as late as possible.

Over the period of the trial, the defense called eleven witnesses each of whom testified the shot was fired after 8:40. For a variety of reasons these people could remember to within a couple of minutes the exact time they heard the shot. Moak was naturally perplexed that so many people had conveniently checked either their watch or clock at virtually the same time as the shot. Hughes tried to make checking the time as natural since at 8:40 the witnesses were preparing for bed.

The testimony relating to time moved slightly each day. If Moak crossed as to reason why the time was fixed in the witness's minds on Monday, then all witnesses starting on Tuesday would testify under direct why the time was remembered. If Moak expanded to what they were doing when the shot was fired on Tuesday, by Wednesday witnesses would all explain exactly what they were doing and why the time was fixed in their mind.

Whether out of exasperation, as a threat to future witnesses, because he was an elitist, or out of cruelty, Moak was universally vicious to these witnesses. He would ask them extremely personal questions as with Miss Houseworth when he asked "did you buy a new dress just for your appearance here?" implying this was a special event.

The witness called regarding the time of the shot were staggered over the remaining days of the trial. They are listed below even thought the day of their testimony may have been later.

1. **Miss Laura Houseworth** a 28 year old domestic servant at the "Old maid's Finne". Who added, "I want justice done in the case, I do." She paused, almost in tears from Moak's assault; barely above a whisper she added, "That is my feeling in the case."

2. **John Calkins** crossed the river with Norton. To Moak's accusation Calkins said, "My watch ain't run down." Although Calkins could not remember any other boats on the river that night, they may " 'ave been

there". Calkins had tied up near the culvert and could not remember any boats being inside, but one "could've fit."

3. **Henry Richardson** had crossed the river with Calkins and Norton. There is an adage taught in law school- "never ask in court a question to which you don't know the answer." This was probably added to the curriculum as a result of Moak's slip. He was pushing Richardson for the reason for his fixation with checking the time on his watch. "I didn't have no watch till the fall. I likes to show it off. It's the best my side of the river."

4 and 5. **Lewis Lee and Edward Lee** lived in the first house across the river next to the bridge. They had not gone to investigate because they attributed the noise to a boys' fooling. Neither brother could recall anyone crossing the bridge after the screams.

6. **Dominique Dumas** was a Canadian with a strong French accent who worked at the saw mill. Dumas assured Moak that he could "tell time." He was able to gain some sympathy when he testified to having slivers in his feet from standing, without boots, on the shore. Unlike many of the others that night he was "very little excited" that night. As he put it, "It takes a good deal to excite me."

7. **Mrs. Carrie Nichols** was the wife of James Nichols. She sat in the door for at least twenty minutes after the shot. The only person to drive by was someone in a wagon pulled by a gray horse [Cramer]. She did not see a boy go by on horseback [Virtue]. Moak asked why she did nothing after she heard the shot. The twenty-nine-year old Carrie answered plainly: "I have a five-year-old child at home."

8. **Margaret Garnsey** was very ill and required medication. Under cross examination Mrs. Garnsey held her ground. When she heard the shot, she had just checked the clock and the time was 8:40.

9. **Frank Dumas** heard a "noise" and screaming afterwards. He went out into the road. Dumas worked across the river, and on one occasion he had seen Mrs. Billings slapping a white cloth against her house and yelling at a great rate.

10. **Mary C. Houseworth** despite the fact that she was in the range of the sound until 8:40, visiting Mrs. Woodworth, she never heard the shot.

11. **Mrs. Sarah Woodworth** confirmed Mary Houseworth's visit and added that she heard the shot about five minutes after Mary left her house.

James Nichols

Dir. A 32 year old raftman by trade, Nichols resided in Northumberland in the first house north of the Washburns. He was a defense witness to provide the sequence of events and his observations of the Washburns. On the night of the murder, he looked at his watch as he left the Union store on his way to Billings's store. It was between 8:35 and 8:40. About five minutes later, he was trading with Sherman when he heard the shot and screams. He followed Sherman to the Billings house. When Nichols arrived, Lockrow as already inside; and Gamash was near the gate. Nichols admitted his recollection of the time lapse was by his best judgment, since he didn't look at his watch after leaving the Union store. While he remained at the Billings's, Carey and Durkee arrived followed a little later by Norton. Before Nichols left for the Union store he saw Billings arrive.

As he approached the Union store, Nichols watched as the last light was being blown out. He saw three or four ladies at the Finne horse block, but no men. He looked up toward Finne's barn and saw Alvinza in the light doorway. Nichols never saw George Washburn in the hamlet. As he continued on toward home, he passed Mrs. Washburn near the blacksmith's shop; she was going south in the direction of the Billings's home. When he was entering his gate, Nichols saw George Washburn, with a lantern, coming out of his gate; a lady was with him.

Cross Despite Moak's efforts to berate him, Nichols could not be shaken to retract any of his testimony. Nichols did say that he and Washburn had compared watches on the Sunday after the murder. According to Nichols the watches were within three minutes of each other. Nichols could not remember which was faster. He would not budge when Moak tried to make him admit that he had told McIntyre in September that the watches were "fifteen minutes different." He had no special reason for looking at his watch when leaving the Union store; "I merely looked to see what time it was."

On re-direct, Nichols testified that he had mislead Thomas Ward on details "Because he was talking too much to everybody and to everything."

On re-cross Nichols testified that he had worked for Billings continuously since the Saturday before the murder. He was employed building boats for Gamash. When asked why he had lied to Ward, he said, "I get him off by lying to him. I tell him the truth - he just keep talking."

On re-direct Nichols said that Ward was quite active in talking with the witnesses in the case.

Lansing Lockrow

Dir. An itinerant farmer, Lockrow lived in a room at the, Old Finne Tavern. He was in his room, reading the paper, when he heard the shot. He had just checked his watch, and it was 8:45. He immediately "raised the window" where he was greeted by the screams. He ran out of the house toward the Billings house. When he got there he saw his brother Clark Lockrow, along with Nichols and George Washburn. After going into the house, Lansing and his brother went into the barn to harness the horse, "as quick as we could." It was approximately fifteen minutes from the time they finished until his brother returned from fetching Dr. Gow. He did not see Billings arrive.

Cross Under Moak's examination Lockrow admitted that he knew Fred Leggett. Despite repeated questioning, however, he would not admit to telling Leggett the time of the shot was 8:30 p.m.. Lockrow said it was true; that he was wearing a hat that night, not because he took the time to put on a hat, but because he was reading a paper in the hat. Lockrow put a twist in the prosecution's questioning when he brought up the fact that he saw a man running south between Billings's and Reed's homes. He called to the man, but the man did not answer. He had not seen the man until they were about even with each other. Moak may have won a point when Lansing refused to say whether he did or did not tell others that the time of the sound of a shot was 8:30 p.m.

Clark Lockrow

Dir. At the time of the shooting Clark was sitting on the stoop of Billings's store talking with Walter Curtis. They had been there for "'bout half an hour." He heard the shot, followed about thirty seconds later by the screaming. He ran to the Billings's house and was the first to confront Jennie. When he left the stoop, Curtis was with him, but Lockrow was not sure where he went. At first, Lockrow assumed that Jennie had been wounded. After Sherman arrived, the two of them helped her into the house where he learned that it was her mother who had been shot. While they were in the sitting room, he heard Jennie say that she saw a man run

163

across the street and behind the lumber pile. George Washburn came in, and Jennie made the remark a second time. As Lockrow was helping Jennie in the house, he saw Curtis upstairs in the southeast window with Mrs. Curtis.

Lockrow was asked to go for a doctor, so he "hitched up" and drove to Schuylerville as quickly as he could. He found Dr. Gow on his front porch. After the doctor got in the wagon, they went up the block a short way then turned around and went back to Citron's Pharmacy. When they got to the Billings's house his brother, Lansing took the horse, while Clark went into the house with Dr. Gow. By that time, Billings was lying down in his bedroom.

Lockrow had reenacted these events since that time, and it had taken him eighteen minutes to travel to Schuylerville. He assumed it would have taken twenty-five to thirty minutes on the night of the murder, because of the time needed to include hitching the horse.

Cross   Moak wanted to know if anyone was in the bedroom with Billings when Lockrow returned. [The question remained as to how the boots got into the Metcalf Office.] Lockrow said that the light in the bedroom was dim, and he could not tell for certain. Clark had not seen Billings's face so he could not tell if there were tears. When asked about Curtis's demeanor, Lockrow said that he "appeared natural as ever" as he walked across the porch of the store to talk with him.

Lockrow said Jennie was excited when she spoke on the night of the murder, but was not "much excited."

Mrs. James Wilson

Dir.   Mrs. Wilson heard neither the shot nor the screams. She had heard about the shooting and went to the Billings's house. When she arrived, Billings was already on the bed. Mrs. Wilson heard Jennie twice tell the tale of a man running behind the lumber pile; one of the times she told it to Dr. Gow.

Cross   Moak was again trying to show that Jennie was extremely upset. Mrs. Wilson said, "I thought she was much cooler than I thought she would have been." According to Mrs. Wilson, there were several people present who heard Jennie say that the man who ran was wearing a slouch hat. Despite Moak's probing, Mrs. Wilson would not admit to telling anyone that Jennie had made "a great fuss" that night.

George Washburn

Washburn's testimony was a classic example of the difference between the handling of the case by the defense and prosecution. The elder Washburn's direct testimony lasted only five minutes, the cross examination more than five hours.

Dir. At the time of the murder, Justice George Washburn had just left Billings's store for home. Upon hearing the screams, he immediately went to the Billings's house. When he left the murder scene for his home, Washburn checked his watch, it was twelve minutes before nine. When the elderly judge arrived at his home, Billings was there. Out of habit, he looked at his watch; it was two minutes past nine. He told those gathered that Mrs. Billings was hurt. Billings left for home immediately.

Cross Washburn admitted that, although not perfect, his "eyesight is not very poor." He did remember that on the Sunday after the murder he had compared his watch with that of Nichols.

To the best of his recollection, Washburn did not believe that it was more than ten seconds between the time of the shot and that of the screams. Upon hearing the scream he turned and ran to Billings's house. He entered the house and went into the room where Mrs. Billings body sat. At the time, he did not think that she was dead. He left the house when "the Mahoney girl ordered" him to go to Finne's. When he got to Finne's, a group had gathered just south of the block. The Squire spoke to Mrs. Finne for less than five minutes, telling her what had happened. Mrs. Finne decided that she would not go to the murder scene until Mrs. Washburn came along. Washburn testified that, he did not speak to Mr. Finne. He then left for home.

The defense objected to a question asked by Moak relating to how quickly the witness sought to assist in the resolution of the crime. Moak told the court, "I want to show that the witness tried to stifle, not forward, an investigation of this crime." To understand the prosecution's perception of the case takes only an examination of George Washburn's answers to Moak's questions. The most significant answers were:

"I did not know of Mrs. Billings's death until the boy, Virtue, came up and told us."

"I heard Finne direct the boy, Virtue, to go get a horse just before I left for home."

"I did not see Mr. and Mrs. Reed that night."

"I will not swear positively that Mr. and Mrs. Reed did not come up to Mr. and Mrs. Finne's."

"When I left for home, Finne was still with the group."

"The boy, Virtue, told my daughter of Mrs. Billings death."

"The boy, Virtue, arrived 'bout ten minutes after I got home."

"Billings left for home within a half a minute of my arrival."

"My wife left for Billings's 'bout eight minutes after I got home."

"I stayed and went down with my daughter."

Washburn explained that he had fixed the time at twelve minutes before nine because he thought that he could be home by nine o'clock. Moak pressed, but the Justice insisted that he was not at home before nine. Washburn swore that he had told two men to "look around for a pistol"; he was not positive that those men were Lockrow and Nichols.

Washburn told the court that he had been a magistrate in the town for thirty years. In this capacity Washburn had often done business with Billings. For the last four years, the Justice had made out several boat bonds for Billings. The squire told the court that on occasions he had loaned money to Billings.

The elder Washburn told the jury that the reason it took his wife eight minutes to leave is that she changed her dress. It was about three minutes after his wife left that Washburn left with his daughter. Washburn added that his son, Isaac, left with Billings.

Washburn denied seeing Billings in the bank the day after the murder. The Justice was adamant that he did not see Billings in his house since the day of the murder.

The remainder of the testimony that day focused on the Squire refuting statements that were attributed to him by Edwin Towne. The judge said that he was not approached by Towne for a warrant. Washburn told Towne to make out a complaint if he wanted a warrant. Washburn did not tell Towne that he wasn't going to allow Billings's enemies control the Coroner's Jury.

Day 13

Interest in the trial had not abated; in fact, the number of spectators increased as the key witnesses to Billings's alibi were to be on the stand. On this day, the court "groupies" received a political surprise. As usual, there was a large group of people waiting on the steps, hoping to get the best seats. When the courthouse doors were finally opened at 9:10, the traditional rush occurred, with the masses hurriedly climbing the stairs. When they reached the courtroom, the spectators were amazed to find half the seats were already filled. People with "connections" had entered through the "underground railroad." The mumbles of the disgruntled multitudes could be heard throughout the entire morning.

Adding to the commotion were the large number of people who had not missed a minute of the testimony. So they would not lose their seats, they ate in the seats; these people had mastered a system of bringing in hampers of food and drink.

George Washburn continued

Cross   The hostility between Washburn and Moak was evident in the exchange of looks between the two as the elder justice was recalled to the stand. Justice Washburn was not accustomed to having his integrity questioned. The offense was considered even more demeaning and unwarranted, since it came from an outsider (Moak was from Albany).

The opening questions by Moak concerned very minute points of contradiction between the justice's statements in court and those he had made before the Grand Jury and/or Coroner's Jury. The questions concerned how many groans he believed had emanated from the house, time for travel, and whether he had told the people in his house that Mrs. Billings was hurt or was sick. Washburn testified that he had tried to whisper in his wife's ear that Mrs. Finne wanted her to come down because Mrs. Billings was hurt. Billings overheard him and said, "Mrs. Billings hurt! How? What?"

Washburn testified that he had passed Billings on the highway about 4 o'clock on the day of the murder. They had passed as Billings was returning from Schuylerville. Although no time had been arranged, Billings told Washburn he would be by later to get a summons.

The justice was adamant that he did not tell Officer Pennick that he had seen people, "playing about the lumber pile."

The final series of questions pertained to the amount of contact between George Washburn and the press. Washburn insisted that he was not the person who submitted the May 9 article to Mr. Elmer of the Standard. He swore that he had not told Elmer that Mrs. Billings had "raised rumpus enough." Washburn also claimed that he had not had any contact with the Republican.

Re-dir. Under Hughes's questions, Washburn reiterated that after he entered his house Billings had said he had been waiting "some time." Billings then asked about a summons. When the justice told Billings, that Mrs. Billings was hurt, Billings left immediately calling out for "Ike." [Isaac]

Seth Lawrence

Dir. Lawrence was the owner of a drug store and the telegraph operator in Schuylerville. On the night of the murder, Dr. Gow had stopped briefly at Lawrence's business; he was looking for Edward Cochrane, to serve as stenographer at the Coroner's Jury. When asked when Cochrane was expected, Lawrence explained that Edward had been fishing all afternoon, then Lawrence looked at the clock and noted that it was between 9:10 and 9:15.

Cross As always, the prosecution sought to find out why so many witnesses were certain of the time. Mr. Lawrence said that he automatically looked at a clock when asked what time he expected someone.

Charles McNaughton

McNaughton was in the store with Lawrence. He collaborated Lawrence's statement regarding the time.

Mrs. Francis Washburn

Dir. On the night of the murder, Mrs. Washburn was finishing a dress in her dining room while her son and daughter were busy writing. The room in which they all were sitting in was about 16 feet square and lighted by a lamp placed on the table in the center of the room. About 8:30, Phoebe asked the time; Isaac called out the answer. About ten minutes later, there was a knock on the door. Isaac answered the door; it was Billings, who asked for the Justice saying he wanted a summons. Isaac said the Justice wasn't home, but that Billings could come in as the Squire was always home by 9:00 "to wind his watch." Mrs. Washburn told the court that Isaac was correct; her husband was "very peculiar about that." After a discussion about the storm damage to the tree and to his farm, Billings sat down and talked with Isaac. Mrs. Washburn concluded her direct testimony by saying that she had known Billings for years as a "near neighbor". On the night of the murder, in her opinion, he acted very naturally.

Cross   The prosecution pressed to find contradictions in her story. The elderly woman held her ground on all points brought out in direct examination. She added details about seeing Billings in church on the Sunday prior to the murder. Mrs. Curtis was there, but Mrs. Washburn did not see if they had arrived together. The two did not sit together; however, they did leave together in Billings's wagon.

Mrs. Washburn was in her house on the Thursday morning after the murder when Billings called on them. He talked to the Squire about Jennie's engagement to Sherman. Mrs. Washburn swore that they did not talk about the amount of time Billings was at their home on the night of the murder.

On the night of the murder, her son, Isaac, had come upon her on the road going to Billings's. He picked her up, and the two went down to Finne's horse block where she spoke to Mrs. Finne and other ladies. The only one she could positively identify was Mrs. Reed. After a few minutes she went on to the Billings home.

When the Squire said Mrs. Billings was hurt, Billings responded, "Hurt? How? Why? Where?" He then ran out the door with Isaac behind him. As Ike went through the door, he told his mother that he would return for her.

Moak's signature cross with regard to time was addressed when the elder lady told the court that she measured time by the amount of stitching she finished. Since the beginning of the trial she had experimented. She determined that Billings was at her house approximately twenty minutes based on the needle work accomplished.

Miss Phoebe Washburn

Dir.   Miss Phoebe's testimony supported that of her mother. She testified that she was nearsighted and had to ask the time. That explained her certainty that it was after 8:30 when Billings arrived. They, including Billings, had joked about her father's habit of always winding his watch at 9:00. Phoebe agreed that Billings acted very naturally in their home on the night of the murder. She remembered him talking to Isaac about the storm damage to his property.

Cross　Phoebe, like her mother, did not falter under cross examination. Her story was simple and uncluttered by minute details. Although she was not able to give any examples of Billings being jovial that night, she continued to claim that he had acted naturally.

The remainder of Moak's efforts were directed toward the issue of the clock and the time. Moak wanted to know how much the clock varied per week (up to 10 minutes). He wanted to be sure that her father wound the clock every night at nine. Her response: "Always. She was the one who went to the door when Virtue called out from the hitching post.

Phoebe and her father had walked to Billings's. To the best of her recollection they arrived between nine and nine thirty. When they arrived, Billings was still at his wife's feet. She saw him helped up and into the bedroom. Phoebe was a teacher in Bacon Hill, so she was not at home on Thursday morning to know if Billings was there or not.

Isaac Washburn

As Hughes lead the direct Moak kept thinking how this was the witness he had been laying in wait for. The prosecutor had merely "breakfasted" on the attack on the elder Washburn. Moak had shown the sexagenarian's memory to be slipping. It would have been unseemly to be any rougher than he had been on the mother or sister. Isaac, however, was a man and a critical element in Billings's alibi. As L'Amoreaux asked the questions on behalf of the defense, Moak found himself salivating, as if awaiting his prey for lunch.

Dir.　Isaac described the events leading up to Billings's arrival at their house, using the same terms as his mother and sister. He told the court that he had glanced at the clock when Billings knocked on the door. He let Billings into the room where the two men had discussed George Washburn's idiosyncrasy, the effects of the storm and his school, and the new bank.

Isaac described the events surrounding the arrival of his father; his description was the same as of the women in his family. When Ike went outside, he discovered Billings had slipped and was lying on the ground. Ike helped Billings into his wagon and drove him to his house. Isaac had not gone in the house this trip; rather he visited outside for a minute and then went back to pick up his mother. He made a third trip to get his sister and his father. According to Isaac, when he and his mother stopped at the Finne's, Isaac told Alvinza that he had just taken Billings home.

When Isaac got in the house, Billings was on the floor. Isaac helped Billings up and to his room. He remained with Billings for a short time, then fetched a glass of wine for Billings, to help him rest.

Isaac concluded by referring back to an earlier time on the day of the murder. Isaac was leaving his school when he met Billings, who was coming out of the National Bank in Schuylerville. Out of courtesy, Billings offered him a lift. When they got to Fort Miller, Billings brought Isaac into the bank and showed him around. Isaac testified that all of their contact occurred prior to the storm.

Cross   As Moak sat in his chair waiting to ask the prosecution's questions, he knew that he was like a man who had finally gotten a date with the woman of his dreams; the greatest probability was that the event would be less than anticipated. Reluctantly, he rose and approached his mark.   The first two questions established that Isaac was a twenty-six-year-old and single. Then the personal credibility hammer fell. Isaac refused to answer as to whether he had registered as man and wife with a young woman at the Millman Hotel on the night of September fourth. He also refused to say whether on September twelfth, he had been in Smith's saloon and won $1.75 from John Donnelly. In 1878, either of these acts would have been the cause of serious concern over a young, single male teacher. Isaac was shaken, but not burned.

On the day of the murder, while he and Billings were on their way back from Schuylerville, they met the elder Washburn; then Billings said he would stop by later.

To Moak's questions, Isaac answered that while he was in Billings's store on September 10 he said that he was willing to be a martyr for the place. He denied saying that they could make him a second Jesus Christ.

Billings got far ahead of Isaac, as they both went for the wagon on June 4 because Ike stopped to put on his hat and a coat. As Isaac helped him up on the front lawn Billings said, "That's bad, that's bad."

Isaac acknowledged that, in the wagon, Billings said that he thought there was a conspiracy against him. Isaac testified that he did not see anyone as he drove to Billings's house. When he got to the scene, he pulled the wagon around to the back of the house.

Isaac was present when Billings arrived at his house on one of the mornings after the murder. On that occasion, he overheard his father and Billings talking about Sherman.

The defense next called a series of witnesses that testified that after the murder they had seen a man a man running south on the tow path.

Stephen LaPoint

Dir.   At age twenty-six, LaPoint boarded in a house next to Gorham's grocery store. He was at home when Julie Gannon (male) came and told him of the murder. The two men left for the Billings's house. They went north on the tow-path. As they approached the intersection of the tow-path and the highway, they saw a man walking south near the sheds of the Finne Tavern. As they approached, the man ran down into the muddy dip between the two routes. The man would have encountered them, but he "shunned" them and turned, surfacing further down the tow-path. LaPoint testified that, he did not recognize the man or see Norton.

Cross   Moak wanted to know why a healthy young man who knew of Mrs. Billings's murder for two minutes made no effort to stop a man running away from the scene. To LaPoint it was easy: "I didn't know that I had any reason to catch him." LaPoint told the prosecutor that the man whom he described as wearing light-colored clothes was the only one he saw running that night.

LaPoint had not told any of the officers what he had seen that night. He didn't know any of the prosecution team or virtually any of the officers, so he "kept quiet".

LaPoint assured Moak that he worked for Gamash building Billings's canal boats. Moak pushed, but LaPoint held firm that he did not work for Billings, although he did get his pay at Billings's store.

Mrs. Selina Passnow

Dir.   Mrs. Passnow, her husband Isaac, and son, Wilfred, lived in the other half of the duplex occupied by LaPoint and Gannon. On the night of the murder she was told of the murder by Mrs. Gorham. Moments later, Gannon and LaPoint left for Billings's. Mrs. Gannon and Mrs. Passnow stayed on their porch. A couple of minutes later, a man without a hat, ran past. The man slowed as he passed the grocery, then began to run again.

Cross Moak went for the detail, Mrs. Passnow countered. LaPoint and Gannon were the first two to leave for Billings's. Later she saw three men, M. Passnow, Gorham and Yott, walk in the direction of Billings's. It was a minute or two later when she was outside and the man ran past. The unidentified man was slowing in his run as he approached the house; he was evidently tired. The prosecution wanted to show that the running man was a new phenomenon created for the trial. Mrs. Passnow responded that, on the night of the murder, she told everyone in her house that the man had run past. Two weeks later, when Medore Passnow and his wife were visiting, she told them about the runner. Mrs. Passnow testified that she told Donnelly of the runner a week or two later even though she did not know at the time that Donnelly was a constable. She thought that he was only the other gate keeper on the canal. When asked why Donnelly missed the runner, Mrs. Passnow pointed out, Donnelly was inside his own home when the man ran past. To the prosecution's consistent questioning, Mrs. Passnow acknowledged that her husband did indeed work for Billings.

Day 14

By this time a critical difference between Hughes and Moak was evident. When Hughes sensed that a witness was less than truthful, he would push until it was apparent to all in the room that the person was not telling the whole truth. When Moak tried to use a similar approach it inevitably appeared as though he was seeking minutiae or was confused.

As had been the case every day of the trial, Billings entered the court exactly at the ringing of the bell. Today, confidence in the direction of the trial was evident in his walk. The papers noted that he appeared "graceful". His father, the venerable doctor, followed along with the husband of his mother-in-law's sister. The Reverend Ford was also in the short parade that announced the beginning of another day of the trial. On this day those in attendance would be treated to the unique spectacle of George W. Jones.

The testimony of the this day would exemplify the intense level of bigotry that existed in 1878 and how openly that prejudice was expressed.

Wilfred Passnow

Dir.   The first witness called was thirteen year old Wilfred Passnow, son of Salina. He admitted that he had never been sworn before, but that he understood what it meant. Wilfred said that on the night of the murder, his mother told him what happened to Mrs. Billings. He also remembered that after LaPoint and Gannon went up the river, he saw a man in light clothing wearing no hat, run past his house. When the man got even with the grocery, he walked. By the hotel, the man began to run again.

Cross   Under Moak's examination Wilfred said that it was common to see men run ahead of the canal boats to be sure that the locks were working. The men always wore hats. During his life, he had seen six or eight hats lying on the tow-path. "My attention was called to the man later that night, and it has been talked about ever since." Moak wanted to know how the boy could see a man in the dark; Wilfred was able to see the man because, "the lights made the two-path light." Wilfred had never spoken to any of the Deyoes, but he had spoken to John Donnelly, "When he subpoenaed me." Wilfred admitted he was not used to judging distance; however, because of all of the discussion that he had heard since the night of the murder, he was sure that the man was 25 to 26 feet away from him. Also, it had been pointed out to him that it was 25 feet from his porch to the light.

Jules Gannon

Dir.   A Canadian by birth, Jules Gannon, 27, stated that he was sitting on the porch at Gorham's when he heard from Norton what had happened to Mrs. Billings. Gannon and LaPoint then went up the road toward Billings's house. As they walked north Gannon saw a man running on the road toward them. When the man saw them, he cut through a hole in the driftwood and on to the tow-path, where the man continued running south.

Cross   It was essential to the prosecution that the witness be discredited; therefore, the examination of Gannon was very difficult. Moak had Gannon state that he worked for Gamash building boats for Billings. Gannon then named the people, his wife included, whom he had told about the incident that evening. At the time of the trial, Mrs. Gannon was unable to support his testimony since she was confined at home and unable to attend court. Jules had attended part of the Coroner's Jury, but had chosen not to speak because he thought it "best not to get into other's affairs." Gannon admitted that he, along with others, had not tried to get Medore Passnow to remember how he had also seen the man. Gannon would not admit, however, that they had tried to get him to remember saying that he had seen the man running.

Charles Yott

In the typically bigoted reporting of the day, it was noted that Charles Yott was a half-breed Canadian Indian. Charles had bright eyes, curly black hair, and an extremely heavy French accent. With his personality and his broken English, he was one of the most colorful witnesses. Perhaps because of its humor, some of the papers carried his testimony in dialect.

Dir. Yott, who worked for Gamash in Billings's boatyard, related that he was at Gorham's when he was told about the murder. He, along with Passnow and Gorham, decided to walk to the murder scene. When they got to Wilson's, Gorham stopped to visit (Gorham was married to Wilson's daughter). According to Yott, when he and Passnow were even with the next barn after Wilson's, he saw a man running toward them. The man passed within one foot to one foot and a half of him. The man was bare headed and running very fast. Gorham rejoined his friend at the corner of Billings's fence.

"In what direction was the man running? This man with his head down?" Moak asked not expecting the response he was about to receive.

"I can no explain, ze norse, ze souse, ze eas' ze wes'. He passy me on ze tow-pass, between ze fence and me."

"What did the man look like?"

"He hed hees head down."

Somewhat exasperated, Moak tried again. "How did he have his head down?"

"I can no explain, but I can myself poot in shape, so" Yott rose and tipped his head down, assuming a posture like a runner caught in a still frame. The courtroom erupted in laughter.

"How many feet was the man from you?"

"He passy me a feet an' a half or two feet." Just the sound of his voice caused a snicker among the large throng.

Moak decided that it was time to take control of the testimony; he decided to redirect the testimony by asking the same question that he had asked all of the other witnesses. "Please look at the map. Is it complete?"

"You no hev everyzing zat was on ze towpass."

Knowing the map was complete, Moak felt he could finally discredit the witness. "Oh, what is missing?"

"Ze man in the gray clothes." The laughter in the court room was deafening.

"And what fixed in your mind on that the man had gray clothes?"

"Because he had on ze gray clothes."

Still looking for a way to show a flaw in the witness's testimony Moak pushed foreword. "Why did you not tell the other attorneys the clothes were gray?"

"Ze cause of zis, ees zey no essky me." Yott was enjoying his banter with Moak. Boldly he continued, "Oh, my storee, she ees true! You no catchy me." Seeing the controlled Moak become dumfounded, even the composed Judge Landon was forced beyond a smile. It took the good judge several minutes to restore order.

"Didn't you have a conversation with Medore Passnow, and in that conversation didn't he tell you that he would not commit perjury for Jesse Billings or anybody else, and you ought not to do it?"

"He did telly me so."

"How often did he tell you so?"

"Eet was no more zan ten or feefteen times." Much to the disappointment of those gathered, Yott's testimony was finished.

John Donnelly

Dir.   On the night of the murder, Donnelly along with Durkee went to Billings's house. They arrived within fifteen minutes of the shot. Donnelly, a constable, spent the night at Billings's. At 4:00 a.m., Donnelly left for Saratoga Springs with Billings's horse and wagon. While driving near the intersection of the tow-path and the highway; he spotted a hat in the grass about forty feet from a puddle. Donnelly was not sure the horse would stand, if he got out of the wagon, so he drove on until he came to Edwards. Donnelly requested that Edwards go and pick up the hat.

John Edwards recalled
Edwards stated that he picked up the hat found on the highway. He saw Gilbert trying on the hat before he handed it to Donnelly.

Peter Davison
Dir. One of Schuylerville's jewelers was Peter Davison. He set his regulator by Albany time. Each week he sent a man to the mill to be sure that the regulator used for the whistle was accurate. Additionally, Davison assured those in the court that, although George Washburn had a good running watch, Washburn was in the habit of checking his watch by Davison's regulator at least once a week.

Cross Davison told the jury that within the last six months he had seen Washburn check his watch at least once every week. "It was never over a minute and usually less than a few seconds out of the way".

Mrs. Elizabeth Smith
Dir. Mrs. Smith had lived in Fort Miller Bridge, in a house near the guard lock. Under examination by L'Amoreaux she related that "one evening prior to the murder" she visited Billings's store shortly before 9 p. m.; while walking home she passed the Billings's house. Crouched on the sidewalk was a man looking through the fence at the house. When she came even with the man, he tried to hide his face by looking away. The man was wearing shabby clothes that, in the darkness, appeared gray. The man was about 10 feet from the fence to Reed's home. From his location, he could have seen into the window through which Mrs. Billings was shot. After Smith passed, the man stood and ran away. Mrs. Smith was positive that the man was not Billings.

Cross Moak's examination was intense, but Mrs. Smith was not rattled. The only new information brought out through the prosecution's questions was that the man had short black whiskers and hair.

Mrs. Hannah Thompson
Dir. Hannah stated that she had been at the house the night of the murder and heard Jennie tell those gathered that "When her mother was shot, she ran to her, then out the front door." Jennie went on to say that when she reached the front piazza she "saw a man run across the road."

George W. Jones

Dir.   Jones had lived in Northumberland for three to four years. He lived alone in a shack just north of the blacksmith shop. On the night of the murder, Jones had been fishing on the river in a boat borrowed from Finne. He was rowing up to the sight of a sunken boat, just north of the Washburn house, when he saw Jesse Billings come out of the lane and pull up to the Squire's house. When he arrived at the sunken boat, he tied up to its hull. Ten minutes after he saw Billings pull out of the lane, he heard the report of a gun. Jones eventually moved to another fishing spot, staying out for several more hours. Jones testified that he was unaware of Mrs. Billings's death until the next morning.

Jones told the court that he was born in the mountains of North Carolina and had moved north at the age of eleven. This was during the third year of the Civil War. He worked at whatever job he could, usually doing day labor. Jones told the court that he did not know Billings personally, although he had worked for him on occasion. He concluded by stating that he heard the shot about five to six minutes after he tied Finne's fishing boat to the hull of the sunken canal boat.

Cross   Moak began his questions by gently nursing the witness. Jones admitted that he could read, but could not write. Moak asked Jones to name all of the places he had lived in Saratoga County. The number was large, but Jones answered promptly and in sequence. The difference in values between witness and attorney was obvious. Moak perceived Jones as a vagabond, while Jones saw himself as a man bent on survival. The level of the conflict was expressed through Jones's answers.

"No, I never worked for a Negro named Brown."

"Oh no! I was not charged for being engaged in a riot at Quaker Springs. I was in the bar room of Wright's Hotel when it occurred"

"Yes, I do collect driftwood, some to burn and some to sell." [Because the quality was low and the product free, those who collected driftwood for a living were perceived as being on the lowest round of a very tall social ladder.]

Moak was able to show that Jones had never been regularly employed. He had moved frequently to places where there was employment. Jones had done just about everything he could to earn a living, from digging potatoes to washing wagons. He earned as much as $10 per week, but usually only about $25 per month. Jones testified that, as a condition of his work, sometimes he was provided room and board, while at other times he worked for higher wages and had to seek his own shelter. His current residence was eighteen feet long by seven feet wide. Although he guessed he was supposed to pay rent, he "hadn't been asked for any yet." Jones wasn't even sure who owned his home. He guessed Finne owned the building, but he had obtained permission to live there from Baucus. Jones guessed that the reason he may not have been asked for rent was because he had added ten feet to the original structure. His furniture was minimal but he was sure to point out that it included a bedstead. It was important to Jones that they not believe that he slept on the floor.

Since the night of the murder, Jones had worked first for Jonathan Deyoe during the haying season, then for James Deyoe (Jesse Billings brother-in-law) and most recently for Dr. Billings, although he was not employed of late. While he was employed by Dr. Billings, he stayed in his house.

The previous spring George Jones owned two sets of clothes. During the summer, "I got a coat and vest at Billings's store and a pair of pants off a Dutchman." He even had four or five shirts, one of which he bought two weeks ago.

Sneering, Moak asked, "Is that the one you've got on now?"

Jones replied instantly. "Do you suppose, sir, that I would wear a shirt for two weeks?"

Jones went on to say that he had attended parts of the Coroner's Jury. He had not come forward at the time because he did not think "they needed me" or that the officers wanted to hear his side. After they took Billings away, Jones claimed, he told Officers Durkee and Deyoe what he had witnessed.

Jones named the numerous other parties who were present at about 8:00 p.m. on the evening of the murder, when he asked Finne for the boat.

Jones closed his testimony for the day by naming various persons whom he had told, over the summer, about what he had seen. He denied ever saying to anyone, "Sometimes I believe Jesse Billings guilty as hell, and other times I think he's innocent."

At 5:55 Judge Landon closed court for another day. Jones was return to the stand the next day.

179

The reporters were more impressed by Jones than by Moak. Jones appeared straightforward, answered quickly, and was totally unrattled by Moak's questions and tone. Moak gave the impression that Jones was beneath him because he cooked for himself and cleaned his own house.

Day 15

So one expert could observe the other and prepare counter arguments, the prosecution paid to have Mr. Leet, the bullet manufacturer, return from Connecticut for the testimony of Dr. Ward.

Deputy Sheriff Shaw was troubled by the laughter heard in the gallery after the attorneys from both sides, made remarks. He was so bothered that he made a statement in court that was overheard by members of the press. The reporters, in an effort to add to public interest, noted that the deputy believed that the use of 'irrepressible adjectives' was inappropriate in such a serious matter.

The court crier E. R. Schureman was unable to perform his responsibility in court this day. It appears he had called "Hear ye, hear ye, all ye gathered The court is now in session" so often in the trial that he had become hoarse. Fortunately, a clerk of the court was able to step in to fill this critical responsibility.

George Jones continued

Moak had had the night to find out as much about Jones as possible. Moak's cross examination continued with an attack on Jones's character.

"Did you go away from Mrs. Smith's without paying your bill?"

Hughes was instantly on his feet, "Objection your honor. The prosecution is trying to imply that a man is prone to lying if he cannot pay his bills." This opening exchange between Moak and Hughes typified the morning.

Jones, the banjo-playing fisherman, was attacked for most of the morning by Moak with a savagery matched only by animals when cornered. He pounded Jones, not only on the story to which he had testified, but also his character. The defense objected vigorously to each onslaught. For one of the only times in the trial, Judge Landon was forced into a corner. Ultimately, he established the position that the prosecution needed to have a wide range in their questioning of Jones because, "If Jones is believed, then the jury will have no choice but to find Billings innocent." Moak's ferocity can be felt in some of the answers that Jones was forced to provide that morning:

"When I worked at Johnson's, I slept in the office, not in the barn."

"No I was not sent away because I was lousy and infected Chase."

"I boarded for a time at Clem Duel's at Bacon Hill but did not understand it to be a house of prostitution."

"No, I do not recall assisting a prostitute named 'Roxy' bury her child."

This line of questions so troubled the editor of the Ballston Journal, that its report stated admirably: Mr. Moak here asked some questions that are not fit for publication, and the court held the witness need not answer.

The prosecution then attacked Jones's account of the events of June 4. Moak was trying to point out that if Jones took the boat at about 8:00 p.m. and "rowed right along as fast as I would ordinarily row," then he would have covered the distance to the sunken boat well before the shot. Despite enormous pressure, Jones never varied from his original story.

Moak then asked Jones if, over the course of the preceding summer, he had not told several people a diametrically opposite story to what he was telling the jury. Now as each person's name was given Jones answered "No;" he had not told them a contrasting tale.

Re-dir. On re-direct Jones explained that he had been to the coroner's jury. He went on to explain that he had heard George Washburn say that Billings was at his house at the time of the shooting. Explaining why he had not come foreword at the Coroner's Jury Jones said, "I figured that if Mr. Washburn said it was so, there was no need for me to say anything." Jones went on to say that he had not spoken to Billings between the time of the shooting and the conclusion of his testimony on the previous afternoon.

Alpheus Davis
Dir. The clerk who replaced Sherman, and who was now in charge of Billings's store, was a young man originally from Saratoga Springs, Alpheus Davis. Davis had worked for Billings as a clerk in the store from

1873 through 1876. He was living in the house when the kerosene affair happened. In court he identified the board that had been on fire. The next day, he asked Mrs. Billings what had happened. She told him that, her husband spilled the lamp on the carpet and mopboard and a small fire occurred. Mr. Billings was not present when Mrs. Billings told Davis what had happened. Davis said that this was the only time the incident was spoken of while he resided in the house. Davis went on to say that Billings was always humorous, but, on occasion, would poke fun at his wife, whom Davis described as medium build and a little "fleshy".

Cross   Despite an extensive assault, Moak was only able to get Davis to add two points. Davis stated that Mrs. Billings was "an active, industrious woman" who supervised the management of the house. He also said that on two or three occasions in the three years that he lived with them the couple had "had words". Despite several questions Davis maintained that he had never told anyone that he felt Mrs. Billings was "shamefully abused." The former clerk was also the person who removed the window from the house and put it in storage. He did this, he said, not to hide it from the prosecution but to keep it way from the curiosity seekers who had invaded the property. Moak tried to establish that Davis was forced to leave Billings's employment for invasion of privacy. Davis replied, "No, I had no trouble with Mr. Billings because I opened a letter from New York."

Re-dir.   Davis's answer to Hughes's opening question on re-direct shows how swiftly the General moved to counter any apparent gains by the prosecution. "I opened all of Mr. Billings's correspondences." Davis went on to say that, when he lived with the family, Mrs. Billings had always been a help to her husband both around the house and at the store. He closed by reiterating that, "Mr. Billings was always very lively and jovial with his family."

Re-cross At this point, Moak's questions were designed to suggest that Davis had tried to hide the window sash. The defense felt Davis held up well to these questions.

Timothy Madigan

Dir.   During the period from 1866 until 1875, Madigan worked for Billings, for a total of sixty one months. As part of his compensation, he lived in the house and 'took his meals,' with the family. Madigan was described as a spicy, lively, touchy 'specimen of an Irishman.' While living with the family, he found Billings to be a pleasant, sociable person who enjoyed his family. Madigan testified that he, "Never saw in word or deed anything improper toward his (Billings) family." Like Davis, Madigan was in the house at the time of the kerosene affair. He stated that the next morning, Mrs. Billings asked him if he could smell kerosene. He said. yes, and she told him, "My husband must have got asleep and tipped the lamp over." Madigan told the court that this conversation took place voluntarily and with Mr. Billings absent. This was also the only time he ever heard of the affair. Like many other witnesses, he told how Billings was always encouraging his wife to get "a girl, use her well and be somebody." Madigan moved back into the Billings house on June sixth, but maintained that this had been arranged prior to the murder.

Cross   In his examination Moak tried to imply that Madigan had told Ormsby that he could not go into the sitting room. Madigan refused to admit to the story. Moak then took a very different line. "Were you ever arrested?'

"Once."

"Any more?"

"Twice."

"When was the first time?"

"In 1866. The second in 1868."

"Was Billings part of your bail the last time?'

"Part of it. I told you four or five times already that I work for Billings during winters. Ask me again and I'll get a spakin' trumpet for ye."

"What were the charges you were arrested for?"

"I shot a man."

It took ten minutes to try to determine whether a jury had found him innocent or was a hung jury. To Madigan it didn't seem to matter; "I got cleared."

Moak then tried to get Madigan to talk about Mrs. Billings's feelings when she would return from her mother's. Madigan testified that she would go to her mother's about four times a month. "She went there when she got ready and came back when she was ready." Madigan would not talk about her attitude upon returning. He absolutely would not speculate about Mrs. Billings having any ill feelings toward anyone, "After all, she never told me."

Alexander B. Baucus

Dir.   With the testimony of Baucus, the trial took a turn by challenging the quality of the prosecution's evidence. Baucus had known Billings for over thirty years. He had served on the Coroner's Jury. On the Wednesday after the murder, he had examined the window and saw smoke on the glass. Most important to the defense were two experiments that he had completed. He had tried to push the ball of a .44 caliber bullet through the hole in the widow pane. The ball would not go through the opening. The second experiment was to discover the effect of weather and water on a gun. In front of Thompson and Chase, on Monday, he placed his own gun in Billings's well. Both men were present when he took it out. There was no rust when it was first removed, but within one half an hour, the gun was very rusty. The Baucus gun was shown to the court.

Cross   Moak was on the defensive, since the Billings gun had virtually no rust, and this one placed in the same well, for supposedly the same period of time, was covered with rust. "Was this gun always in paper since its removal from the well?"

"It was opened twice, but always in paper."

"Do you have a Ballard Carbine yourself?"

"Yes, I bought one since the murder, in New York City."

"Why didn't you use the Ballard in your test?"

"Because it was new and this gun (referring to his gun that was in the well) is old like that of Billings.

Re-dir.   Hughes led the witness to establish that he was an engineer and surveyor and had measured the hole in the window. It measured six sixtieths one way and seven sixteenths the other. (A .44 caliber ball is .44 of an inch in width. Six sixtieths is .375 and seven sixteenths is .44)

Later in the trial Baucus was called back to the stand to examine the window sash. He stated that the hole was larger than when he first took his measurements. The difference was explained by the missing pieces of shattered glass around the edge.

George Thompson

The extent of Thompson's testimony was that he was present when the gun was taken from the well on September 5. He identified the gun and stated it was a rusty then as it was now.

184

Dr. B. Halstead Ward

Dr. Ward was president of the American Microscopical Society and a member of twenty-five other scientific societies in America and Europe. His testimony focused on four points: the size of the hole in the window, the existence of substance on the glass, the amount of powder left on glass by various types of guns and the damage that would result from a bullet fired from a Ballard .44.

In preparation for the trial, he had field tested a Ballard .44 Carbine. According to Dr. Ward, the Ballard fired with great velocity which should be evident in the hole in the window. The faster the bullet, the larger the hole as the bullet pushes out more glass. He went on to say that he had never known of an incident where the hole was smaller than the bullet.

When Ward examined the window, he noticed small black particles. The spots were about the size of a pencil point. The particles were on the glass and in the paint of the frame. He tested one of the particles on a piece of glass to see if it would light, and saw where it ignited. The glass was admitted into evidence with the residue clearly visible to the naked eye.

The doctor tested a Ballard .44 rifle and a pistol to see how much residue they left on a window. The rifle was tested at point blank range and at four feet. In both cases it left no residue. A pistol fired at three and at four feet left a residue, but only occasionally when fired at five feet. There were never spots from a pistol fired at nine feet.

After a very significant debate, the witness was allowed to answer a defense question as to his belief that the bullet was fired from a .44 Ballard. He testified that he did not think so, because of the deficiency in the weight of the ball.

Dr. Ward then went on to say that he believed the bullet had not come from the Ballard, since it had not gone completely through the head of the victim. According to the doctor, the Ballard fired with such velocity that, at the distance in question, the bullet would have passed completely through the head of Mrs. Billings.

Dr. Ward's testimony was interrupted due to the time of the day.

Day 16

Court was delayed until 9:35 because the train from Albany, which carried most of the prosecution's team, arrived late.

Those gathered in court this Friday illustrated the prestige that the trial had attained. Among the audience were New York City's District Attorney Phelps and his Assistant District Attorney, Russell. They had made the trip to Ballston Spa to witness for themselves the "trial of the year".

For one of the first times since the opening of the trial, there were seats available during the morning session. Despite the knowledge of those following the trial that most of the testimony would be technical, the room was full in the afternoon.

Moak had experienced a series of unfavorable performance reviews in the various newspapers carrying the trial. At last, Moak was able to turn the tables and poke fun at the press. He began the session by pointing to an article in the <u>Troy Press</u>. The article he questioned carried the testimony of Captain Nelson Lewis of Troy. According to the newspaper, Captain Nelson had testified on Thursday afternoon. Moak pointed out that he was in court the entire day, and, to his recollection, the good Captain had not taken the stand. Moak asked to have the testimony read from the official transcript. Judge Landon pointed out that the attorney for the prosecution had not forgotten any testimony. He then cautioned all the reporters present to only report the happenings, not to create them.

Gilbert Elcock

Dir. Since so many witness testified that they set their clocks by the whistle at the paper mill, Elcock was placed on the stand. Part of his duties were to ring the whistle on the hours of 7a. m., 12 noon, 1, 6, and 8 p. m. He was on duty the day of June 4. Elcock assured the court that the clock in the engine room is regulated by Mr. Davison and never varies by more than three minutes per year.

Cross Elcock told Ormsby that the whistle was not automatic, but had to be hand blown. He went on to say that, on occasion, he held back by up to three minutes, if there were numerous "teams in the street."

Dr. Ward (recalled)

Dr. Ward's testimony occupied nearly the entire day. The evidence was very technical. Because of the nature of his testimony, it is difficult to assess the doctor's impact on the jury. Moak asked some very specific questions which the doctor could not answer. The degree to which these questions related to the specific case is arguable.

In concluding his direct examination, Dr. Ward made two additional observations. The more rapidly a bullet is fired, the cleaner the hole. As a bullet slows down, it leaves jagged edges in glass. These jagged edges point toward the center of the hole. Examining the window that he stated he believed the bullet was "thrown at a slow velocity." Dr. Ward also pointed out that it is difficult to aim a gun at night unless pointing from the dark to a lighted space.

It was now time for payback. Moak was fully aware of how Hughes had treated Leet, the prosecution's expert. Moak attacked Dr. Ward's credibility. Dr. Ward admitted that this was the twelfth time that he had appeared as an expert witness. Dr. Ward, who had first become involved in the case one week earlier, was paid $50 per day as a witness.

Despite Moak's allegations that Ward was not an expert in firearms, he answered some very specific questions with respect to the velocity of a bullet and the heat that the bullet would generate. The doctor would not yield as to his position that there would be very limited loss of weight of a bullet due to the friction of air. He pointed out that a bullet continues to gain speed as long as it is contained in a barrel; therefore, a bullet fired from a rifle would be faster than the same bullet fired from a pistol. He also assured everyone that the longer the barrel, the more powder is burned; so smoke could exist from the same caliber pistol, but not the rifle.

The only real "scores" that Moak was able to make regarded the depth to which the "powder had entered the paint" in the Billings pane. The doctor said that it was unusually deep; he pointed out that this depth may have been the result of uneven paint. Ward also said that when he removed the particle and tested it, he heard a slight explosion. The doctor also conceded that he was unsure but that it may be true that the ball would have melted into the skull of the victim if it were sufficiently hot.

187

Dr. Reed B. Bontecou

Dir.   Dr. Bontecou, a physician, had served as a surgeon during the Civil War and had treated many head wounds. He explained, at length, the effect of a bullet on the skull. He pointed out that the human skull has varying thickness; effect would differ based on the location of the entry point. One of the thinnest portions is near the ear, where the bullet entered Mrs. Billings. Dr. Bontecou concluded his direct examination by saying that in his opinion a bullet from a Ballard .44, fired at the distance assumed by the prosecution, entering Mrs. Billings skull, should have gone through the other side.

Cross   Moak pushed for an estimate of the number of times, out of 100, a bullet might not go through the skull. Attorneys for the two sides went back and forth several times with the witness. Ultimately, the doctor admitted that the odds were about 50-50 that the ball of a Ballard .44 would go through the skull.

Captain Nelson Lewis

Dir.   Having been a gunsmith for 47 years, the last 25 of those in Troy, Nelson was considered to be an expert. He had first testified to the effect of bullets in the Strang-Whipple murder. He testified that, in his lifetime, he had fired over ten tons of lead. He had fired a Ballard .44 at a pane of glass. He shot the bullets through the glass at four feet and at nineteen and a half feet; both times he had fired at a 25 degree angle. In both cases a bullet of the same caliber fit smoothly through the hole. According to Lewis, "The fractures in glass are always larger than the bullet." In his store, he had not carried cartridges for the Ballard in seven or eight years. On June 20 he examined the shell from the carbine in evidence. The shell matched those that he had carried. With a pistol he could get residue on the glass by shooting up to four feet away. With a Ballard .44 Carbine, he could not get residue at any distance. He had fired the Ballard into wood; it never keyholed. The only way to get it to keyhole, he theorized, would be to lighten the charge. The greatest loss of weight of the bullet in any of the test shots was 9 grams.

The remainder of the examination of Captain Nelson was postponed until Monday morning.

Amanda Ormsby, the sister of the district attorney, had died on Thursday. At the request of Moak, for the prosecution and Hughes, for the defense, Judge Landon adjourned court for Saturday so that Ormsby could attend the funeral.

Knowing that this would be a long adjournment, Judge Landon took extra care to remind the jurors that they should not discuss the case with anyone, including each other. Landon pointed out that the trial had reached a critical point and they, "should not in the least be governed by influences or pressures." After three weeks, the men of the jury were beginning to feel that they were prisoners as much as Billings.

Day 17

For the jurors, the funeral day meant an extra day off. About one month after the trial, it was revealed, through a sworn statement by one juror, that they used this time to demonstrate their humanity. On Saturday afternoon, one juror consumed so much alcohol that he had to be walked around the grounds of the American Hotel by a deputy sheriff and another juror to sober him enough to have dinner in public.

According to the same statement, there were worse offenses then mere drunkenness. Two of the esteemed body were seen playing pool. Even the behavior of the pool players was surpassed by three other jurors. It seems that on Saturday night one of them had played the piano, while two others and one deputy sheriff danced with girls who worked at the hotel. Under the prolonged stress of the trial, even these twelve good and fair men tainted their images.

Captain Nelson Lewis (recalled)

Dir.   Lewis told Hughes that on the ninth of August he had tried to gently propel a .44 caliber bullet through the hole in Billings's window. The bullet would not fit through the opening. He went on to say that, in removing the bullet, he had knocked off some of the small filament of glass that had surrounded the opening. In all his years Lewis had never seen an instance in which a piece of glass had been penetrated by a bullet and a bullet of the same caliber could not pass through the hole.

Although he could not be absolutely sure, Nelson believed that the bullet used in Mrs. Billings murder was a .36 caliber fired from a Colt revolving pistol. In part, his reasoning was based on the weight of a .36 caliber bullet, which is 168 grams.

Captain Nelson was with Dr. Ward when he tested the residue from the Billings widow pane to see if it was unexploded gunpowder. In court he reported only that he saw a flash and heard a report. The defense was finished with the witness, and turned him over to the prosecution.

Cross   Although it took almost a full day of questioning, Moak tried, and was somewhat successful, in raising some level of concern about Nelson's ability to claim that he was an expert in firearms. Nelson underwent a very long and extremely boring cross examination. He told those gathered that the guns he fired were mostly muzzle loaders. Nelson continued to maintain that, as a gunsmith, he could possibly be an expert on guns. He admitted that he was not much of an expert on modern shells. Nelson claimed that he had fired a Ballard .44, but could not remember when, for whom or even where he was when he fired the rifle. Nelson also testified that, throughout his career as a gunsmith, he had sold .44 caliber cartridges manufactured by seven or eight different companies. He went on to confirm one of the prosecutions key points that there were slight differences in the sizes of bullets of the same caliber, depending on the manufacturer. Nelson was careful to point out that these differences were in length, not in dimension of the bullet.

Captain Nelson also said that, although he did not know for sure, wet glass might have some elasticity. He did hold firm that the bullets he fired through glass always fit through the hole in the window.

When Moak asked personal questions of the witness, Nelson noted that he was able to see as well as ever with his "specs." And assured everyone that his hearing was fine.

William Hagan

Dir.   In mid afternoon, Hagan, a self proclaimed expert in chemistry applied to the arts, took the stand. The 52-year-old Troy man had been present for Dr. Ward's experiments. He concurred that the Billings window and sill contained particles of powder. In the experiments with Ward, powder was never found on a surface more than five feet from the end of the muzzle of any gun. The limit on smoke was seven to eight feet. Like the other expert witnesses for Billings, he noted that, because of the length of the barrel, all powder for a shell is consumed in a rifle. A pistol shot may have unused powder after the bullet leaves the gun.

As those in the court room watched, Hagan examined the bullet used in the murder. Hagan assured L'Amoreaux that he could see no evidence that any portion of the bullet was missing or had fragmented.

Cross   Cross examination was another attack at both the personal and the investigative level. Hagan assured the court that he had been engaged full time since 1865 as an expert witness. His career was to examine evidence in cases and to determine the causes of events. His original studies were in chemistry. From 1848 until 1851 he was employed by the arsenal at Watervliet to examine and test gunpowder.

Moak decided to test the reactions of the jurors to hearing the fees paid to a full-time "expert witness." Hagan was forced to testify that his standard fee was from $25 to $50 per day for days spent in court and $10 per day for days spent preparing to testify. Over the past ten years, Hagan had testified in more than one hundred cases. He also admitted hat he was on annual retainers with several law firms.

The farmers, who comprised the majority of the jury, work long hot days in the summer and in the frigid cold winter of Saratoga County to earn $500 to $600 a year. It is reasonable to assume that they were impressed, though not favorably, by Hagan's career and earnings.

The prosecution also wanted to note that L'Amoreaux read his questions. They asked the witness if he felt that his answers were either impromptu or responsive. Hagan answered that they were. No one else in the court agreed.

Moak scored a point when it was brought out that the last particle of powder from the Billings's window was tested on the previous Wednesday. Moak's next question was important to show the defense misused evidence; he asked, "Didn't you feel the people should be able to test the powder?"

Because of his experience on the stand, Hagan was a match for Moak. This was evident from mistakes made by the prosecutor in his questioning. Moak was convinced that he could show the jury that there was elasticity in glass when it is wet, such as by the storm on the night in question. Hagan said he had run a damp cloth over the glass before he fired a bullet through it. He noted the size of the hole did not vary if the glass was wet or dry. Hagan countered Moak claiming if glass is wet, would it make a difference whether it was from a damp rag or a torrential rain. In either event it was wet. The other problem occurred when Moak handed a particle of powder to the witness on a piece of glass asking him to cause it to explode. It was obvious to all of the farmers on the jury that some form of heat or fire was needed to explode the powder. Moak would pay several times for this error before the trial ended.

The effect of expert witnesses on laymen was evident in the number of persons present when the court adjourned at 5:45. One reporter noted that between the court room and the reception area outside there were only twenty-seven people present as the Judge closed the trial for the day. Most of these people were the ladies who had become court "groupies". Those ladies who had suffered through the day had a "tried appearance."

Being able to claim any attendance at the trial of the century had become such a social status symbol that, Douglas Levien of the New York Herald brought a young lady to court to hear an hour of testimony.

L'Amoreaux announced that Hagan was to be the final expert witness. It was uncertain how many witnesses were to follow, so Judge Landon informed the prosecution that they should have their rebuttal witnesses on hand first thing the next morning. Even announcing that the defense was close to resting its case did not prevent the court from having to reassign the special term that was to be heard by Judge Landon to Judge Bockes.

Day 18

Charles Taylor, an artist for the New York Graphic, was in the court room sketching the "celebrities" created by the trial. The attorneys, knowing of his presence, were sure to have what they perceived as their "best side" toward him as they were sketched. Humility was not a color warn well by any of the egotistical lawyers.

Although the reporters were not able to find data to substantiate the assertion, the trial was already being called the longest criminal trail in the one hundred year history of the United States. The press appreciated the extended hours imposed by Judge Landon, since the trial would have been even longer if a less decisive Judge were presiding. One of the few professional people in the room, Judge Landon was not above asking for assistance, turning to Judge Crane for input on a debate.

Professor Hagan recalled

Moak demonstrated his adversity toward Hagan when, after having the professor called to the stand, Moak told those assembled he did not wish to ask the witness any more questions. Moak's decision amazed the patrons of the trial. Hagan, who had matched adjective for adjective with Moak on the previous day, rose from the witness chair. The knowing counsels for both sides noted a glint of triumph on the face of the professor from Troy.

Daniel Deyoe

Dir. Daniel Deyoe had participated with Baucus in the defense's forensic experiment. The rifle was clean when it went in and rusted over within minutes of being taken out of the well.

Cross Moak asked Deyoe if the gun had been oiled before it went in the well. Deyoe responded that he did not know.

Jonathan Deyoe recalled

Dir. The watch, used to time Norton and others as they crossed the river, had been maintained by Deyoe. He had fired a shot and then watched as Norton and others crossed the river, entered the Billings's house, then went down toward Gorham's. The time was 8 minutes 35 seconds from beginning until Norton was back in the house.

Cross Moak wanted intermediate times, such as how long to simply cross the river, to go to Gorham's and back. Deyoe was unable to provide answers to these interval questions.

George Bates

Before Hughes called George Bates, he announced to the court that he had intended to call him earlier but could not because Bates had been suffering with measles. Hughes believed him to be entirely safe; and there would be no further "breakout if the counsel treated him well."

Ormsby tried to counter with "I hope the witness does not have small pox."

As was nearly always the case, Hughes won the exchange by adding, "I don't think we will get small-pox, although we are all to be pitied."

Dir. A resident of Tompson's Mill, Bates was at Finne's store the evening of the murder where, at about 7:30, he saw Billings drive by in his wagon going north toward the lane. Later, Bates went to his parents house by way of the bridge. After he had been at his father's house "for a while", he noticed it was eighteen minutes before nine. About three minutes later, he heard the shot and screams coming from across the river. He took a boat and went to the scene.

Cross   Moak asked how Bates knew that it was 7:30 when Billings went by in the wagon. Bates assured him that he didn't; know it was just his best recollection. Following up on why the time was so well fixed in his mind, Moak asked, "Are you sure it was eighteen minutes before nine?"

Cocky, like many young male workers of the time, Bates responded, "It may have varied two or three seconds."

Re-dir.   Hughes wanted to show it was late as possible when Bates saw Billings. Hughes asked George to talk about his evening. Bates said that he had worked until six. He had taken his supper, changed his clothes, then he walked the half mile from his home across the bridge to Finne's. He had been at Finne's for a while before he saw Billings.

Recess for the defense

The judge allowed the counsel for the defense and the prisoner to withdraw to the law library. After a brief consultation, they returned to the court. Hughes advised the court that the defense had only two witnesses remaining. The two were not present, but would be arriving on the noon train that day. Judge Landon asked Hughes about the nature of these witnesses's testimony. Hughes assured the Judge that the two would talk about the relations between Billings and his wife. The Judge turned the case back to the prosecution for rebuttal.

Rebuttal Testimony

Under the rules of law in 1878, rebuttal, was restricted to countering testimony or facts already in evidence. New lines of inquiry were not permitted. Based on the issues raised by the defense, the prosecution may have wished to change directions, but they could only counter on points already in evidence. Despite the fact that they knew there would be instant objections, Moak and his team were able to use questions to make assertions not allowed under rebuttal. The effects of the questions are uncertain. A jury may be told to disregard a question, but its effect is not erased from the mind. Moak banked on the fact that the minds of the jurors would retain all the questions.

194

E. G. Cochran recalled

Cochran was the magistrate who had taken the minutes at the Coroner's Jury. From those minutes Potter read portions of Isaac Washburn's testimony. The portion that the People wanted were where Isaac said that his father had looked at his watch and said it was 9:02. Cochran assured the court that the minutes were accurate.

The voracious animosity between the counsels was evident in the next exchange. General Hughes stood and suggested the entire minutes taken by Cochran be read for the jury.

Mr. Moak responded, "That is just another clever piece of claptrap intended for the jury."

Mr. L'Amoreaux began to answer when Moak interrupted. "Ah, the gentleman with the singing voice, like the wind before a storm, is beginning to speak. That voice stands well for a few times, but becomes monotonous after a while."

Hughes countered, "Mr. Moak is trying to explode another atom of gun powder", a reference to Moak's error in asking Hagan to explode an atom of gun powder without a source of heat.

Judge Landon calmed the two sides, and the cross examination of Cochran began. Cochran recalled that, when the testimony was first shown to Isaac, he had objected; saying it had been taken down incorrectly.

James Whalen

Dir. Under direct examination, Whalen told the court that Jones was at his house on the day after the murder. Jones told him that, at the time of the murder, he was fishing up near the brick yard. Jones told him that he didn't know a thing about the murder. Whalen informed the court that the abandoned brick yard is about fifty feet north of the sunken boat.

Cross Hughes was in his glory as he cross-examined this witness. Whalen started by saying that it was two Sundays after the funeral when Jones had made the remarks, not the next day. He went on to say, "I didn't have no conversation with Jones, not at all. I know what I say; I had no talk with Jones." According to Whalen, Jones had come to his house "separate together" with two other men. Whalen could not remember the identities of the other two men, but he claimed to "know's em well." "I know what I knows and Jones said it." Whalen closed with, "I been friendly enough with Billings. Our difficulties are all settled up." One newspaper went so far as to describe Whalen as "a very stupid witness."

George Jones recalled

Jones swore he never told Matthews, "that sometimes I thought Billings guilty as hell and sometimes innocent."

James Matthews

Dir.   Matthews was brought into court to contradict Jones's testimony. Matthews said that he was hoeing corn with Jones during the summer. Matthews related that, in a conversation, Jones told him that he had seen a horse at Washburn's on the night of the murder, but he wasn't sure that it was Billings's.

The defense raised objections based on the competency of the witness. Judge Landon reminded attorneys for the defense that he would have to charge the jury that, if Jones were to be believed, then Billings could not be guilty. The prosecution could, therefore, raise issues of Jones's character and comments.

Cross   Matthews contradicted himself under cross examination. He wasn't sure of dates, or even the month, of his conversation with Jones, but he claimed to be able to quote the exact words used.

James McCarthy

Dir.   An employee of Ward's blacksmith shop, McCarthy had seen Jones at the shop within a few days of the murder. Jones told him that he had been fishing at the old boat when he had heard a shot. Jones said that a few minutes later he heard a horse go up the hill at a gallop.

Cross   The questions asked by Hughes led only to the admission that Jones's domicile was near the shop and that McCarthy saw him frequently.

Frederick Leggett recalled

Dir.   About four weeks after the murder, Leggett claimed that Lansing Lockrow had told him that the shot was heard at 8:30. The scene of the conversation was in front of Goldsmith's Hotel in Schuylerville.

Leggett's testimony was to contradict Lockrow's claim that the time of the shot was at 8:45. Looking at the records, it was clear that Lockrow had never testified to a conversation in Schuylerville. He only spoke of Fort Miller Bridge. Landon said that, in order for Leggett's testimony to stand, Lockrow would need to be questioned.

Nelson Morey

Dir. Morey's testimony was to report comments that Reuben Woodworth had made about the speed of Billings's horse when coming down the lane. Mr. Morey was at Gorham's Grocery on June 11th. He claimed that, in a discussion, Reuben had used the term "break-neck gait" to describe the length of the strides Billings's horse had made on the night of the murder.

Cross After a brief series of questions regarding Morey's decreased ability to hear, the witness admitted that he and Billings had experienced "business difficulties some time ago." The division within the community was apparent in the question concerning Morey's contacts since the murder. Morey admitted that since the murder he had visited William Harris, John Harris, and Alvinza Finne on more than one occasion.

Re-dir. The prosecution tried to explain the numerous contacts with this group as directly related to Mr. Morey's responsibilities as town assessor.

James Burton

Dir. At 8:00 p.m. the night of the murder, Burton had gone to visit Drew Lang. He heard screams up the river, but did nothing about them. Burton "sot" on the stoop for six or eight minutes, then went home. As a result of a remark he made to his wife, he was sure it was quarter to nine when he spoke to his wife. Burton also said that he was present at Finne's store three or four weeks prior to the murder when Jones borrowed the boat.

Cross The gallery was squirming in their seats as Hughes attacked this witness. Hughes pressed and pressed, holding the witness for what seemed like hours. Burton claimed to have been at Finne's Union Store for three to four hours on the day he saw Jones take the boat. He could not recollect anyone else who was present at any point during his stay. He thought he went to Finne's store to purchase sheep shears. He did not buy shears. He said he didn't trade at Billings's store but refuted suggestions that the reason was that Billings had denied him credit. Those in attendance were visibly relieved when the man who earned his living hoeing potatoes and shearing sheep was allowed to leave the stand.

Dr. Reed B. Bontecou recalled

Dir. With Bontecou, Moak was attempting Hughes trick of turning the opposition's witness into his own. Dr. Bontecou was asked if, according to the literature on gunshot wounds to the head, it was not possible that part of the bullet could come off upon entry. He said it was possible, but that the portion of the bullet should have been found at the entry point. Naturally the defense objected to virtually every question asked by Moak. In exasperation Moak called upon the court; "I know something about how these examinations are done."

To which Hughes commented "I would like to know something that you do not know 'something' about."

Mr. Moak countered, "Well I know you mind your business only half the time." Judge Landon had heard enough; he ordered both men to speak only the question before the court.

Hughes argued that a discussion of the loss of a portion of the bullet was not rebuttal but rather new evidence and, therefore, inadmissible. Judge Landon agreed and the jury was directed to disregard the questions.

Hughes did not bother to cross examine Dr. Bontecou.

The defense noted that their final two witnesses had arrived and asked the Judge if they could proceed with the end of their case. Judge Landon so ordered.

Rosanna Paine (witness 100!)

Dir. A dressmaker by trade, Rosanna Paine had spent several days at a time each year, since 1869, working at the Billings's home. She had been employed by the Billings family two to three times per year. On the occasions of her employment. she had, "taken her meals with the family" and slept at the house. Mr. Billings was always pleasant toward his family, at times humorous. Rosanna said she had never seen Billings appear angry.

Cross In response to Moak's cross-examination, Mrs. Paine said that Jennie was usually at the home when she was employed to make dresses for the two Billings women. Mrs. Paine, at twenty-eight, was a first generation American of German descent. She was reasonably attractive with blonde hair and blue eyes. According to Mrs. Paine, Billings joked

198

with everyone in the house, including her. "No, he did not joke with me more than the others." Moak was trying to elicit some suggestion of impropriety in Billings's relations to other women, namely Mrs. Paine.

Clarence Coon

Dir. The ladies in attendance this day were in for a visual treat when they looked at the unusually handsome Gansevoort resident. Coon had been a clerk at Billings's store from November 1876 through March 1877, Coon testified regarding the Billings family's relations. Like the other clerks, he had taken his meals with the family. He assured those present that Mrs. Billings could and would come to the store as she wished, taking anything that she needed for personal use. Coon added that he often saw Mr. and Mrs. Billings riding off together for lectures in Schuylerville.

Cross Moak was able to make Coon admit that the Billings only once went together to a lecture. Coon would not budge on his assertion of positive relations between Mr. and Mrs. Billings. Coon maintained that Billings's humor was well intended. Despite Moak's question suggesting the contrary, Coon had never seen Mrs. Billings leave the table as a result of Mr. Billings's comments.

The case was returned to the prosecution for rebuttal.

Edwin Towne

On the night of the murder, Towne was present when George Washburn talked about setting up a coroner's jury. Towne said that he (Washburn) was not 'going to allow Billings's enemies to come in and run the thing.' Towne added that the statement was said in the presence of Dr. Gow.

Edmund McIntyre

Dir. A resident of New York City, McIntyre was staying in Fort Miller Bridge for health reasons during the summer of 1878. McIntyre had known James Nichols for at least eight years. McIntyre testified that he had spoken to Nichols who said that he and Washburn had compared watches on the Sunday after the murder, and there was a fifteen minutes difference between the time of the two.

cross The "distinct sides" in the community were again evident during Hughes's line of questions. McIntyre had been staying at Finne's for ten weeks and had spoken to him frequently about the case. The reason for

Hughes's question is not recorded, but he did have McIntyre state that his family had not been with him the entire time of his stay.

D. T. Elmer

Dir. In March 1878, fewer than three months before the trial, Mr. Elmer purchased The Saratoga County Standard from Mr. Ford, one of the counsels for the prosecution. Mr. Elmer was both the editor and publisher of the small weekly paper. He stated that: in May, Mr. George Washburn came into the paper, alone, with a manuscript that he wanted to have published in the May edition.

Cross Under cross examination, the editor continued to assert that he was handed the article by the elder of the two Washburn men. He was so adamant that, when Isaac Washburn was asked to stand, Elmer claimed that he had never seen Isaac before. Mr. Elmer had no recollection of any member of the Washburn family saying that, if the article contained anything slanderous, it should be scratched. According to Mr. Elmer, what appeared in the Standard on May 9 was the entire transcript given by George Washburn.

Re-Dir. Before Judge Landon closed the court for the day, Moak was able to get the editor to say that the composition was written on a half sheet of paper.

Day 19

Mrs. Brisban, a clairvoyant from Waterford, joined the spectators. On the steps of the court house, she took the opportunity to enlighten all who would listen that she could tell if Jesse Billings was guilty or innocent by studying him. At the lunch break, she informed all that, in her belief, Billings was innocent.

The trial was so long that one of the jurors became a father during his sequestration. Since the judge hoped that the trial would end within a day, he would not allow the young man to visit his wife and "treasured" child.

D. T. Elmer recalled

Cross The day opened with Hughes continuing his cross examination of the editor. Elmer insisted that he was not particularly nearsighted, although he did wear glasses around the office. Having thought about it overnight, Elmer would not swear that there were not two people present

200

when he received the article. He did hold absolutely that the article was handed to him by George Washburn. Reluctantly, Elmer confirmed that the newspaper was under a mortgage to one of the prosecutors.

Madore Passnow

Dir.   Passnow was employed by Gamash in the Billings Boat Yard. At the time of the murder, he was with Yott, Gorham, and Palmer at Gorham's grocery. He left the store for Billings's house with Yott and Gorham. Along the way, he saw Gannon, but not LaPoint. He was aware of the place where Yott claimed to have seen a man running, however, even though he was with Yott, Passnow said he did not see any man. Asked to repeat his statement, he swore that he did not see or hear anyone going south while he walked between Gorham's and Reed's. Moak asked if he had given anyone advice regarding their testimony in the trial. Passnow said that he had told "Yott not to commit perjury for Jesse Billings or any other man."

Edwin Towne recalled

Dir.   Towne told Moak that on the night of the murder, he examined the window through which the bullet had entered, looking specifically for evidence of smoke. Towne told the jury that the window was dirty from natural dust; however, there were no signs of smoke.

Cross   Towne testified that he formerly worked in Finne's store. He also stated that it was at least 10 p.m. when he checked the window. He admitted that he never looked at the window in daylight.

Darwin Dean

Dean, a neighbor, was at the Billings's house on the day of the Coroner's Jury. He examined the panes of glass in the window and saw no discoloration on either pane.

William Wolf recalled

Dir.   Wolf testified that when he first found the gun there was enough rust to necessitate that the shell be removed with a ram rod. Although the gun was not overly rusty when he first found it, there was some rust which had now decreased due to the handling of the gun. The gun had be touched by; the grand jury, officers of the law, witnesses, and the trip to Connecticut where Leet had conducted his examination. Wolf assured the court that between examinations, the gun was stored in a leather case.

Cross Examined by Hughes, the witness was requested to take a piece of paper and to rub the inside of the leather case for rust stains. None appeared on the paper. Wolf claimed that the gun was now almost bright.

Lansing Lockrow recalled

Lansing testified that he had no memory of being in Schuylerville four to six weeks after the murder or saying to Fred Leggett that the shot was fired at 8:30 p.m.

Fred Leggett recalled

Leggett's testimony contradicted that of Lansing's. He said that they met and Lockrow had said the shot was heard at 8:30 p.m.

John Sherman recalled

Dir. Sherman testified that he had sent Clark Lockrow for Dr. Gow. Lockrow had first tried to use one of the Billings's horses. Finding they were all out he took one of his own. One of the jurors asked if there were any boots in the store like the ones worn by Billings the night of the murder. "We had that kind two years before. At the time of the murder, we had a different kind with a different marking in the sole."

Cross L'Amoreaux asked, "Do you know whether you had any of the same kind at the time of the murder?"

"I think we had a pair of eleven's."

"Who asked you about eleven's? Were there not boots of this same kind in the store?"

"There might have been."

Young Sherman went on to repeat that on the first two nights after the murder, he slept upstairs in the Billings's house. He did not sleep much but had, "lopped down on a bed some." He had given up the keys to the store on Friday. He could not remember being alone in the store with Jennie after her mother's death. He said he would swear that there was not a pair of 7's in the store at that time.

Re-dir. Moak asked if Sherman had any knowledge of how the gun came to be in the well. Billings's former confidential clerk asserted: "I have not the slightest knowledge or idea how the gun came to be in the well. I was not west of the garden that night."

Re-cross L'Amoreaux's questions dealt with assertions by others; Sherman claimed not to have handled the gun after Brumagim handed it to him. He was vehement that he never measured the gun for the size of bullet that it required. He never told Charlie Cramer where the gun was. Even more importantly he had never heard Cramer say that the gun was not upstairs.

Edwin Hammond recalled

Dir. Early on the morning after the murder, Hammond was in Billings's store where he met Mr. Woodworth. They decided to go look at the evidence. Between 9 a.m. and 10 a.m., they noticed two sets of tracks near Reed's property line. One set of tracks came down off the hill, and one set went up the hill. After an objection was filed, Judge Landon determined that the testimony would be disallowed because during the course of the trial, Woodworth had testified to going twice to look for tracks and to seeing two sets of tracks. The prosecution, therefore, was attempting to open a new area. Landon did allow questions regarding the fitting of the Billings's boot into the tracks. Hammond said that they had tried the boots. Later he saw Gilbert try the boots west of the hole in the garden fence.

Mrs. Mary Finne

Dir. Mrs. Finne testified to the following sequence of events: She had not heard the shot, but she did hear the screams. At the time of the shot, her husband was at the store. She left the house and joined her husband out near the block. The two Finnes were joined by their daughter, Julie, and the hired girl, Sarah Ray. Soon after, Thomas Virtue and George Washburn joined the group. Washburn stayed with them ten to fifteen minutes. Virtue went to the barn alone. The Reeds joined them at the block. About three minutes after the Reeds arrived, Washburn left for home. About seven or eight minutes after the Squire left, Mrs. Finne started for the Billings's house. Along the way, she was passed by two men in a wagon. She was unable to determine the identity of the men. Mrs. Finne was certain of the following chronology: Virtue went to the barn; minutes later her husband went to the barn; the Squire left for home on foot, Thomas Virtue left on horseback, headed north; the wagon went by with two men in it; the wagon went by again in the opposite direction. Mrs. Finne then went to the Billings's house. She said that George

Washburn was in the house when she arrived. She also saw Billings helped to his feet by Isaac Washburn.

Cross Hughes's examination was grueling. Mrs. Finne said that she could not remember whether Virtue's horse was saddled or not. She claimed, however, she was certain of the order of events. "Yes, there was one wagon that went north, but that was before the wagon with the two men went south." She saw Mrs. Washburn arrive in a wagon driven by her son, Isaac. Mrs. Finne was certain of the order because she was waiting for Mrs. Washburn before going to the murder scene. Mrs. Finne went on to say that it had been many years since she had been in the Billings's house.

Julia Finne

Dir. Julia Finne assured the court that she was with her mother at the horse block on the night of the murder. Her testimony mirrored that of her mother with two exceptions. Like her mother, she remembered that the two men went by in a wagon, going south. The wagon went north again about six minutes later. The third time she saw the wagon, it was going south again with Mrs. Washburn and Isaac aboard. The other difference was that Julie remembered Mrs. Palmer joining them at the block. Her mother had omitted Mrs. Palmer as one of the group at the horse block. Julie said Mrs. Palmer eventually walked south toward the Billings's house.

Cross Hughes only pursued the issue of time in his cross examination. Julia admitted that the times she gave were her best judgment. She had not looked at a clock or tested to see how much could be done in a minute. Hughes did go a little further in pressing the issue of the conflict within the hamlet; he solicited from Julia that she had talked about the incident with her family throughout the summer.

Charles Leet recalled

Dir. On the witness stand, Leet testified that because of his previous testimony, he had shot three bullets through a glass window. Each time he shot at an angle to the glass. He then took a bullet out of its shell and was unable to push it through the hole he had created. He went on to say that, until six years before there were a great many .44 cartridges manufactured which fired a round ball. Before the court, Mr. Leet then weighed the bullet that killed Mrs. Billings. It weighed 165 grams.

204

Cross   Hughes was exasperated as he went to the witness.   His frustration was apparent as he spoke, "How many times have you been before this court previously?"

"Twice."

"And how much are you paid as an expert?"

"I am paid $25 a day plus expenses."

"Did you fire the shots through the window?"

"No, I caused them to be fired."

The witness went on to note that the hole in the glass of the Billings window was more ragged than those in his window.   Leet also stated that his windows were thinner than the Billings's window.

Alvinza Finne

Dir.   At the time of the shot, Alvinza Finne was sitting on the steps of his store, talking to Thomas Virtue. Hearing the commotion, he went into the road.   He watched as several people ran by.   He told Virtue to go down to Billings's to see what had happened.   After Virtue left, his wife called and joined him at the block.   The Squire joined the Finnes at their block.   Virtue came back in about three to five minutes, telling those who had gathered that Mrs. Billings had been shot.   Finne told the court that he thought Virtue should go for J. Howard Thompson; he told him to get a horse and to head for Bacon Hill.   Unlike his wife, Finne was sure that it was Isaac Washburn and Billings in the first wagon to pass by.   Finne said it seemed like only five minutes, ten at most, between the time George Washburn left and the time Billings came by in the carriage with Isaac.

Finne told the court that Jones had borrowed the boat two or three weeks prior to the murder.

On the same day that he was leaving to testify before the grand jury, Finne saw Jones.   Finne asked Jones if he were going to testify before the grand jury.   Finne remembered that Jones had responded, "For once I'm lucky and don't know a darn thing about it."

Cross   Hughes had awaited this opportunity to examine the person whom the defense had painted as the root of the problems in Fort Miller Bridge.   The cross examination was to be a spectacle for those gathered in the court room.   The banter began with a debate about Mr. Finne's business.   On direct examination he had said that he was a farmer.   Now, he said he had been "a farmer on a small scale for twenty years."

Farming was not his only business; it was his "legitimate business." For five years he had railroaded, providing the Adirondack Rail Road, running between Saratoga Springs and Rockwell Flats, with horses, wagons, tools and carts. He also had an interest in the Union store for many years. While he was on the railroad, he stayed at several hotels. Hughes smiled when he asked, in play-back for Isaac Washburn, "Do you know Room 33 at the Marvin House in Saratoga?"

Without hesitation Finne answered, "I do not."

Finne admitted that he and Billings were the two biggest property owners in the town. He also said that they were not the best of friends. Their differences included a "personal encounter once," and "litigation more than once."

Reluctantly, Finne acknowledged that he had fired a pistol at a person. Although he maintained that he had no interest in the case, he had gone to Waterford to meet with the district attorney. Since June, he had been to William Harris's house, and John Harris's gate, and had seen "Old Mrs. Harris" in his store.

Although he had no way of proving that Jones had not borrowed the boat on the night of the murder, Finne assured the court he had loaned the boat to Jones only once during the summer. He was unable to give any details about Jones having the boat. He was not sure of the month or the day of the week or who else would remember. He was unable to think of anything that he did the on day that Jones borrowed the boat.

On the night of the murder, Finne was in his barn between 7 p.m. and 8 p.m., long enough to take care of two horses. To the best of his recollection, the only person he talked to early that evening was Virtue. Finne was unable to state whether Bates, Norton and Nichols were at his store on the night of the murder.

As to the incidents related to the case, the defense had little success making him change his story. Finne had been in attendance for the entire trial. As one of the last witnesses, he had watched others and had a good idea of how to respond. To the best of his knowledge, it was about twenty-five minutes between the firing of the shot and Virtue going for Thompson. Hughes kept picking. He was able to get Finne to change his testimony on minor points like the estimated time between events.

One new twist was Finne's acknowledgment that Cramer had driven by "like lightning".

Finne resisted when Hughes asked if Finne had told Reed Peck that he was at his wife's side when he heard the shot. He also could not remember whether John Donnelly was with Peck. Finne had no idea how Phoebe or Mr. Washburn had gotten to Billings's house on the night of the murder. Unlike many of the witnesses, Finne had not looked at his watch all evening. Finne admitted he had previously shot at a man.

Re-dir. Moak suggested that Finne should have his picture taken for being a witness who had not looked at his watch. Moak tried to have Finne explain about his own shooting incident. Finne was awakened one night by someone banging on his door, screaming that he was being robbed. Finne got out of bed and opened the door. There were two men outside who began to stone him. Finne threatened the persons with a gun.

Re-Cross Hughes wanted the difficulties between Finne and Billings to appear in the record. Finne admitted that he had a personal encounter with Billings sixteen to eighteen years earlier. At that time, he had lost an eye when Billings hit him with a shovel. There had also been litigation six years before, and had been some "pretty high words" three years before.

Day 20

Portions of the final day of testimony could be characterized as a trip into the bizarre. That evening, as the attorneys for both sides went to dinner, they wondered whose witnesses were whose. It was truly a day of some astonishing occurrences.

When the day ended, the stenographers had transcribed approximately 450,000 words. Each day of the trial it took the entire overnight hours for six copyists to transcribe the transcripts into four copies in "normal hand" for the attorneys and the court.

A. S. Finne

Cross Demonstrating how the witness's memory for detail varied, Hughes was able to get Finne to state, that at the time the shot was heard, he was standing on the ground in front of his store with his left foot on the step and his hand clasped around the post. This was in contrast to Finne's vague memory of pertinent facts on the previous day.

Hughes was able to make Finne contradict himself when Finne claimed that, on the day prior to his testimony to the grand jury, he had spoken to Jones about the boat.

Thomas Virtue

Dir. Finne's hired man for the two years prior to the murder was 18-year-old Thomas Virtue. Virtue had been held in reserve by Ormsby to offset the testimony of witnesses summoned by the defense. Virtue related how on the evening of the murder he brought a cow up to Fred Hilton's to be serviced. He brought the cow back to Finne's barn, arriving at 8:20 p.m. About ten minutes later, while sitting on the stoop at Finne's store, he heard the shot. Virtue told the court that he was within six feet of Terhune, Finne and Reed at the time the shot was heard. When Virtue heard the screams, he said, "Someone is hurt down there."

After some bickering between the attorneys, Virtue continued, "I ran down there and saw Cramer going into Billings's store with a lantern." Virtue reported that he went into the store, and talked with Cramer, then came out. The two young men went to Billings's gate together where Virtue talked with Joe Passnow. He then returned to Finne's carriage block, where he talked with Mr. and Mrs. Finne for about four minutes, until the arrival of George Washburn. According to Virtue, Washburn stayed approximately eight to ten minutes before leaving for home. After Washburn left those at Finne's block learned of Mrs. Billings's death from Mrs. Palmer.

Virtue and Finne then went for a horse so that Virtue could go for Mr. Thompson. First he harnessed the carriage horse, then Mr. Finne came in and told him to saddle the cream horse. He unharnessed the carriage horse and hung up the livery. He then got the cream horse from near the gate. Virtue believed that this took five or six minutes because the horse was out in the lot. Virtue then rode north, stopping at the Washburn's. According to Virtue, when he stopped at the hitching post, no horses were there. Virtue called out twice before Mrs. Washburn came out the side door. Virtue asked, "Do you know Mrs. Billings has been shot?"

"Yes, George has juss come." Virtue said was her reply.

"She is dead now," Virtue told Mrs. Washburn

"Is she?" Mrs. Washburn replied. Virtue, like Revere, rode on in his mission to tell the news to the country side.

Virtue also supported Finne's testimony that the day Jones took the boat was two weeks before June 4th.

Cross   Hughes's examination did not challenge much of Virtue's testimony. Like Lizzie Hill, Virtue was able to retell the story about the entire evening in virtually the same words he had used on direct examination. With respect to Jones and the boat, Virtue admitted telling Jones to see Finne about the boat that afternoon. Virtue swore that he never saw Jones with Finne's boat. Virtue added that he, along with Durkee and Finne, launched the boat about two weeks before the murder.

Mrs. Washburn recalled

In one of the more bizarre acts of the trial, the prosecution recalled Mrs. Washburn so that Moak could testify through his questions. The incident was short, but painful.

Mr. Moak walked to a position directly in front of the witness. He stared into her failing blue eyes and called forth the deity. "In view of your solemn oath to tell the truth, the whole truth, and nothing but the truth, is it not true that Jesse Billings came to your house on the night of the murder *after* your husband came home." For emphasis, Moak had virtually shouted the word 'after.'

Mrs. Washburn, remaining naturally humble, answered, "No, sir."

Moak continued his harangue at the witness. "Isn't it true that your husband was telling you that someone down the street was shot when Jesse Billings burst into the room and made this exclamation, 'What's to pay? Who is shot? Who's hurt?'"

Mrs. Washburn's face was red, but her demeanor never changed as she said, "No."

Moak would not, or could not, back off from his assault on the defense's witness. "And after your husband told him about Mrs. Billings, didn't he exclaim, 'O conspiracy, O conspiracy!'?"

"No, sir. Nothing of the kind ever occurred. " Mrs. Washburn, the humble wife of the towns justice, had not yielded an inch to Moak.

Cross   Mrs. Washburn stated that it had to be later than the time to which Virtue testified when he arrived at their home. She was sure because she had already changed her dress when she went out to respond to his call.

Charles Leet recalled

Dir.   At the request of Moak, this witness had telegraphed Connecticut asking for cartridges to be expressed by train. The package, which contained two boxes of shells, was opened in court. Moak created high drama with the arrival of the mystery package only to find that they were the wrong cartridges. The shells were for a .44, but were made for a Howard rifle and had a flat base. The prosecution was embarrassed. Recovering quickly, Leet testified that he had also purchased a box of cartridges in Albany. One of the Albany shells was then measured and found to be one one-hundredth of an inch shorter than the Billings shell. Leet testified that this amount of difference was normal in manufacturing. He went on to say that the Albany shells would fit the Ballard .44.

Cross   Mr. L'Amoreaux asked Leet to take a bullet from the Albany box. Leet was asked to calibrate the bullet. He placed a calibrator around the bullet and tightened until it fit perfectly. Leet was then asked to put the Billings bullet through the calibrator. The undamaged end of the Billings's bullet would not go through. Leet was forced to testify that the weight of the Billings bullet was 165 grams.

Re-dir   To explain the difference in width, Leet was asked to explain the effect on a round heel bullet when it is fired through a rifle. "It would tend to flatten out." Leet was provided two .44 cartridges that had been test fired. Even these shells were one one-hundredth of an inch smaller than the Billings shell.

Charles Bullard

During the months of May and June 1878, the man responsible for the whistle at the paper mill was Bullard. He testified that he never blew the whistle before the appropriate time, but would on occasion blow it up to three minutes late if there were many teams of horses near the mill.

The prosecution rested.

The defense began recalling witnesses.

Dr. Gow recalled

When questioned by Mr. L'Amoreaux, Gow restated that, at the time of the post mortem, he had found two parts of the bullet, with a combined weight of 165 grams.

William Hagan recalled

Hagan testified that when he weighed the bullet used in the murder it weighed 164 grams.

Mrs. Allen Lewis sworn

Mrs. Lewis was the composer for the <u>Saratoga County Standard</u>. Mrs. Lewis swore she saw a "tall young man, twenty four to twenty-five years old" handing to Mr. Elmer the May article concerning the lawsuit against Mrs. Billings. Mrs. Lewis added that Mr. Elmer had struck out the last paragraph which would have stated, "We are glad Mrs. Curtis has at last taken this matter in hand, for peace will now return to our little village."

Albert Ellis sworn

Albert also worked for the <u>Standard</u>. He went further than Mrs. Lewis in identifying the man who had handed the article to Mr. Elmer. Ellis stated that he had known Isaac Washburn for ten years. He was positive that it was Ike, not his father, who had handed the article to Mr. Elmer.

David Mosher sworn

Mosher lived in one of Billings's houses and worked for Gamash in Billings's boat yard. Before his testimony was interrupted, he was allowed to say that he was present when Billings was taken away by the officers. The rest of his testimony, which was going to corroborate Jones's, was objected to on the grounds that he could add no knowledge of the facts. The defense wanted him to be allowed to testify that, on the Saturday after the murder, Mosher had spoken to Jones who told him of seeing Billings at Washburn's. The court ordered the testimony struck from the record. Despite the order, the jury heard the arguments.

William Palmer sworn

Dir.   William Palmer, in addition to working at the lock, was the town clerk. In March he was in Billings's store while inventory was being taken. He saw the gun in the hands of Brumagim.

Cross   Moak was able to get Palmer to admit that this may not have occurred at the time of the inventory. William, however, would not yield about having seen the gun in the hands of Brumagim.

George Bates re-called

Dir.　Bates was called to corroborate the testimony of Jones. He was able to confirm that Jones had used the boat on June 4. While Bates was at Finne's store, the discussion was about the storm. Bates also remembered Billings driving by in the wagon, so it had to be the fourth. He was sure of the date and that it was 'darkish' when he was leaving the store because he passed Virtue, who was returning with the cow. To support Bates testimony, Hughes was also able to get him to say that, on the night of the murder, he had spoken to George Norton about Jones having gotten the boat.

Cross　Moak was unable to get the witness to establish a time when he heard the shot. Bates said that it was ten to twelve minutes after he got home, but he had no idea what time he had arrived at his house. More importantly to Moak, some doubt about credibility had been raised when Bates admitted that on the evening prior to his testimony he was 'in consultation' with the defense counsel. He then went down to Billings's cell and met with Billings.

Re-dir.　Bates said that he knew Billings by sight and that his visit to the cell the night before was with others. In the cell, no one had spoken of testifying.

George Norton recalled.

Norton's only contribution was his corroboration of Bates's testimony regarding the time Jones picked up the boat. Under cross examination, Norton appeared to be confused by his own testimony. Norton also admitted to being in L'Amoreaux's office the night before and to visiting with Billings in his cell.

John Terhune re-called

Terhune, who had not been at L'Amoreaux's office or Billings's cell the night before, continued to appear nervous as he confirmed the testimony of Norton and Bates. He was with Finne outside his store at the time he heard the shot. He followed Virtue to Billings's house. When asked by the court, he said it was about two weeks after the murder before anyone raised the issue of the date that Jones picked up the oars. The final comment made by Terhune was a direct contradiction of Jennie's testimony. According to John he, "...never knew of Billings's dog to bark at anyone, not even strangers."

212

James Nichols re-called

Dir.   Nichols confirmed the statements of Bates, Terhune, and Norton, with one modification. Nichols added that he had seen Jones and Finne go together for the oars. He was certain of the day because, while at the Union Store, Finne remarked, in talking about the storm, that he once heard man being blown away along with his horse and wagon.

Cross   Nichols claimed that he was first aware of the date because Finne was saying that he had not loaned the boat to Jones on the night of the fourth. Moak changed his strategy to a more personal level by asking, "Have you been drinking today?"

Nichols was incensed as he answered, "Yes."

"How often?"

"I've got no idea."

"Can't you tell us within fifty or sixty drinks?"   The sarcasm in Moak's voice was missed by no one.

Nichols was indignant as he said, "No." The court room rang out with laughter.

"Oh you can't! That's all."

Re-dir.   L'Amoreaux was obviously surprised as he rose to try to shore up his witness. He asked the obvious, "Mr. Nichols, do you mean to answer that you can't tell us within fifty or sixty the number of drinks you have had today?"

Nichols leaned back and looked casually at the jury. "That is what I said."

The room roared even harder with laughter. L'Amoreaux used the moment to regroup his thoughts to get out of this dilemma. When the room became quiet, he asked, "What did you think he meant when he asked you that question?"

In school Nichols must have been the little boy who got bolder when he was in trouble. Confidence evident in his smirk, Nichols answered Billings's attorney, "I don't know what he meant."

"Well what did you mean when you answered that you couldn't tell within fifty or sixty drinks the number you have taken?" L'Amoreaux felt that he had things back on track.

"Well, I meant that I've drank within that bounds." The room was totally out of control; the laughter was harder than at any time in the trial.

L'Amoreaux tried one last time. "Well, how many times have you really drunk today?"

Nichols seemed almost disappointed as he was forced to admit that he "Took a small glass of beer just before breakfast, and that is all I've had today." The court buzzed for a final time.

Re-cross Moak asked, "Then you have just done a little promiscuous lying when you told me you couldn't tell within fifty or sixty drinks how many you have had today?"

Nichols was adamant, and everyone in the court heard his resounding, "Yes, sir!"

Geradus Deyoe sworn

Dir. Deyoe swore that he had seen Jones return the oars to Finne's barn on June fifth. The witness added that he had known Jones for about four or five years, having employed Jones as a day worker on occasion.

Cross Moak pressed to have Deyoe state that Jones suddenly found regular work with Billings while he was only a day worker in the past. Moak also tried to get into evidence that Deyoe had, on one occasion, gone up to Mrs. Curtis's rooms with Mrs. Billings and found Billings there. The Judge ruled against the line of questioning based on order.

Both sides stated that they had no further witnesses. Judge Landon declared testimony for both sides closed. Court was adjourned until the next morning at 9:00 a.m

Part III

Closing Arguments

Hughes for the Defense

The anticipation in the court on the morning of Friday, October 4, was for the beginning of the defense's lengthy, emotional diatribe. The trial had already consumed twenty days when State Senator, Civil War veteran, and State Militia General Charles Hughes stood to begin the closing arguments. As a result of his performance at this trial, Hughes had become a celebrity for his wit and oratory. Now it was time for him to demonstrate his ability to summarize a series of disjointed testimonies. In all, it would take him the better part of three days to give a complete proclamation of his client's innocence, along with his interpretation of justice and of the law.

Calmly, and with the polish acquired after many years in front of a jury, Hughes began his comments at 9:20 in the morning. He walked slowly up and down in front of the jury as he spoke. "I am impressed with the idea that you will perform your duty. The duty of a jury is that of highest responsibility." He paused, placing his hands on the rail that constituted the boundary of the jury box. "The case is now closed. You, as men of integrity, will weigh well the evidence which was accumulated to a voluminous degree. I will not wade through every detail of the evidence, but will give you the salient points."

Hughes, with the tact of a master, decided it was time to redefine himself as a humble professional. His hands opened and closed as if inviting each juror to embrace his client. "I am bowed down this morning. It is one of the most eventful moments of my thirty years experience, as I am now uttering the last words on behalf of one who stands charged with a terrible crime. If I should overstep my bounds in addressing you, I hope you will excuse me. During this trial there may have been asperities between counsel, but I hope you will forget all that."

"Gentleman of the jury, you are autocrats and despots in that box; the court is powerless, for it is your power, and yours only, to pronounce the verdict in this case. It is with you to say whether my client shall live or die." The general allowed the impact of their power to settle in before he began to remind them of the obvious problem with the prosecution's case. "There is no direct or positive testimony as to who committed this offense. No one saw the crime committed."

"We shall not deny that guilt may be established by circumstantial evidence. With this character of evidence, just conclusions must be drawn and deductions must be free from prejudice and partiality. All proof must be reasonable and morally certain."

Pausing for a dramatic breath, Hughes continued to admit the obvious to the jury, as if to show that the defense had nothing to hide. "We shall not deny that on the evening of June 4th last a cruel and deliberate murder was committed, and the unfortunate victim was the wife of the prisoner. All we dispute with the prosecution is who committed the deed. The simple question is whether the prisoner committed the deed, and whether the Ballard carbine was the weapon used."

"The law panoplies a prisoner with several buttresses." Hughes was going to attack the way that the prosecution had treated his client and had violated his rights as a citizen of the United States. "On the 5th of June, his wife dead in his house, his daughter like one who would not be comforted, the prisoner was called by the Coroner's Jury and swore to his whereabouts on the previous evening." Implying that Billings's rights had been denied when he was called to testify the previous June, Hughes pointed his finger at the prosecutor and continued, "Ormsby was there, knowing that death had come, like lightning from the clouds, to the house of the witness he called. Billings was put on the stand after a sleepless night, in which he heard the moaning of his old father and the pitiful cries of his daughter; he was called, without any preparations, before the jury. If, under these conditions, Billings made a minor mistake in tracing his tracks, it should be interpreted as just that and nothing more. It was only the mistake any man might make in the same woeful circumstances."

"The tracks made from the Reed fence point toward the Billings house. It is argued by the counsel for the people that Billings went by this route to the Metcalf Office and there fired the shot." Hughes was about to attack the problem of an expert's testimony as disposed to what was actually seen by the neighbors. Hughes wanted the jury to catch the full blow. "And the strangest thing about all these stories of tracks is that the very tracks that we swore were made by the accused, Chief Markham, with all his years of experience, could not make the Billings rubber boots fit in them. Not in a single instance. I place little reliance on the testimony of detectives. It is no wonder they are frequently crucified by lawyers. We have two or three witnesses who saw Billings take out a measure and, by wagon, go to the back part of his farm. Terhune, on his sacred oath, told you the truth. Mr. Terhune saw Billings go up the hill, and, on leaving the Metcalf Office cross his garden. These are the tracks which the people wish to show were made after dark. Terhune swears that Billings made that line of tracks before dark."

Walking to his table, Hughes took a swallow of water. His next point was important to him, he wanted it to stand separate in the jurors' minds. "Unlike the prosecution, it was impossible for Billings to have the professor of a college note to the court his footsteps on the night of the 4th of June. He needed no expert to sustain him. He has called the persons living in the vicinity. He had only people who know whereof they speak."

Hughes was sure that the prosecution was going to claim Billings used his fortune to buy the testimony of witnesses. He summarized his point in one sentence. "Despite allegations and innuendoes, there is nothing to show that witnesses have been called to swear for a purpose."

Hughes needed to be sure the jury understood the sequence of that fatal night. "On that fateful evening, Billings had intended to repair the fence near the oat field with a hammer and nails which he had left at the bars. He had left them there several days previous. Orson Garnsey testified that he found the hammer and nails at the fence in late May after Billings used them."

"We have produced witnesses who saw evidence that the cattle had been salted and another who swore that he saw Billings in the act of salting them. This evidence is not contradicted, and it has been shown that he left his house after a late supper, went three and three-tenths miles, salting his cattle and doing other chores, which must have consumed much time. Busy as he was that evening, he arrived at the Washburn house at twenty minutes to nine o'clock."

Keeping in mind that the jury was comprised of farmers who had to work hard for their incomes, he brought his point home. "These rural detectives are ready to swear to any tracks and that any boot will fit them, as the case may require. These detectives like nice slick jobs and fat fees. They will swear to anything that will bring a conviction." Shaking his head as if in disbelief, Hughes continued his attack. "If I had a decent dog accused of sheep stealing, and there was no better evidence against him than these tracks, as sworn to by these rural detectives, I'd stand with pistol in hand and defend him against all comers."

Hughes was never one to let a point be missed. True to his reputation and wit, as a defense attorney Hughes had turned the testimony of many of the prosecution's witnesses against their own case. "One of the principle arguments of the prosecution was the fact that every person who was in the Billings house when he entered, and first saw his wife dead, alleges that the prisoner got there in less than twenty minutes after the homicide occurred. Several young men in the prime of their lives have claimed to make it in this time. Could Billings? Of course not."

With the dramatic flair of an actor in summer stock, General Hughes traced on the Potter map the outline of the path claimed by the prosecution. The strong finger illustrated the trip, the fields and hills where the horse was hitched, and even the well. "I declare it would be physically impossible for any man to make that distance in the dark and stop at the Washburn house as did Billings and be at his own home in under twenty minutes. It consumed all Billings's time that evening attending to the cattle, mending the fences, and visiting the Washburns for twenty minutes. That is all he or any man could do in that space of time."

A segue was needed between the discussion of time and the question of Jesse's state of mind. Hughes continued. "Another thing-Billings was at Washburn's house for twenty minutes and did not act at all like a man who had been running hard or was excited, but seemed perfectly calm and natural, chatting pleasantly about commonplace subjects."

"Maggie Mahoney says that the accused made certain statements. Maggie says that Billings told her that she need have no fears of the hole in the window, as the shot had hit the one intended." Hughes moved his arms simulating an embracing hug used to calm someone in a state of trauma. "Billings had merely told her that to quell her fears." Hughes pointed an accusing finger at Moak. "The opposing counsel will attempt to distort his language."

"He came to his home; he has been told his wife was hurt. He enters and finds a corpse confronting him, with a gaping, red dyed wound in the left temple, from which the life blood yet oozes. His wife has been murdered. What does he do? Shrink away like a guilty man? No; he falls and clutches at her feet, murmuring, "Oh, wife! oh, wife!" and faints there." Hughes slowly turned away from the jury and walked slowly toward Billings. He nodded at the accused and pointed to members of the gallery as he said, " Presently some of his neighbors (men) raise him from the floor, lift him to a bed, and there he tosses all night long, muttering "Poor Jennie! Poor Jennie!" Looking directly into the eyes of each of the jurors, Hughes said, "Could his ideas have been guilty ones when they were fraught with solicitude for his only child?" Hughes' voice dropped to just above a whisper. "They say he is guilty on that account."

Hughes paused not to collect his thoughts but to give the jury time to digest what he said. Assured they had accepted his points, he continued to stress the ways in which Billings was solicitous. "As soon as he is permitted to leave the Coroner's Jury, he enters the room where his wife's corpse is lying." Hughes drew from mythology, "We all know the ancient test of a person's guilt or innocence by taking him into the presence of the killed and ordering the laying of a hand on the corpse. If the accused is guilty, it is said that the blood would flow from the death wounds. Billings did not act as if guilty. He approached the form of the assassinated woman, placed his hand on her cold brow within a few inches of the bullet hole in her temple, and moaned. 'Too bad! too bad!' He did not know that a human eye was near. He supposed himself in the solitude of the dead and his conscience only." Giving several seconds for the picture he had just created to develop in their minds Hughes continued, "Would a murderer have acted so? Did his words or deeds indicate that he cherished a hatred so deadly that he could put that weapon to his shoulder only a few hours before and deliberately send a bullet crushing through her skull? No! No! No!"

It was now time for Hughes to destroy what he envisioned as the feeble motives the prosecution had put forward. "The 'Curtis feature' of this case is the most odd one, to my mind. Mrs. Billings's jealousy did not begin with her husband, but with John Sherman and the clerks. Here was the curse of a blind, overwhelming jealousy that stung her heart, warped her mind, distorted her womanly instincts so much so that it fired and heated her brain. She applies to her husband all sorts of harsh opprobriums. What does he do? Goes quietly to her mother and asks her to check the erring and unkind woman."

"The prosecution will pronounce that on the day of the shooting he visited his mother-in-law for the first time in years. Is this any reason that he went home and shot his wife? Was it the typical mother-in-law that caused him to commit the deed? John Harris, his enemy, was away, and he took this opportunity to visit Mrs. Harris, with whom he did not agree particularly well." General Hughes took the opportunity to draw a visual picture of the two sitting at the table and the conversation that ensued. "Mrs. Harris drew up a bill of indictment against him there at that dinner table. She was sure that there were several counts in it. Mrs. Harris was the typical mother-in-law, drawing her son-in-law over the coals. She accused Billings of certain improprieties. She swore on her best, but dusty, Bible, her husband in heaven, about her own virtue; that then she asked him to do the same. He told her she had him where the hair was short." Hughes let the impression of this delightful little discussion set in. "Nice talk. But the mother-in-law was arraigning Billings for all she was worth." [Hughes's sarcasm still rings out from the words more than a hundred years later.] "She was the estimable, the typical, the much adored, mother-in-law, and he the jocose and pleasant son-in law! Is it any wonder Billings's visits there were not more frequent?"

Humor and sarcasm aside, Hughes drove the nail into the argument that the visit was a precursor to the planned murder. "The sole object of his visit there was to have Mrs. Harris talk to his wife, who, by her talk was injuring his business. That was all. Had he had murder in his heart, would he have gone to see Mrs. Harris? Was he afraid some disclosures would come out of the slander suit brought by Mrs. Curtis against Mrs. Billings? No!"

"The people have brought no proof that he was guilty of illicit intercourse with women." The General broached carefully the topic of sex; he wanted it eliminated as motive without challenging the values of the conservative farmers who were sitting in judgment, "and, except the bill of indictment brought by Mrs. Harris, there is not a breath against him." Hughes had the advantage of knowing that most husbands had, at some time, been unjustly accused of some offense by their mothers-in-law. "Mrs. Curtis was a young married woman and a respected member of her church. Mrs. Curtis's husband is in ill health, and she endeavors to be a helpmate. Has this age become so corrupt, that because a woman is poor and compelled to work she must necessarily be unchaste?"

It was time for Hughes to turn his venomous attack on the character of the prosecution and their description of the murder. "The counsel for the other side will compel you to swallow everything. They will test your gullibility. They will override improbabilities and picture them as facts. Because he had a pair of rubber boots on, they say he must be guilty. Had he made elephant tracks, they would have said the same. They place his hands on a gun that he was never seen to handle. It is absurd to think that Billings, known to everyone there, should walk up to the window and shoot his wife. His daughter was there. The daughter was the apple of his eye. You can't believe that, with all these facts, he would commit this deed."

"As to the difficulties between this man and his wife; the pocketbook story is simply a playful skirmish easily explained. The kicking story told by Jennie is of little account; the woman ran through the house, and he followed her to the door, and as it was closing, he reached out his foot to prevent that, and struck his wife. The chloroform and kerosene affairs are found to be the most groundless exaggeration, and you should pay no heed to them. No evidence is brought of any injury to the delicate flesh of this woman. Who told you this; Jennie told you. She was brought here and placed on the stand, as the drapery is placed on the stage, she was paraded here in her habiliment of mourning; she was brought here in her drapery of woe and mourning habiliments to influence the minds of you twelve men. The counsel on the other side had no need to drag her here. They had studied its effect and her production in court was only a part of their programme. The courtroom effect, the escort in and out, the fainting, and hysterics were a part of the programme. You probably fathomed it as we did. It was a terrible thing. It was a cruel act. Even now she is loved and worshipped by the accused with all the tenderness, love and forgiveness of a father's heart. She added nothing to the testimony of Maggie Mahoney. Why did counsel need to put her on the stand? Gentlemen, it will take years and probably a lifetime to heal her own mind and conscience. But what care the prosecution, if only they succeed in convicting an innocent man."

Hughes, because the defense is required to go first, knew that this was his only chance before the jury. He attacked what he believed would be the prosecution's characterization of Billings. He proceeded pointing-open handed to Billings, as he faced the jury. "It is shown that Mr. Billings was never cruel to his family; he was not a brooding man, but he was light-hearted and jovial. The evidence shows that of all the numerous people who have testified here, but one ever saw him angry, and this anger was a matter of business. Is this the man who prowls about in the night to shoot his wife?"

"What did Billings have to gain by committing this murder? His mother-in-law testified that she had made arrangements to take her daughter back into her home. If Mrs. Billings had died on June 4 as she did, what would he get: one third of $900 and life interest on her estate. That's all. What, shoot Mrs. Billings so he might possess Mrs. Curtis? Why? They tell us that he already had possession of the body and soul of Mrs. Curtis. The prosecution would have us believe that Billings 'capers nimbly in a lady's chamber to the lascivious pleasing of a lute.' But there is Mr. Curtis in the way! Would he have to shoot, him too?" Hughes then attacked the basis for the jealousy. "It all originated in the brain of his wife, who was crazy with jealousy. Does a man bring a harlot under his own window, where sits his child? Does he set up a house of assignation in his own door yard? No! It is unnatural and impossible." Hughes knew by the reactions of the jury that he had made his point.

It was now time for the defense to question the weapon. With characteristic showmanship, Hughes moved to the table where the evidence was placed. "The detectives said they found the carbine in the well on the Friday after the murder. They immediately concluded that Billings shot his wife." Picking up the .44 carbine he said, "We say he did not do it, and that it was not done with this carbine."

Hughes continued drawing on the imaginations of the jurors, "Maggie Mahoney was sitting in the room with Mrs. Billings, a little to the east and north of her. She testified that she saw the flash. Now, it has been proven that a carbine will not show a flash, but a pistol will, which proves that the shot could not have been fired from a long-barreled gun." He walked back to the enclosure that divided the jury from the others assembled. "From the nature of the wound, the shot must have been fired point blank, and, if from a gun of the strength of this carbine, it must have passed entirely through." Knowing that these jurors are farmers, all of whom have some weapon with which to free their fields of varmints, Hughes continued. "The character of the wound proves that it must have been made by a bullet of slow velocity. It is claimed that the ball, with which this wound was made, fitted the gun, and weighed 220 grains, but the learned doctor who made the postmortem examination could find, after a careful investigation, only 165 grains of lead." The implication in

223

his voice made the next question rhetorical. "What happened to the balance of the lead?" Hughes answered the question, as he hoped each member of the jury would later. "They have not accounted for its loss, and we say that it was never there; the ball fired was of a smaller caliber and of less weight."

"They tell us that the gun lay in the well fifty-seven hours and then came out as bright and clean as it is today. We assert that it had not been in the well that length of time." Holding the Billings gun in his right hand, Hughes moved to the evidence table. He picked up the Baucus gun in his left hand. "We show you the Baucus gun, and upon this you see the rust made by the action of the water of the same well." Hughes held out toward the jury the rifle that was supposed to be the one used in the murder. "That gun was put in there for the purpose of intensifying suspicion against Mr. Billings. Who had a motive to do this? Who had stolen the affections of this man's daughter? Who had hard words with Mr. Billings? John Sherman. I can hear the splash of that gun in the well on that Thursday night as John Sherman goes up there after his discharge by Mr. Billings; he thought, I have done nothing wrong; this will be found in the well, and Jesse Billings will be hurried off to Ballston before a jury and will be put out of the way. Then Jennie will be mine, the darling of my heart, the possessor of her father's wealth. I have done nothing wrong; I have shot no one: But when Officer Chase shows this gun to John Sherman, John faints; he asks for brandy; he is overcome."

"On Wednesday morning Durkee went up the lane to see if anybody had crossed that lane. He found nothing. The theory of the prosecution is that Billings must have deposited the gun in the well. But Durkee found no tracks, no mud on the fence or trampled grass, nothing to associate the accused with this horrible crime was found."

It was time to attack Ormsby's decision to put the case before a jury. "Soldiers fight for all; priests pray for all; but farmers pay for all. As you will find when the costs of the prosecution of this case are made up."

In 1878, the United States had not adopted standard time zones; this would not happen until November 18, 1883. Hughes, therefore, needed to address the discrepancies in the reported time at which the murder occurred. "There is a great variance in time, a difference in the time of different villages, Glens Falls, Sandy Hill (Hudson Falls) and Fort Edward each have different times; but in this hamlet the time is regulated by an unerring whistle which is carefully watched and regulated. This whistle is something to fix the time. The paucity of the People's time is noticeable. Maggie Mahoney fixes it at 8:35; William Durkee fixes it at 8:30; Mr. Burton makes it six or eight minutes before 8:45. That is all the prosecution's witnesses prove about time. We bring Lewis Gorham, who looked at this clock at 8:30, and heard the shot fired fifteen minutes after. Miss Houseworth heard the shot and looked at the clock, and it was 8:45; James Nichols, 8:35 to 8:40; John Calkins, 8:40; Mr. Richardson, 8:42; Louis Lee 8:48; Edward Lee 8:40; D. Dumas 8:43 to 8:47; Clark Lockrow, 8:52, George Washburn soon after 8:48." Hughes took the opportunity to review the testimony of the Washburn family regarding time. Billings arrived at about 8:40 and waited at their table twenty minutes. "Margaret Garnsey places the time at 8:46; Frank Dumas 8:50, George Bates 8:40." The General took a breath, letting the discrepancies set in. "If time can be established by human testimony, it seems that we have proved that this shot was fired from 8:45 to 8:50. A great deal is made of it being dark. It is not to be supposed for a moment that any man will commit a murder in daylight, and you all know what 8:30 is like in the month of June, with its long days and short evenings."

"You may say that we are struggling to prove that Billings did not fire the shot and that the shot was not fired out of the carbine. It was sought by my esteemed opposition to deny that Jennie did see anybody that night. But she did. She saw a man rush across to the lumber pile. They tell us that Jennie was confused and did not know what she said. Maggie ran out on the south stoop, and she says that Jennie ran out the front door. If a man rushed out to the lumber pile, she saw him. She did see the man, and she said so. She described the man and his hat. The prosecution will say that you must not charge Jennie with saying that she saw a man, that it was too dark to see anyone. The river furnished the background of light which enabled her to see the man. Who was the man? It is not pretended that it was Billings, for the prosecution theory is that the accused ran another way. Terhune went to the lumber pile, but did not see a man. Terhune had 'flushed the game.' The unknown man saw boats coming across the river and passed down to the old Finne shed. He struck out in front of the shed and crossed over to the tow-path. On the tow-path the stranger met two men, LaPoint and Gannon, who both said so to you."

"In reviewing the evidence in this case I have endeavored to show that when the prosecution rested, they had not made out a case against the defendant." Now Hughes needed to assure the jurors that the reason they had not heard directly from the defendant was the fault of the prosecution, not the defense. "As they put in his testimony before the coroner's jury, there was no need to put the prisoner on the stand, to swear him a second time."

It was now time to make the prosecution appear evil for their unrelenting attack on the Washburn family. Voice soft, Hughes continued. "Mr. Washburn is an old gentleman above suspicion as a true and just man. A man who has had a seat on the bench of this court, and been otherwise honored by his fellow citizens. Mr. Washburn had given testimony which must be regarded as decisive in favor of the accused. The testimony was so clear as to secure his acquittal from the grave crime with which he is charged."

By this time, Hughes was enjoying his ability to twist perceptions; especially as they related to Ormsby and Moak. "The prosecution regarded Mr. Washburn's testimony as decisive; for what other reason would they have subpoenaed him? Why then did the prosecution not bring either Squire or Mrs. Washburn to the stand? Because, as their own witness, they would be prevented from any attempt to discredit them. Washburn's testimony comports with the whole evidence in this case. He finds Billings at his house engaged socially with his wife, son, and daughter. As a witness, he admits that he spoke to his wife telling her that Mrs. Billings had been hurt. Billings started up, rushed out, is followed by Isaac Washburn, and helped into his buggy and driven home as fast as possible. All this was at 9:00 o'clock at night."

"Miss Washburn's testimony shows that Billings came at twenty minutes to nine or before, and they had a conversation on various points. Remember, Billings had spoken to Esquire Washburn in the afternoon about getting a summons." Again, Hughes addressed the points that he anticipated his counterpart would put forward. "Now, opposing counsel will say Billings planned all this with murder in his heart. Then you must believe that he planned to have his wife at the window just at the right moment, and planned to have Washburn absent when he should rush up to his house, also to have Mrs. Washburn, her son, and daughter together in her house, waiting for the coming of Billings. Believe it! Then believe Musschausen and Sinbad the Sailor."

"It will be said that there are discrepancies in the testimony of the Washburns as to the subject matter of their conversation on that evening." Hughes relished his own ability to use the Bible as a vehicle for his clients. "Well, gentlemen, you should recollect that the eye witnesses at the crucifixion do not agree as to the words inscribed on the cross. But there is nothing in the testimony of the Washburns that is conflicting or damaging to their credibility. Everything said and done in their testimony is entitled to implicit belief."

"Now gentlemen, if any of you were in circumstances requiring you to show where you were at a given day and a given hour, how could you do it better than by producing four credible witnesses who could tell just where they saw you, and just when they saw you? You would consider yourselves impregnable, fortified against all attempts to locate you in a different place. As it would be in your case so it is in the case of Mr. Billings." Both sides personalized the argument asking the jury to consider the events as if they happened to them.

"The attempt of opposing counsel to make Mrs. Washburn forswear herself came from a depraved mind and ought to be rebuked by the jury. She is brought back upon the stand and counsel, with a preliminary flourish, and a tone of awful premonition, asks Mrs. Washburn, 'Now is it not true that Mr. Billings came to your house that night after your husband had gotten home?' She, astounded says, 'No Sir!' This solemn effort to make the old lady perjure herself is unprofessional and should be discountenanced."

"Now, without abating anything from the just merits of Mr. Finne, who had for years been the sworn enemy of Billings, I shall name a witness, a truthful man, in advance of all the Finnes in the case, and it is George W. Jones." Hughes wanted the jury to see the humble, hard-working Jones, so he walked to the rail separating the gallery from the court. This move placed Jones in the seat behind him. As he spoke, each juror saw Jones as they watched the great orator deliver his blow to the prosecution. "Every effort has been made to break down this witness, because the court said, 'If this witness is believed, I shall have to tell the jury that the accused is innocent.' Opposing counsel saw the necessity of destroying Jones, and they have brought to bear upon him every engine in their power. They say he is a liar with perjury on his soul." Hughes fixes his stare on Finne who was seated in the second row. "But he had Finne's boat and only once. Jones says the night he had it was on the fourth of June. Finne puts the time a week or two previous. Jones is corroborated as to the day and hour by three witnesses who can be assailed in no other way than by giving them a bad name, because they are working with their hands to earn a living. But it will be said, some of them had, at some time or other, worked for Billings, or for contractors who ran Billings's Boat Yard, and therefore they have an interest to swear falsely. This presentation of facts is too weak to be thrown into the scales against a man's life, and the jury will so regard it." Hughes was again playing to the jury, each member of which earned his living by the honest sweat of his brow.

"I speak of Jones, not as an important factor in this case. Blot him out and our case is not weakened. But we called him, and they sought to destroy him. No one says he has a character for lying. Thirteen years he has lived at various places in this county, during a formative period in his career, when, if ever, he was open to temptations and blandishments, without the restraints of family, home, or a mother's voice and influence; but, after a most searching examination, not a wrong thing, not a mean thing, is found against him. We claim that his story is truthful, and that he was in a boat in the river where he could see Billings at the time he says he did." Hughes was not finished with how the prosecution had attacked his witnesses. With these words, he showed the clear division in the community. "Counsel will say Billings bought him. If this were so, why should Jones swear that he went to Finne's to get his boat, and thus go right into the camp of the enemy?" This simple direct logic had to strike into the heart of the jurors.

Hughes then claimed that, if the jury were to look at all the evidence produced by the prosecution, it was altogether insufficient to criminate and convict the defendant. Hughes pointed out that the prosecution's case was too weak, even if left without any evidence by the defense. But with the defense's evidence to be considered "I do not permit myself to doubt, for a moment, that the verdict of the jury will be an acquittal." Ever the politician, Hughes took a few minutes to speak tenderly of Mrs. Billings and her daughter. Hughes claimed that he would not say an unkind word about Jennie; however, he then alluded to an incident in Roman history in which a daughter rode in a triumphal car over the dead body of her father. In words that would never reach a courtroom today, Hughes said, "A woman has possibilities in her nature which no one could understand."

Hughes had presented his last argument; it was now time to emphasize to the jury their ultimate responsibility to deliver justice. "I ask no sympathy for my client. I simply ask justice for him. I have no wish that this jury should do anything but what right and justice demands. Left to me, I might have asked the court to discharge the prisoner at another stage of the trial, but he (Billings) desired to have all the evidence passed upon by the jury."

His final words spoken, Hughes turned his back to the jury. Hunched slightly, drawn as if from the exhaustion of presenting what he hoped was the obvious, Hughes walked slowly back to his chair.

While driving home from court, the most noble parent in the court, Dr. Billings, had had a buggy accident on October 5. At 84, he, along with a passerby, righted his overturned wagon and he drove home. His minor injuries were the talk of the court.

The Prosecution Closes

It was two o'clock on Monday afternoon, when Moak was finally able to stand before the jury, intent on beginning the prosecution's summation. For the next four days Moak's comments would be constantly interrupted by the defense, claiming that he was manufacturing evidence. During the course of the trial, which began with his opening remarks, until now, the mood of the courtroom, like the weather outside, had changed from abnormally hot and steamy to damp and chilly. It was now late enough in year that the leaves had gone from greens of summer through the magnificent reds and orange of autumn. By the time Moak finished his discourse, the color of the leaves, like the temperament of the room would be burned and brown.

As if trying to emulate Hughes, Moak began with his voice thundering the opening line. "That shot went where it was intended!" He paused and regrouped as he walked to the front of the jury. "On the night of the 4th of June somebody knew whether it did or not. That somebody was Jesse Billings, Jr."

"When Jesse Billings, on the night of the 5th of June, told Maggie Mahoney he assumed that the bullet hit the one for whom it was intended, he told the truth. It was the fact he stated, not an assumption. It was one of those slips which any man may make. He told a fact that no person but one on earth knows and that person is Billings."

Moak, although not Hughes's equal in charisma, was very adroit in the ways of juries. He knew he needed to thwart the effects of the denunciations Hughes had leveled on him for the presentation of witnesses. "We are not here to turn this court of justice into a circus. We are here not to enact scenes of tragedy." Turning toward Hughes, he spoke again. "We are not here to put on a show or a performance the knowledge of which are acquired in early youth." Moak now turned his discussion to the power and responsibility of the jury. "The law says that the only safeguard of the community is that the taking of a life be met by the death penalty."

"This case has assumed an importance which is seldom attained in criminal jurisprudence. This case will decide whether the testimony of a few truthful witnesses are to be offset by perjury and money." Hughes and L'Amoreaux were both on their feet objecting to the implication that money was used to influence anyone. "The length of the trial has, perhaps, never been equaled. In the presentation of this case, I ask you not to consider me as the representative of the Harrises, Miss Jennie Billings or the Finnes." Moak had found himself in the unenviable position of defending himself, rather than his position. "I come at the request of the district attorney, and by designation of his Honor who presides here. It has been heralded abroad that I came upon the retainer of the Harrises and the Finnes. The learned gentleman says I came here because I have my reputation at stake. I have never in my life tried but two capital cases, and I have nothing to gain personally in this case. I hope that I have reached such an age and such a degree of experience as to enable me to discard any hope of convicting an innocent man for what little credit it might add to my reputation. I am not here to play the part of the mountebank."

Moak went on endeavoring to turn the perception that the use of the courtroom as a base for personal gain, was in reality, Hughes's objective. "Neither have I graced Congressional halls and the Senate chamber of this state, and there gained a reputation to defend. You have heard the tragic rendering of the story of the priest, the soldier and the farmer, and you know that it was an appeal to the sordid natures against the prosecution in the cause of justice on account of its expense. Why did counsel allude to the large amount to be paid to settle all the criminal trials? He thought he could reach you in this manner. Criminal trails are expensive. But if the laws were not enforced and criminals brought to justice you could not lay down your heads at night"

"I wish to say nothing against Saratoga County, but it is, by word in the city of Troy, the headquarters of crime in the United States. It is reported in their papers that when a crime is committed, criminals should go over into Saratoga County and be fined $250." (The value of this argument is hard to weigh in the context of an outsider - Moak - using it to disparage the local persons of the jury.) "I know that you have a district attorney who has done his full duty, but, if he is not sustained by public sentiment, you may as well resign your county to anarchy and confusion. If the county does not assist in the administration of justice, criminals will run at large among you."

Like his counterpart, Moak was always one to play on the ego of the jury. "It is obvious that we have an intelligent jury, one of good understanding, and, therefore, there is no use to apply to your sympathies. In judging between truth and falsehood, you, the jury, are capable of determining between the two. We must judge the truthfulness of a statement from what we know of a man. The character of Jesse Billings is before you in the evidence of the witnesses, and from his appearance here. We are told Billings is a pleasant and jovial man. Why then, only a few months after his wife's death, do you see him appearing in a crowded assembly with a white vest, and not in the semblance of mourning? (For the remainder of the trial, Billings wore a black vest.) Have you seen a tear drop from his person? Even my friend Hughes, in the kindness of his heart, showed emotion when he referred to the murdered." Moak's sarcasm was missed by none in the room. "My pious friend over yonder," Moak pointed with his whole hand in the direction of L'Amoreaux, "who thanked God seventeen times for something in his opening, brought tears to his own eyes. But who has seen the first tear in the eye of the prisoner?"

Moak knew it was time to press the attack on Jesse at the most personal level. "Did you not hear him say, 'it is all put on!', when his daughter was carried from the courtroom fainting. That's the kind of affectionate father the accused is." Pointing directly at Jesse. "Look at him, as brazen as a post. The witnesses have told us that Billings would smile at home. Billings has smiled here. You have seen that smile; it is a terrible smile."

"Hughes called me a Moloch, a Big Injun, and several other things, this morning, and I thought I would say something mean about him, but I can't. Hughes said this was the first time he had looked you in the face, but if he secures a verdict from you, the next time he meets you, he will laugh at how he influenced so many 'soft-heads.'"

"You remember when L'Amoreaux, in his opening remarks, asked, if any one of you had been 'approached'? Why did the defense ask this if it was not in their heads." The issue of the cost of this trial could not be ignored. "You see the prodigality with which money was spent here. Billings may spend his money liberally where his life is involved. If it were me accused of such a horrid crime, I would do the same."

"It is the duty of a jury to find the truth and to render a verdict in accordance with the truth," A long pause followed. Assured he had the jury's attention, Moak lowered his voice and continued, "Simply declare the truth."

"Where a chain of circumstances is repeated by several witnesses, pointing to a certain individual, and there are no circumstances pointing toward another individual, it is stronger proof than that of the positive evidence of one witness. Suppose that some enemy of Billings had come here and stated that he saw Billings fire the shot; it would not be as strong as the chain of circumstances which show that Jesse Billings perpetrated the crime." Moak continued his admonishment, pointing out that the decision should be based on the quality of the witnesses, not their sheer numbers. "One man might perjure himself, but it is not likely that the several would all perjure themselves."

Turning to the ability of the members of the jury to disregard the spoken words in favor of their impression of witnesses, Moak addressed the need to read people through their actions and behavior. "When we read nature aright, she never deceives. When a man commits a crime and thinks he will never be discovered, he will learn that nature through circumstance, will find him out. A man who is weighed down with the consciousness of having committed a crime is never natural. Even the shrewdest burglars and other criminals make mistakes that lead to their detection. The shrewdest man, if he becomes a criminal, will prove the veriest fool."

Moak segued his argument from a general statement, that people need to be read, to how to read Billings. "They tell us that Billings is too shrewd to have committed this crime, and that it is improbable that he could have done it; but to whom do the circumstances point? Every circumstance points toward Jesse Billings, and they tell us that he is a respectable, church-going citizen. Respectability doesn't make honesty. Those values do not prevent a man from committing a crime."

"To deal the fatal blow and to escape with his life is often all that a criminal can accomplish. The murderer forgets that his feet are making the impressions which are to lead to his discovery. You can always show, after a thing is done, that the man was a fool who did it."

At this point in the prosecution's summary the reporter from the Saratoga County Standard had to leave to meet his deadline. The following paragraph appeared in the Standard, Schuylerville's weekly paper, as they closed their article on the trial.

As we go to press on Wednesday afternoon, Mr. Moak is still speaking. The judge's charge will be given tomorrow, and we shall be able to give the verdict in our next issue. We sincerely hope the jury may find Jesse Billings, Jr. not guilty.

Moak continued: "Our friends say that, 'There is a Divinity that shapes our ends'; we believe that is true. And Divinity points out the guilty party. Motives prompt men to commit a crime. Men are sometimes murdered for merely a few dollars. Men have and will be murderers. It is humanity. We should judge, when a murder is committed, whether or not the motives are adequate. In this case there is nothing that will cause a greater motive than that which leads from illicit love. Passion's manipulations lead to some of worst crimes known on the criminal calendar. Illicit love is a degenerating passion on both men and women. It is based on shared lies. It is rooted in deceit. When Billings married the young Eliza Harris, she was, in every way, his equal. He may have, since that time, surpassed her intellectually and by experience with the world, while she was plodding in her little home. He finds himself attracted to another woman, and, naturally enough, the wife becomes jealous. Between Billings and Mrs. Billings there had been estrangement for years, as they had occupied separate beds. They say Mrs. Curtis was chaste. That may or may not be true. I have an opinion of my own, which I will be compelled to throw into the jury box before I am through. We are told Billings called on Mrs. Curtis and was repeatedly in her company. They say he was under a contract to let them live over the bank, but there was no contract that allowed him to pass a portion of his time up there. We all know that Mrs. Billings was jealous. Whether or not her jealousy was well or ill founded, Billings knew she was jealous, and, if he loved his wife, should have properly governed his conduct. Perhaps we all know the state of a jealous woman. But Billings would laugh at her and then call upon Mrs. Curtis, where he has been seen by a number of witnesses. When he could not be found during business hours, his clerks would send up to Mrs. Curtis's rooms for him. Is there any wonder that Mrs. Billings was jealous." Moak then entered the dangerous, but ever so pleasant, dark area known as speculation. "Mrs. Curtis may have drawn Billings gradually into her power, with the same subtle influence that other women have ruined other men and crushed their families."

"Testimony should be weighted, not counted. One truthful witness will offset a hundred of another kind. The defense came here with numbers, but without credibility. One only need consider of what character are their witnesses made. There are only a limited number of people who live in a hamlet such as Fort Miller. In this canal hamlet, Billings was 'the autocrat.' Billings, they would have us believe, and we do, was the power of the place. Billings calls for his foreign laborers to swear for him. As a Counsel, I ask if a man working for another must sell his body and his soul to him? We say, 'no'. But what do we find among the ignorant French Canadians who are in the employ of this prisoner? Billings claims, through his demands, to own them." Hughes was on his feet screaming there was no testimony given that in any way implied that Hughes felt he "owned" anyone. The point already made, Moak continued. "And there is Jones whom Hughes has pictured as a saint. They all swear, just as Billings wanted them to." Despite screams and objections, Moak had made his point. He had personalized the assaults on the individual characters of some of the most important witnesses for Billings.

"The Coroner's Jury was public, and counsel for the other side were there. The defense has tried to make capital of the fact the District

Attorney was there. He was, and he did his duty. This Ormsby did, not withstanding the sneers and insinuations of the opposite side." Hughes, in his argument, had impressed the prosecution, if not the jury, that early in the case the district attorney was acting on the outer fringes of his responsibility.

In their summation the defense had attacked several of the prosecution's witnesses; Moak was not to be outdone in assaults on character. "Deyoe and Baucus are friends of Billings; about their testimony, I have nothing to say. They did their duty as friends of the accused. They cling to him, the same as I would cling to a friend who was similarly situated. Terhune, Nichols, Norton, Garnsey, Dumas, Lockrow and Jones have been their witnesses. Their friendship to Billings has been shown here. All of these witnesses should have known at the coroner's jury what they know now. Instead they let their neighbor, their friend and employer be arrested on suspicion and incarcerated here for months. What do you think of these witnesses? These men say they told what they knew to Deyoe and Baucus. But still, with such information as they had, they allowed Billings to be dragged to a felon's cell. Have the witnesses lied, or have they colored their testimony? Billings knew he could use these men, and he has - most emphatically, he has. This is one of those little things that point out the manner in which the defense has managed its case. These are the little trifles that make the whole - the leaves that make the book."

"The day after the murder, Mr. Billings charged Sherman with the crime." Facing the jury, Moak points backward to Billings. "Sherman boldly and honorably faced this man. Billings then responded by discharging Sherman. I would rather have Sherman's old boots than Billings's whole body. Billings was a man intent on crushing everything he could not rule. Sherman, in this case, has shown himself to be an honorable man! Has Billings?"

"The defense tells us that Jennie played the light tragedy, and Finne the high tragedy in this case. They say we dragged Jennie in here in all the habiliments of woe and sorrow and draped the court stage with her." Moak believed he was compelled to clear up the issue of the prosecution's need to have Jennie testify. "It is sometimes necessary to drag forth the 'family skeleton' to ascertain the truth. They tell you that Billings, as a 'loving father,' ordered his counsel not to traduce his daughter. Did you not hear the base insinuations, their sneers, their comparisons and flings at her? God hates a coward; and if a man traduces by insinuations and smears the character of a young girl, he is the meanest coward on the face of the earth. Had Jennie been the person the counsel would have you believe she is, she would not have fainted in this room. You saw Jennie here with dropping eyes. The eyes of the assembled were upon her. What a dilemma she faced. She sat in that chair, knowing she must tell the truth or commit perjury. Can you appreciate the circumstances and her position? She saw her mother's life taken by a wretch. She told what she knew, and then, when the excitement passed away, she fainted. Then the 'affectionate' father says 'she is only putting on.' With the most utter repugnance, Jennie had repelled his offers to put her mother in an insane asylum."

"Mrs. Billings told Jennie that Billings had tried to take her life, first with the kerosene and then with the chloroform. Others have heard of the kerosene affair. The story was not the creation of Mrs. Billings's imagination, but even if it was, it was the result of her belief. I don't know if it was true or not, but it does speak to the relations within the family. Mrs. Billings, it appears, had anticipated what occurred. Jennie, in turn, tells her father that, if anything happens to her mother, she would spend her last dollar to ferret out the perpetrator."

"Mrs. Billings had lived with this man for twenty-two years. They had what our friends call 'spats', but which one of the newspapers truthfully calls 'shots.' Billings had attempted to use his daughter as a shield. Billings says he loved his wife and daughter, yet he surrounded them with the drunken and debauched Sam Philo and Tim Madigan. This is what the 'highly respectable' Billings did."

After the trial, Jennie lived out her life as a recluse. The cause of her extreme introversion may have been the next line uttered by Moak. "The child kept them together; and the child may have been, indirectly, the cause of the death of his wife. For if she had not existed, Mrs. Billings, years ago, would have left the company of this 'affectionate husband.' Gentlemen, you have all seen the instances when a daughter should cling to her father. Jennie could not; his conduct, for years, had torn from him the love of his only daughter, who turned her affections toward her mother. It is for you to decide whether she told the truth or perjured herself that her father might be sent to the gallows. Jennie has not told you all. If

236

I were to picture to you what I know, it would make your hair stand on end." It was lines such as the preceding that caused the defense to repeatedly object to the comments, saying that Moak was creating testimony. "Gentlemen, Jennie is a noble woman and possesses all the characteristics of a noble woman. You can, and I am sure already have, judged that for yourselves."

"They say that Mrs. Billings was a jealous woman. Yes, she first complained of actions of the two clerks, Sherman and Brumagim, toward Mrs. Curtis. Mrs. Billings suggested to Sherman that they should not visit Mrs. Curtis. Sherman, at her reasonable request, ceased his visits. When Mrs. Billings spoke to her own husband he continued his visits. Billings paid no attention to his wife's fair words, and continued to flaunt Mrs. Curtis in his wife's face. Men have called on the bank, when Billings and Mrs. Curtis were there, and found the door locked. If Mrs. Billings is a demon, as the defense would have us believe, who made her the demon, if it was not Jesse Billings?"

"How to get rid of his wife filled his brain. He had tried kerosene, chloroform and threatened her with drowning. Billings had called her 'work away Becky.' He had asked her why she did not 'get a girl and be somebody.' That is a trifle, but it speaks volumes. Billings would insult her by calling her 'one of those damned Harrises.' Remember when Jennie testified that he hit them with a whip and exclaimed 'where are you delfers going?' Grose's Dictionary of Vulgar Terms defines 'delfers' as 'lewd women.' Billings compared his wife with that 'splendid woman' at the Washburn's. Which one of the Washburns he meant, I don't know or care, but I don't believe old hawks go after old hens." Moak had once again demonstrated his ability to use implication where there was no testimony.

"You have heard what the clerks, Brumagim and Davis, said about his behavior. They were witnesses for the defense, yet they spoke of how Billings's jokes would bring a tear to Mrs. Billings's eye. They admitted no more than what they were compelled to. Tim Madigan shot at somebody, and Billings stood by him; Billings shot at somebody, and now Tim stands by him. Tim Madigan is here reciprocating a previous kindness."

"Now for the 'typical mother-in-law' as Hughes styled Mrs. Harris. Jesse Billings swore that he had not been to her house for two or three years. He said he let the horse have its own way, and it went naturally to her house. Jesse Billings had challenged her to swear on a Bible. At her house, Mrs. Harris swore to Jesse Billings that she had lived a virtuous life. Just imagine in your mind Jesse Billings serving as the august judge. When asked to swear the same, the 'highly respectable' Jesse Billings told his aged mother-in-law that she had him 'where the hair was short.' Billings had traduced his mother-in-law and then had the cheek to go see her. He had assailed her chastity with the most sardonic grin. He assailed her most sensitive point - her chastity - and then he invited himself to dinner at her house. He told Mrs. Harris that Mrs. Billings was injuring his business, and that he would kill Mrs. Billings and Jennie with trouble. You see he was already thinking how to get rid of Mrs. Billings. Billings was afraid of the slander suit, fearing his acts would be spread out with a public disclosure." Having pursued motive, Moak took a few moments to take a sip of water and catch his breath.

"You heard the defense talk of Mrs. Harris's girl as 'little pitchers have big ears.' This is a homely phrase, but there is a great deal of truth in it. This defense to protect the 'affectionate father' and 'highly respectable' prisoner compelled a young girl, one of the witnesses here before you; they forced her to state in public that she was taken out of a poorhouse. So forced were they in their defense that this young female witness was compelled to whisper a portion of her testimony in the ear of the court, who clothed it in other words and gave it to us."

"We may assume that on that fateful day, Billings left Mrs. Harris's on an assurance that she would not take her daughter home and that the slander suit would continue. Jesse knew also that Mrs. Harris took supper at Mrs. Billings that night. He must have guessed that his wife knew what he had said to her mother. Billings had been told that fateful day that, if he didn't improve his conduct, litigation would follow. And he knew that his mother-in-law felt that, at the litigation, some disclosures would be made about his behavior."

"What frame of mind was Billings in when he left Mrs. Harris's that day is for you to consider. The main matter for you to consider, however, is if Jesse Billings, that day, desired to get rid of his wife. When considering motive, you are honorable men who will want to know: Was her jealousy well or ill founded?" Moak wanted to be assured that the jury would separate Billings's motive from the possible contention that his wife also acted inappropriately. "We are not dealing with Mrs. Billings's expressions."

Moak continued with a rhetorical question. "Does the evidence point to any other man having a motive except Jesse Billings? Clearly, we have shown he had a motive."

. "The defense would have you infer that possibly Sam Philo might have committed the murder. We have proved he was at Hammond's, a clear alibi. They then pointed a finger at Sherman, but we have shown he was selling goods in the store when the shot was fired. Sherman's alibi is clear and positive. Now, about the man whom the defense says ran down the tow-path - the 'Tom Collins' in this case. Jennie and Maggie both saw Mrs. Billings shot before their eyes. They both ran out of the house when the shot was fired. It doesn't make any difference which door they ran out. The counsel for the defense would have you believe that the man who did the deed ran out the front gate, and that Jennie saw that man. Jennie didn't." Picking and choosing testimony to suit his argument, Moak proceeded. "Jennie does remember that she said that night 'three times and out.' Jennie knew what she meant, and so does Jesse Billings. That comment meant the kerosene, then the chloroform and then the shot. Jennie is very near-sighted; for you to believe this near sighted girl could see a man, to distinguish a form or clothes, is nonsense to any fair-minded person. Coming from a lighted room to the dark, what could any near sighted person see?"

"Upon the supposition that she could see a man's hat as far away as the lumber pile, they have built their 'Tom Collins.' Hughes says, Terhune 'flushed the game from the lumber pile.' Terhune, the valiant, went clear around the pile. He looked for tracks, but he couldn't find them. Wilson said he found some tracks leading around the lumber pile. Norton and others came over the river and landed near the lumber pile and made tracks. Is it any wonder they found tracks there? Then their 'Tom Collins' runs off down the tow-path." To add to what he believed was the irony of the tale Moak contributed sarcasm. "It is possible he is now running along the line of the Champlain Canal somewhere. The defense would have you believe that the murder was committed by the man running south on the tow-path. There is no evidence the man was ever under that culvert. That man was the creature of my friend's imagination. That man was an improbability, an impossibility, and the theory they present is unreasonable." In 1878, there were some beliefs that today are rejected. "A murderer is always suspicious of the casual eye. To say a man was running down that highway is absurd. Let us look at the place. There was the tow-path, the canal, constantly passing boats, adjacent houses, and a number of lights that shone across the canal. That man would have to run the gauntlet of all these obstacles and past the lock where people are always standing. These men, the defense's witnesses, knew that Mrs. Billings had been shot, and yet they made not a single attempt to arrest the man running away from the scene of the murder. You cannot make me believe that these French Canadians - for such they are - are such cowards as to make no attempt to arrest a fleeing man or to raise an outcry at the time. You heard these men equivocate and stammer, but little Wilfred Passnow says that it is not uncommon to see canal men running on the line of the tow-path. The boy has heard the 'shabby gray clothes' talked about until he actually believed it to be a reality. The story is not a creation of the boy's fancy or imagination, but he was instructed to say it, and you must know the source from whence those instructions came. Gentlemen, I don't believe that you believe that credibility can be imposed with this 'Tom Collins' theory."

In changing from those who testified to the existence of the runner on the tow-path to those who said he did not exist, Moak added the implication for the indifference and the vindictiveness of Billings. "Medore Passnow was on the towpath and saw no one. You have heard Passnow say he would not perjure his soul for Billings or any other man. But Passnow's companion, Yott tells the improbable story that he did see a man. Passnow has been discharged from the boatyard; but Yott, is still retained there. Gorham went up to Wilson's house and he did not hear anyone pass."

"It is not fair to assume this runner was a stranger in these parts; a stranger does not kill a stranger. There must have been a motive. No one had a motive except Jesse Billings. Jesse had a motive, he and no one else! Not a single circumstance has been developed by his defense to point truthfully to anyone else."

"Let us look at some of the principal witnesses for the defense! I would not say that they were lineal descendants of Ananias; but gentlemen, it must have been plain to you that they colored their testimony. These men did not disclose their story to the officers of the law. There must have been some motive that led them to keep their mouths closed until the time of the trial. The defense carefully concealed the names of their witnesses until they were placed on the stand. It shows the art of the defense and their manufactured testimony." The testimony indicated that the small hamlet of Fort Miller Bridge was divided into two camps before the trial. With attacks like this, mending the open wounds would take generations.

"Gentlemen you may believe that a man with blood on his hands would run down the tow-path; and if you do, I might as well stop now." Even with this comment, Moak had no intention of stopping for anyone. "They say that Gilbert saw and reported the hat; but no-one told the officer that a man was seen running away. If a man running was a fact, and I doubt it, the defense witnesses purposely kept it from the public officers. The story was concocted for the jury. Their story is so thin it shrinks before the light of truth and investigation."

"Mrs. Smith says that on a certain night previous to the murder she saw a man in shabby gray clothes, shabby soft hat, crouch before the Billings's fence. She can't tell the night, week or month. I won't say that she committed perjury! She may have heard that shabby story until she actually believes it. That is for you to say. She says that she could tell the color of the clothes even though it was dark at the time. Mrs. Smith may have seen a drunken man, for it is fair to assume that liquor is drunk in Fort Miller Bridge. Let us for a minute assume it is not impossible or unreasonable to accept that the "crouched man" may have been the murderer. This was before the murder- she thinks a week or two before. If that man did commit the murder, he must have been hanging around the hamlet a week or two before the shot was fired! Can you believe that a stranger could hang around a canal town of twenty or thirty homes, and nobody now be able to describe him. The whole story about the man at the fence looks to me as a regular 'cock and bull story.'"

"Gentlemen, on the night of June 4, a murder was committed in Fort Miller Bridge. The whole village was aroused. The defense says a man ran down the main and only street, and yet we cannot find any one who attempted to arrest him." Just imagining the prospect, Moak shook his head as he walked back to consult his notes.

"The defense would have you believe the tracks were made by some other person. Is Northumberland so corrupt that some man up there made the tracks and now allows the finger of suspicion to point at Jesse Billings? I doubt it, and I know you don't believe it. We know that Jesse Billings put the rubber boots on that night. Some person may have seen some tracks, and another person other tracks. But that doesn't change the fact that there were tracks made." The prosecutor was persistent in his assault on the logic of the defense's position that the tracks were neither made, nor observed by, one person.

"When Terhune says that the door to the Metcalf Office was open, he fastened the halter tighter around Billings's neck. Terhune was there, and Terhune was their witness, yet he says he never knew that door to be open before. The day before, it was fastened with a nail. Billings asked Maggie for a hammer. What use for that hammer except to pull the nail? The door had been opened as part of his premeditated plan. It was opened some little time before the murder. Billings had laid out his plan before he went up into his lots. Only somebody who had a motive would have opened that door. It was not spirits. No one not familiar with those premises could have arranged such a plan. A stranger would not have hazarded himself in such a place." Moak continually attacked the stranger concept as it was important to the prosecution that the 'Tom Collins' theory be blown completely out of the water.

"You have all heard Terhune's story. He knew suspicion was pointed against Billings, and he knew he was arrested, yet this Terhune kept as silent as a tomb. What do you think of such a man? Terhune was willing to shape his story in any form he might to make the jury believe him. Detail is one of the greatest mistakes of liars. Inevitably, they try to remember too much. It was impossible for him to remember all the minor details that he pretended to give here. Could you remember all those details?" Time for Moak to launch another assault on Hughes. "My learned friend has thrown everything into this case but testimony and truth."

The turning of the accused's words against him was necessary in a trial based on circumstantial evidence. "Billings told the Coroner's Jury, under the sanction of oath, that he left the house between 6 and 7 o'clock, and probably nearer 7 o'clock. The shot was fired at 8:30, over one hour and a half later. The defense says he walked over 3 and 3/10 miles in that time. Well, that is easy enough. Even if you believe he salted his cattle, which is entirely improbable, even a poor traveler would have had time to get back by the fatal time." For effect, Moak, paused he wanted the jury in its deliberation to remember his next line. "At 8:30 o'clock Billings had traveled the distance and was back at the house, ready to commit the murder."

Believing that he had clearly established opportunity, Moak shifted his remarks to the prosecution's theory of how the act was perpetrated. "Billings took the route any man would have taken who wanted to be obscured. He was sneaking into the Metcalf Office so that he might reconnoiter and commit his hellish purpose. His motive compelled him to do this. Billings crouched along. He was bent down until he got to the hole in the fence, and then he crawled through it like a hog. Down the south side of the garden he went until, like a treacherous Indian, Billings came to the grape arbor. Why did he sneak like a hound unless he had a motive and desired secrecy? It was what a murderer would do to conceal his purpose. He went to the Metcalf Office, possibly to reconnoiter. Within a minute or two before the shot, there is no light in Mrs. Reed's window. He stole out of the office door. He crawled out into the darkness and saw his wife sitting in the window. He raised his weapon, and the shot went where it was intended. While this was going on, Mrs. Reed came into her room with a light. Billings saw he could not escape back along the Reed house. The way was blocked."

"As soon as Mrs. Reed heard screams, she raised the curtain and looked out. How long would it take Billings to vault over the fence and escape? Would it take as long as for Mrs. Reed to turn down her lamp and raise the curtain and look out? Would it take as long as the frightened girls to run out on the piazzas? Billings vaulted the fence with the agility of a murderer - that he was - making his escape. If he jumped into the flower bed, he would make no noise, as he had prepared himself well with rubber boots on. Up along the fence, the fleeing man had stopped to see if his aim had carried the messenger of death to her head. That man had a nerve; the same nerve that makes him sit here like a stone. The man sits there who fired the shot, and he says it hit the one intended. Billings, like all murderers, avoided the highway, avoided public gaze. He did not drop the gun, for that would have pointed to him directly. He thought to put it in the well, thinking nobody would look for it there. We have all heard the testimony that the horse stood within thirty feet of the well."

"One thing is certain. On Wednesday there were tracks there, and the boots were measured with the tracks." Moak had heard that the tracks were considered to be in conflict by some of the jurors. It was necessary that he complete an explanation of the tracks. "It was Wednesday when Gilbert, in pursuit of knowledge and the murderer, found the boots. He did not know if they would fit the tracks, but afterward found that they did. As you remember, his brother officer disputed him; Markham, the big city detective, could not work with the 'Wolf' and a 'howling hyena' and slunk back to Troy. Wolf, Gilbert, Teft and McConakey say they saw the 'frog' in the tracks." Having conveyed his message about the boots to those jurors who believed in them, Moak then refocused on those jurors who were concerned about the tracks. "I do not attach much importance to these tracks, except they form a link in the chain of evidence. Reed says he made one of the tracks in the garden, but not the tracks near the rear of the house."

There could be no pause now. Moak had the visions he wanted flying through the jurors' minds, and he did not want them blurred. "There were tracks around the barns. Why did Billings go around the barns, if not to visit Mrs. Curtis? On Sunday, Billings and Mrs. Curtis rode to church together. His wife was jealous, and he thus flaunted the Curtis woman in her face. Officer Durkee says that on the day he served a summons on Mrs. Billings, Jesse was seen talking with Mrs. Curtis." Admitting these are only small parts of the big picture, he went on, " All these are links in the chain of evidence against Jesse Billings."

"How came the Metcalf Office door to be open, except for the purpose intended by the murderer? Billings must have opened the door after Terhune left. Billings prepared himself for the murder. All murderers do."

"There is something about the commission of crime that is strange. Human nature seems to move in a circle. Billings had spoken of getting rid of his wife - drowning her, offering her to an asylum. His mind continually harbored thoughts of how to get rid of her. Her demise consumed him."

"On the Saturday before the murder, Billings asked Sherman where the gun was. On Monday and part of Tuesday, Billings was away at Whitehall and other places. While away, did he purchase a missile for the gun, or some other weapon?" Again an objection was made as no testimony had been offered to support this allegation, indicating that again the prosecution was fabricating evidence.

Moak was undaunted by the objections; he seemed to almost enjoy provoking the defense to react. "Where did he get all the mud on his clothes? The tell-tale mud that he had to lie away. He says he fell down several times. Fell down several times -Yes- when he was escaping, and his wife's ghost was chasing him! Where did he fall down? Ike Washburn says he fell down, but that was on the grass. How and where had he fallen down several times? Do men fall down in daylight, or when running in the dark? Billings, at the Washburn's, rolls on the green, but not till he calls Ike so he can have a witness. What made him fall on the bank at the Washburn's? We are told that, at the time, he did not know his wife was shot."

"The day after the murder, Billings did not see his wife's remains until his attention had been called to it by the district attorney. Then he enacts the tragic scene of putting his hand on his wife's head, in what the defense calls 'a spontaneous outburst of feeling.' On the night of the murder, he got down at his dead wife's feet and pretended to have fainted, but he was only carrying out part of his plan. They say Billings lay in a faint for fifteen minutes at the feet of his wife. A person in a faint for fifteen minutes would never recover from it. Billings overdid himself; he acted unnaturally. He lay on the floor waiting for the lovely Ike, his own witness, to lift him up and assist him to the bedroom."

"Jennie said to Billings 'three times and out.' Billings knew what she meant. Jennie, a weak girl, charged him with this fearful deed. The accusation was too true, and, fearing Jennie would have the sympathy of those present, he asked that she be taken from the room. He could not stand the charge of the expressive eyes. Jennie told the truth. He did not want to look her in the eyes, for he could plainly see that she knew he was the murderer of her mother. Jennie knew that her father, Jesse Billings Jr., had coldly, cruelly and brutally murdered Mrs. Billings."

The prosecution had determined that it was important to give the perception that Billings had not tried to apprehend the felon. "Did Billings offer a reward for the apprehension of the murderer? No! Did the sheriff offer a reward? No! Billings, eighteen hours after the murder, told an officer he would contribute and send for a detective. His wife dead and he - this rich man - said he would contribute with his poorer neighbors to send for a detective! He was afraid of the sharp eyes and knowledge of a detective and wanted it postponed for a day. Billings did not want Gilbert to send for a diver, but wanted it put off for a day or two. Why did he want to wait? I leave that to you."

"Billings said that he went up to his back lots and there he found the gate shut, but when he came down that night, he left it open. Why? Because he was in a hurry to get to Washburn's. He came down that lane at break-neck speed. In his mind, he knew that Washburn's was his only hope and salvation. Anything - anything - anything that he might get to the Washburn's."

"The old man, George Washburn, says that when he got home, Billings told him he had been waiting for him some time. Now see how the old man acts. Old Squire goes in to the room where, he says, the husband of the murdered wife is waiting. Before he enters the room, he stops and winds his watch. Picture the scene." Taken as Moak was telling it, the story lacked plausibility.

"We find Billings again the next morning at the Washburn's house, manufacturing evidence. If you can rely on the evidence of the Washburn's, when Billings left their house on June 4, he did not know how or where Mrs. Billings had been shot. He did not know but that she had met an accident. In the face of all this, Billings rushes out and rolls on the grass in agony, calling for Ike. Ike helps him into the wagon and, according to Ike Billings says, 'it's too bad - too bad - there must be a conspiracy.' A general charge of conspiracy, drawn to throw suspicion off himself. This is not the first case on record that the criminal tried to claim a conspiracy. Billings knew when he left the Washburn's who fired that shot. He knew that the shot went where it was intended, and he knew the head into which he had sent the missile. He spoke of conspiracy; that was subterfuge. Billings's own words tell us that he was rolling on that bed that night moaning 'poor father,' 'poor Jennie.' The name of his wife, whom he murdered, never escaped his lips. He was afraid that, if he spoke her name, her shadow would then and there haunt him at the bedside." Moak throughout the summary seemed to enjoy implying spiritual involvement.

"The morning after the murder, Billings confronts Sherman; he attempts to suborn that young man. Let us look at Billings's magnanimity. He tried to barter away the affection of his daughter that he might influence Sherman and suppress some material facts. He called Sherman a traitor, discharged him and demanded his keys. He did not want anybody around who 'would help those damn Harrises.'"

"I shall assume that the gun found in the well was once in the possession of Jesse Billings. I don't care if the gun were upstairs or down, it was in the building owned by Jesse Billings. No matter where it was, it was easy enough to get the rifle out of the store. Counsels say Billings did not have a key. The store was open almost all day. Billings could have carried the gun out at any time and put it in the Metcalf Office. The gun is 1 1/2 inches wide; the witnesses said the opening in the well was 2 1/2 inches wide. One witness says the board was disturbed; the other did not notice it. Men put down grappling irons and pulled up the gun. Our learnered friend would have you believe that Sherman stole up there in the night and put the gun in the well. He would have you believe that Sherman thought the gun would be found, Billings would be hung, and then Sherman could marry Jennie and come into possession of all the property. If Sherman had put the weapon in the well, how did he know that anybody would find the gun? The defense would say that Sherman turned pale and asked for brandy when meeting with Chase because he was the guilty party. What really happened was that Sherman was overwhelmed with the startling fact that the gun belonged to the father of the girl to whom he was affianced. He was overwhelmed with the fact that suspicion pointed directly to Billings as the murderer of the mother of the girl he loved. Had Sherman put the gun in the well, he would have been on his guard and would not have exhibited any faintness. The defense would have you believe that Sherman is a wretch, and Jennie worse than that." Emotions. Moak knew to always go for the emotions of the jury.

"On June 4 somebody knew who fired the shot that hit the one intended." Referring back to the transcript of the coroner's jury Moak repeated. "On June 5 Jesse Billings testified that his wife was killed by the effects of a 'gun shot', not a pistol."

"The wound in Mrs. Billings was made by a key-hole shot. The Ballard .44 shoots just that kind of shot, and Leet said that the ball was a .44 long." The window was held up by two of the prosecution's attorneys and shown to the jury. "The hole is clearly a key-hole shot. Gentlemen, there is an elasticity in glass, and you may try it when you get in the jury room."

Turning his comments to the availability of bullets for the gun, Moak alluded to work of the officers in the case. "Brumagim and Davis had been looking for cartridges for this gun and could not find any. If this gun was discharged after the night in question, as the defense would have you believe, the people of the hamlet would have rushed out of their houses fearing repetition of the affair. If, according to the evidence, the bullet that was found in the head of the murdered woman was not fired from this gun, then we do not exist!"

"The defense says this gun was not in the water sixty hours. They say this because it did not rust. There is no rule about the amount of rust that will accumulate on iron or steel." Holding before the jury the casing that had been removed from the rifle, Moak stated: "This shell had to be forced out of this gun, showing there must be some rust. They say there was no evidence of anybody having been at the well. Billings was in the vicinity and owned the gun. He could have put it in the well and, unlike Sherman, Billings had a motive to put the gun in the well."

"Durkee committed perjury with a motive. Let me give you a sample of his deceit. Durkee says he went pawing around in the grass looking for a pistol or a gun. Yet, at the same time, he had no suspicion of Billings! I don't believe it, nor do you!"

"They say the bullet could not have been a .44 caliber, because they only weigh 220 grains. Dr. Grant said he would not like to say that they had found all the particles of lead that were fired into the head. As a consequence of the impact on entering the head, there must have been particles of lead at the point of resistance, and all the experts on earth cannot prove to the contrary. It is idle to say the bullet contains all the lead it did when it was fired."

"Juries should not give too much weight to the evidence of experts." It would have been more apropos for Moak to say, 'Juries should not give much weight to the evidence of the opposition's expert witnesses.' "The courts state that experts have been dishonorable to the courts. Hagan is a professional expert and, for a retainer of $50 a day, will find out and swear to anything that is wanted of him. If wanted, Hagan would say he had been to the moon, and would give you all the particulars. Hagan is a knave; he burned off the one spot and destroyed the rest, so we could not experiment with them."

Walking to the evidence table Moak picked up the Ballard .44 Carbine. "Maggie saw the blaze of the gun, but doesn't indicate if the gun was near or fifty feet away from the window. She was facing the blaze so fifty feet would not make a difference with this carbine. The man who fired the weapon did not get near enough to the window to expose his face. Billings stood back in the dark, and hit the one he intended. In the light of all circumstances, it is only fair to assume that the ball that killed Mrs. Billings was fired from this carbine and hit the one intended."

Explaining to the jurors why he had been so rough on the witnesses, Moak explained, "A false alibi can only be detected when it is subjected to a strong cross examination."

"Perhaps persons are easily mistaken as regards the matter of time. Billings reached his home in twenty to twenty-five minutes after the shot was fired. From the time the shot was fired, it took Billings ten to twelve minutes to get to the Washburn's, and then three minutes to get to his house. You may give him ten minutes at Washburn's, and then he has time to get back to his house within the time frame. Billings had arranged well his plan. This man, fleeing for his alibi, would have made the trip more rapidly than the young men. The murderer would be spurred on by the thought that his life was in danger. The younger men made it in nine minutes, and they were not spurred on by motive to save their lives."

"I am not going to abuse all the Washburns. But remember, they are only human. There is Ike; we can go whole hog on him. Billings knew the old Squire's peculiarities. He told Washburn that he wanted a summons - as part of his plan. Promptly at 9:00, after he had heard of the murder, the old Squire got home. In regard to time, Fort Miller Bridge is simply immense. I saw the Hughes Light Guards (reference to General Hughes's Militia) handle their guns with the "perspicuity of accuracy." General Hughes commanded and up went the guns - all at once - simultaneously. The same at Fort Miller Bridge. Hughes commands, and everybody pulls his clock or watch and swears positively to the time. Phoebe is near- sighted, and the old lady says it was 8:30 o'clock. By and by, in came Billings. She did not look at the clock, then but thinks Billings was there ten to twenty-five minutes. Ike looked at the clock when Billings came in, and it was 8:40 o'clock. Ike - the lovely Ike - said he is positive about the time. There was nothing to fix the time in his mind, but he comes here months later and swears to it positively. The old lady and

Phoebe merely guess at the time Billings came in. But Ike, the lovely Ike, is positive. Ike is like plastic material, and Billings has used him. Upon Ike depends the matter of time, as the others only guess at it. There are other circumstances connected with the Washburn family that night. Ike picked up Billings; the old lady went afoot toward the Billings house; Phoebe stopped to put on her best clothes; the old man stopped to wind his watch; and, finally, they all got down there. Phoebe saw smoke on the window. The old man, the 'grand old oak tree,' managed to look after the Coroner's Jury. Ike held on to his boon companion, Billings. Mrs. Billings was dead, but there is no evidence that they loaned the dead woman any of their kind offices. They were friends of the murderer, but not the woman. They were part of the general plan. Billings went up to their house on Thursday and talked with the old Squire. Billings would have you believe he only talked of Jennie and Sherman. I don't believe it; do you? I don't say that the old Squire is corrupt, but we all know the weakness of age and its influences on his family." Moak had poked, but not thrust, at the Washburns.

"We have put on the stand Mrs. Reed, and she put the time at 8:35. Durkee puts the time at 8:30. Reed is an honest man, and he is unbiased. He didn't want anyone hung on the track he made in the flower bed, so he told the officers of his track. He said that they have reenacted their events that night, and it was fourteen minutes until he and his wife were up at Finne's horse block. Virtue puts it at 8:30 when he heard the shot. Benton heard the screams, and, in a few minutes, went home and looked at the clock and saw that it was 8:45. We say it was twenty-three to twenty-five minutes between when the shot was fired and when Billings returned. We may allow ten to twelve minutes to get to the Washburn's, and he has got ten minutes before the 'grand old Oak' arrives. The unreliability of Mrs. and Phoebe Washburn as to time, should not bear a feather weight. Ike, lovely Ike, says Billings got at the Washburn's at 8:40. I would not hang a dog by its hind legs on Ike's testimony." The level of personal attacks made by both sets of attorneys made the division of the community even deeper. There is the continued wonder if they were seeking victory or justice.

"The sun set at 7:32 that night and one hour later it was as dark as it was at any hour of the night." There was no testimony to the hour of darkness quoted by Moak, in fact many of the prosecution's witnesses said that it was still twilight when the shot was fired. "They say the moon was in its quarter on June 4th. The moon would not furnish as much light as a respectable star. Some of the witnesses say it was twilight when the shot was fired and not as dark as it was afterwards. All these are part of the testimony you will consider. The true issue is that, according to the time, Billings could make the round trip by walking!"

Referring back to the testimony, "The Old Squire had been Billings's confidential advisor for years. To give this relationship the mantle of charity, we are apt to think this would color, if not bias, the testimony of the 'grand old oak'. We do not find that the Washburns were friendly to Mrs. Billings. Once she called the old squire in to her home. She told him of her troubles. Mrs. Billings confided that she could not endure Sam Philo and Tim Madigan, both drunken brutes, about her and her daughter. The 'grand old oak' remained as silent as a hitching post. He offered her no relief; he was Billings's friend and advisor, not hers. They say the old Squire was all excitement and edged around to tell his wife that Mrs. Finne wanted her to come down, as Mrs. Billings was hurt."

"There is another circumstance in the case that could escape unnoticed. Billings, all of a sudden, cultivates a friendship for the Washburns - something more than a business acquaintance." Moak was implying that Billings was conniving even months before the murder.

"The old Squire's eyesight is not very good, for, when the copy of the Standard was handed to him here, he could not read it; and the presiding justice had to read it for him. If the Squire could not read the paper, could he see his watch accurately?"

"There is another minor point: the article in the Schuylerville Standard. Elmer, the publisher, says it was the old man who handed it to him. The defense goes one better and puts on two witnesses in a feeble attempt to show it was the 'Lovely Ike' that took the communication to the office. I would rather think it was Ike, and not the old squire, who wrote and handed the article, as Ike has been mixing in this affair a little too much." At this point, Moak stopped and stared at Ike, silently driving his point home.

"Billings took care to surround himself at every point with the Washburns. How convienent it is that Phoebe relied on Mrs. Washburn to tell the time, and Mrs. Washburn relied on Phoebe to recollect it. You recollect, we recalled Mrs. Washburn and put to her certain information,

251

not yet made public, that led me to do this. This information I have not given to all my associates, as I received it under a pledge." Understandably, Hughes was out of his seat screaming objections. Moak had made a critical gamble, the comment had either made the impression that there was incriminating evidence not in the record, or the converse; it was adding to the jury's rejection of the prosecution's arguments.

Calmed and remanded, Moak smiled at the jury. "Now for Isaac, but I will not spend much time on him, for 'small birds require small shot.' I asked the young man an important question, and he refused to answer. Ike denied the old man pulled out his watch, fumbled with it, and said it was 9:02 o'clock, and nobody had even asked him. Before the Coroner's Jury, he swore to the contrary. Another thing that shows the animus of Ike was he was asked if Jennie was weeping and he said she 'was pretty well strung up.' With these demeaning words, Ike showed his spite for Jennie."

"Now for Jones. Gentlemen you all saw him. My learned friend said he was a waif, a sand hiller from North Carolina. There is not much stability about Jones. Jones did not do anything when there was plenty of work, but now when the work is scarce, he appears to have plenty of work and a domicile. Jones was there when the inquest was held and told the people nothing. Jones's memory is not much better than his honesty. Jones says that he got Finne's boat on June 4. Finne, Burton and Virtue all say it was not on June 4. Jones is either mistaken, or he willfully perjures himself. A liar is always caught, or, at best, Jones may have confounded some other time with this. The boy, Virtue, knows it was June 4, as he had put the date down. I would match this boy Virtue to any number of Joneses. Jones, if he is to be believed, must have known that Billings was innocent, but he kept his mouth closed, except to the Billings's crowd. Evidence shows that Jones told a man that, 'sometimes I think Billings as guilty as hell and, sometimes I think him innocent.'" Moak paused for a sip of water allowing the jury time to absorb his words. "Jones, if he is to be believed, knew if Billings was innocent or not."

"The fact is, Billings never got to the Washburn's that night until after the boy, Virtue, had passed. When Virtue told them that Mrs. Billings was dead, the Squire had got home, and there was no horse at the hitching post. It was after this that Billings and Ike went down the road. This alibi of Billings is a pure fabrication from beginning to end, Jones was included and thrown in as a dessert. The truth is simple, while a liar attempts to tell too much. They have reached out to get too many circumstances and have got caught at it. The witnesses for the defense have been manufactured and paid."

Moak now rose to the high road; leaving argument and evidence for the jury to review, he now talked of justice. "General Hughes told you, gentlemen of the jury, that public sentiment demanded that Jesse Billings ought to be released. Gentlemen, I can hardly turn any way, but I hear the public expression that Billings is guilty."

Putting Hughes's assessment aside, Moak added, "Gentlemen jurors, public sentiment has nothing to do with you; you must decide on the evidence. The words of counsel must not influence you. It is for you to say whether or not, in your judgment, Jesse Billings, Jr., the prisoner, murdered his wife on the night of June 4th. If the circumstances in this case do not point to Jesse Billings, you might as well abolish the courts. I now leave it to you. I thank you for the courtesy extended to me on this occasion. Do what you think truth and justice will require. Gentlemen, the case is now with you."

Moak was humble as he walked back to his chair. Circumstantial evidence is the hardest to prove. He had done his best but would it be enough?

Judge Landon Instructs the Jury

In his closing remarks, General Hughes had spoken at the rate of 105 words a minute. In contrast, Moak had blasted forth at 175 words per minute with gusts recorded at 200. The stenographers glared at Moak when he finally resumed his seat.

It was widely felt that Hughes had done a masterly presentation of the defense's case. As the reporters waited for Judge Landon to complete his notes, they all agreed that Moak had been compelled to attempt a Herculean task. Moak had presented the information like a forensic expert. The prosecutor had done his best, and better than most, but there were issues that defied logic.

On the afternoon of October 12, the courtroom was brimming, not just in capacity, but with anticipation. It was obvious by the expanding throng in the courtroom, that the message had gone out over lunch. Everyone in Ballston Spa knew that Moak had brought to a close his four days of summation for the prosecution. With the beginning of the end at hand, the room, which was crowded in the morning, was packed. There was a natural buzz when, at 2:00 o'clock, Judge Landon began his address to the jury.

This day, as in each of the days when the spectators felt that something significant was going to happen, many of the people arrived in the morning and didn't leave their seats until the end of the day. The reporters had named this group the "immovable stayers". They fed their appetites with food carried in picnic baskets. They fed their minds with the comments of the attorneys, and the constant debates, during the breaks, among those in attendance. One of those people was the maid, Maggie Mahoney, who had not missed a moment of the trial.

The roar decreased to a murmur as Judge Landon stood, faced the jury, and began to address the twelve men who would decide the fate of Jesse Billings, Jr. The first sounds from his mouth caused the room to go silent. His baritone voice, which had controlled the courtroom for twenty seven days, rang out again. "Gentlemen of the jury, on the evening of the 4th of June last, Mrs. Mary Eliza Billings, the wife of the prisoner, while quietly sitting in a chair in her own house in Northumberland in this county, received a gun or pistol shot wound in her head, which caused her instant death. Death thus caused is called a homicide. That homicide is charged in this indictment to be murder in the first degree, and the prisoner is therein charged as the murderer. The truth of these charges you must determine."

"In this case it is not improbable that your minds will naturally be led, in considering the circumstances, to the conclusion that whoever caused the death of Mrs. Billings was guilty of murder in the first degree. The time, the place, the weapon employed, the deliberate accuracy of the aim, the stealthy secrecy of the deed, will, I suppose, naturally lead you to the conclusion, in the absence of any excusing or explanatory circumstance, that the actor, whoever he was, with both premeditation and deliberation intended to take the life he did take, and therefore, was guilty of murder in the first degree. Indeed the counsel for the prisoner frankly conceded that such must be your finding. The grave question with which you are confronted is: did the prisoner do the deed? The People, by their indictment, charged that he did. You have carefully listened to all the evidence bearing upon the charge." With these words, Judge Landon removed from the jury any choice. The finding must be on a charge of murder in the first degree.

"The burden of proof rests upon the People. That proof must be such as to be inconsistent with his innocence and consistent only with his guilt. Every other reasonable hypothesis than that of his guilt must be excluded by the evidence and excluded beyond all reasonable doubt. Your minds must be thoroughly and completely convinced of his guilt as the result of the evidence. Otherwise, you must acquit him."

The justice had charged numerous juries before. He was aware of the concern that members of juries had when trying to decide what to do with testimony they do not believe. "When I say evidence, I mean that testimony which you believe worthy of credit. In a case like this, where so many witnesses have been sworn, and in which the passions and the interests of so many persons have been enlisted, it is not impossible that some witnesses have given testimony which you cannot, as fair men, believe to be true, and which you may see a reason for disbelieving. You see at once that you ought to decide this case upon the testimony which you do believe, and not at all upon the testimony which you cannot and do not believe; now when I say that the proofs must be consistent only with his guilt and inconsistent with his innocence, I mean those proofs which are the result of the testimony which you do believe and can find no just ground for disbelieving."

Judge Landon knew the jurors were concerned over the level of proof required for conviction, so he addressed their concern. "Not withstanding the favorable rules with which the law shields and protects the prisoner, the law, nevertheless, resorts to such methods as are just and reasonable in eliciting its proofs. In the case of secret murder, it does not require that any eye should have seen the act or have seen the accused commit it. From the very necessity of the case, the law is compelled to resort to circumstances. You see at once how necessary and reasonable this is; otherwise secrecy would be safety, and the assassin need only to seek the darkness of the night and the solitude of the hillside to commit his crime and defy detection."

"This leads us to the consideration of circumstantial evidence. In this case, that Mrs. Billings was killed is proved by direct evidence; as I have no doubt you will find. The fact that it was a murder is an inference. The fact of murder is proved by the circumstantial evidence attending to killing. Whether the prisoner did the deed, depends upon circumstantial evidence."

"When a secret murder has been committed, and we are seeking to ascertain whether the prisoner is or is not guilty, we naturally inquire:

1st.   Whether the prisoner had any motive to commit the crime?

2nd.   Whether he had the means or weapons with which to commit the crime?

3rd.   Whether he had the opportunity to commit the crime at the time the crime was committed?

4th.   What are other circumstances pointing toward the guilt of the prisoner?

5th   What facts has the prisoner been able to establish in his defense?"

"No man committed a crime without some motive leading him to commit it. That motive may seem too strong or weak. You are not to inquire whether the motive is one that ordinarily would   lead to the commission of the crime charged. It is difficult for the mind that is fortified by the consciousness of its own recitude to conceive of an adequate motive for any crime. No motive will lead the entirely just man to the commission of any crime. You could not be moved to take the life of your fellow man except in the defense of the lives and right or just defense of the lives and rights of them who it is your duty to defend. Just defense is no crime." Judge Landon explained that the motive would not need to be one that they would accept for themselves to commit the crime, just one that the criminal, whoever that was, would hold as a reason.

"If, in this case, you find some motive which, under all circumstances, might have lead this prisoner to this crime, you will not convict him on the ground of motive alone. You will set it down as one of the circumstances and look for more. If you find other circumstances which lead your minds to the conclusion that the prisoner is guilty, then if you are satisfied as to the cause which led him to commit the crime, your assurance is made still surer. If you believe the prisoner committed the crime, your belief is stronger if you know why he did it. But this is not all. If you believe, from all the circumstances, that he did have a motive to kill his wife, that motive may have an important bearing upon all the other circumstances. If you believe the prisoner had such a motive, that fact will render such an important aid in constructing the circumstances which surround this crime, and may color your doubts when nothing else will."

"Now, in this case, a large amount of evidence has been given on the question of motive. This evidence bears upon the relations existing between the prisoner and his wife. That the relations had been unhappy you will doubtless be constrained to believe. From cause, real or imaginary, the wife seems to have been intensely jealous of her husband. She charged him with repeated attempts on her life and criminal relations with another woman. These charges she made in the presence of her daughter and their servants. The victim took no pains to conceal her jealousy. You may find that she believed she had cause. Perhaps you may find that the prisoner took too little pains to dispel her fears and allay her suspicions. The difficulty, for weeks before the homicide, seemed to be growing day by day, and to be becoming more pronounced and offensive. The prisoner's daughter took sides against him. He appealed to his mother-in-law on the day of the murder to try to calm her daughter and to give her some good advice. She resented his overtures, and bitterly denounced him. A slander suit had been commenced. The wife had sought the assistance of counsel to compel the prisoner to repay the money she had brought him."

The judge then put before the jury the prosecution's position on motive. "What was the state of the prisoner's mind on the afternoon and evening preceding the homicide? It is a proper question for your consideration. Is it true that he then thought that this scene of domestic discord must end; that he found every member of his wife's family against him; that a slander suit to which he was a party, but by which he must be disgraced, was pending, that his wife sought the aid of counsel to compel him to pay the money she had loaned him; that wife, daughter and mother-in-law would no longer be silent either upon his own account or their own; that discord and disgrace were on every hand and peace and comfort nowhere. And if it is true that he thought of these things, did he resolve that his wife should die by his own hands, and that he would seek whatever refuge could be found in the secrecy of the act, the concealment of the weapon, and the semblance of an absence from his home in the discharge of those duties which the storm made necessary upon his farm, and a visit at his neighbor's house at so instant a time, as to appear in the confusion that must ensue, almost identical with the shooting itself."

"I must not omit to put before you the other side of the case. Is it true that, notwithstanding his wife's jealousy, he had become accustomed to it; that at his age, with his business interests, his surroundings, his life long character, his regard for his position, his intelligence, his interest would lead him and did lead him to bear all these burdens as things to be regretted, but yet to be borne with that patience which nature had given him. If not for the sake of his wife, yet for his own sake and the sake of his daughter - that he is no fool, and none but a fool in his circumstances would have committed such a murder. If Mr. Billings desired illicit connection, Mrs. Billings living was scarcely an obstacle. If he sought matrimonial connection, Curtis was living; and are we to believe that his grave was also to be opened and covered? Later, you will find but little evidence that Mrs. Curtis was not a true woman to her own husband."

"Next, to the means. By what weapon was this woman killed? The People claim it was done by the prisoner's gun - a Ballard .44 carbine, for a long time in the store, for which the prisoner inquired on the Sunday preceding the murder. That on Friday after the homicide, the gun was found in an old well in the prisoner's meadow, up the lane so often spoken of, opposite the red gate. If the bullet found in the woman's head was a .44-100 caliber, the claim of the people is a very important one; for if that bullet came from the shell that was found in the carbine, then it is quite plain that that gun was the weapon used, and also that the gun was placed in the well after it was used and perhaps by the man who used it." Judge Landon went on to instruct the jury that it was important to the case that, "you as jurors remember that, the prosecution claimed that the ball found in the head of Mrs. Billings was a 44 caliber."

The judge's voice was beginning to get dry, so he took a sip from his glass. The courtroom, despite the throng assembled remained silent until he resumed his comments. "The defense claims that the lead found in Mrs. Billings's head, the hole in the window, and powder grains in the stile, and the marks of discoloration on the window proved the bullet used was not a .44 caliber. They also claim the added fact that the range was short, and the bullet did not go through the head. Based on these facts, the defense claims that it is beyond reasonable doubt to accept that the gun was a Ballard carbine, but instead a pistol carrying a much lighter ball."

258

"You will be likely to inquire how came that empty shell to be in the carbine. How came that carbine to be in that old well, if some other fire arm was used? Why hide the gun that was not used? If you find, on the whole, evidence that the carbine was not the weapon used, but that the bullet must have been fired from a pistol, then the link in the chain of the people's case, namely that he had the means, remains unproven, and their case is, therefore, not strengthened by any evidence that he had the weapon used to commit the crime, but is weakened by the loss of it. If you conclude that the carbine was the weapon used, then your minds will naturally recur to the evidence by which it is sought to be proved that the gun was the property of Billings and also as to its probable whereabouts on that fateful day. The people have submitted their evidence on that subject, and the defense has offered none. If this gun was used, you will agree that it is a fact of the highest importance in this case; especially if you also find that Billings knew where the gun was." The judge had placed before the jury that, since there was no witness to the actual crime, the most significant decision for them in the case was to determine if the gun was the weapon used in the murder.

"The People's theory is that Billings fired the shot from the garden, then ran to the old well where he disposed of the gun, and then, by buggy to the Washburn's. The defense holds that Billings was having a conversation at the Washburn's at the time the shot was fired. The question then becomes important: what minute was the shot fired? At what minute did Billings reach Washburn's? Was he at Washburn's when the shot was fired? If not, did he have time enough between the time the shot was fired and the time he arrived at Washburn's, to pass from his house, over the route indicated by the People's theory, to the old well and from there to Washburn's? How much time elapsed between the firing of the shot and the time Billings returned home after the shot?"

"Mrs. Reed, Durkee and Burton, place the time at twenty-five minutes to 9 o'clock; Virtue at 8:30; Lansing Lockrow, Mrs. Garnsey, George Bates, and Miss Houseworth, at 8:45; D. Dumas and John Calkins, at 8:42; Lewis Lee and F. Dumas at 8:48; Nichols at 8:43 to 8:48; G. Norton at 8:49; Isaac says that Billings reached his house at 8:40. If Washburn's clock was the same as his watch, and there is some evidence that it was, and Isaac tells the truth, then, by the same clock, Billings would have been at Washburn's 9 minutes before the time George

Washburn says the shot was fired. It took the map-maker Cramer 8 minutes 50 seconds and Hodgeman just 9 minutes to pass over the route the People claimed Billings must have taken. It is scarcely probable that Billings made the journey in any less time. If these witnesses are all to be believed, there was considerable discrepancy in the watch and clocks that were all regulated by the same whistle. Perhaps this can be accounted by the fact that the whistle was not automatic, but was blown by hand."

"The statements of the Washburns would make it three minutes past nine when Billings left the Washburn's house. If it took Billings five minutes to get out of the house, into his wagon, and home, 99 rods, this estimate would bring him home at 8 minutes past 9 o'clock; according to the defendant's theory that the shot was fired not earlier than 8:45, 23 minutes after the shot. If instead, we assume Washburn's time of the shot to be 8:49, about 18 minutes after the shot."

"At what time did Billings arrive at Washburn's? Isaac swears it was 8:40. He looked at his clock and is positive. How long did he stay at Washburn's? Is it probable that he reached home about twenty minutes after the shot? George Washburn says that he reached home at 9:02 or 9:03. Phoebe thinks Billings was there about twenty minutes before her father came. This testimony is to the effect that he came in at 8:40 and stayed there twenty-two minutes. Add nine minutes to get to the Washburn's from the time the window shattered and three minutes to get back to his own house, and you have thirty-four minutes from the time the shot was fired until Billings reached home. This, Gentlemen, is fourteen minutes longer than the estimates made by the witnesses who heard the shot and saw Billings arrive."

"Sherman says he came in twenty minutes after the shot. Durkee puts the time between eighteen and twenty-three minutes. Gorham testified it was eighteen minutes. Mrs. Garnsey stated she thought it was about twenty minutes. Donnelly thinks it was about fifteen minutes." Judge Landon provided a caveat that should be considered in the estimation of time. "All of these are estimates made under the highest state of excitement."

"The people boldly challenge the accuracy of the Washburns. They do not deny that he went to the Washburns, but they deny that he went there so early and stayed so long. Billings himself went before the coroner where he said he was there from ten to twenty minutes. Isaac's testimony was challenged on account of his manner upon the stand. No inference against his character is to be drawn because he refused to answer certain questions. George Washburn is sought to be discredited by other testimony which the People claim directly contradicts his statements in some important particulars, and the testimony showing his eagerness to protect Billings."

"The defense seeks to confirm the testimony of the Washburns and to establish a complete alibi for the prisoner by the testimony of Jones. I must say that if the testimony of Jones is to be accepted as true, the corroboration is complete, the alibi is established and the prisoner cannot be convicted. The People seek to discredit Jones. First by his own account of his method of living. He led a lazy and shiftless life, you will perhaps believe. Whether he is a vagabond and a scapegrace and unworthy of credit is a more serious question. But the defense come to the support of Jones by several witnesses. The People claim that, if Jones in court is stating the correct time when he started for Finne's with the boat, it took him one hour and forty minutes to go from Finne's to his fishing ground - that is, if he started with his boat before Virtue started for Hilton's with his cow, about 7 o'clock and was gone until 8:20, then Jones statement is confronted by this remarkable circumstance that he was one hour forty minutes in the journey of sixty rods." Landon chose this time to review the quality of witnesses. "The witness is produced here that you may see and believe him, observe his manner, and measure his intelligence and fairness. Something there may be in the tones of his voice, in the expression of his eyes or face, in his eagerness or indifference, and convincing, which will satisfy you in regard to his trustworthiness."

"In reviewing the testimony, this question will occur to you. If Billings was not at Washburn's when the shot was fired, could he, in from fifteen minutes to twenty-two minutes, have gone from his own house, after the shot was fired, over the route claimed by the People, to Washburn's house and thence back home? Nine minutes to get to Washburn's and three minutes to get in and out of the house would make twelve minutes, and leave the rest to be spent at Washburn's, five minutes to get in and out of the home would make fifteen minutes, and leave the rest, if any remained, to be spent at Washburn's. I only give the estimates to illustrate the methods by which you may examine this question, not at all to impress your minds with this idea that I have correctly stated the exact time."

"You see that the defense of an alibi is one that does not rebut the fact of the circumstances against the prisoner, but simply affirms that the prisoner was elsewhere. An alibi merely establishes that he was not at the place the crime was committed at the precise time it was committed. There is no defense of an alibi which requires it to be more minutely scrutinized, than for opportunity, for there is none more easily fabricated."

"Perhaps, after considering the evidence, you will come to the conclusion that when the shot was heard, it did not of itself arrest much attention. Rather, that it was not till the screams were heard that attention among the community was excited. And then the people were excited to learn the cause of the screams and not the precise minute when they occurred. It probably was not till after Billings and Washburn gave their testimony before the coroner that attention was strongly called to the precise minute it occurred. By the time that time became an issue, it might have been too late to find, with exact accuracy, the moment the watch or clock was really looked at. By then it may have been difficult to determine the precise things that were done by each witness at the minute the shot was fired and the minute that each really looked at the clock."

Judge Landon took this time to talk about the effect of a witness's perception on his testimony. "Again, when witnesses testify as to their estimate of time, when they do estimate, it is not unreasonable to expect their estimates will not be hazarded so as to be unfavorable to the side they wish to succeed. Therefore, if all the evidence in the case, other than evidence as to time, points with certainty to the conclusion that Billings did not reach Washburn's until ten minutes after the shot was fired, you should not overlook the evidence in your estimate of the fact of his having the opportunity to fire the shot. But if the evidence does fail to point with such conclusive certainty, then the evidence as to the time should add to the doubt you entertain of his guilt, and he should be acquitted. If Billings did shoot his wife, the time when he did it is of little moment. If the facts other than time fail to convince that he did shoot her, then the exact moment is unimportant. Time is important, if you are satisfied that it is so fixed that he could not have shot her." Having finished with the issue of the time, the Judge paused to look at his notes.

"What are the circumstances pointing to the guilt of the prisoner, as the People claim. A most important circumstance is the tracks that lead to and from the house. Rubber boots have been produced here. They were produced by the coroner. The prisoner there said they were his, and that he had worn them on the night of June 4th. Maggie said he had them on before supper. Isaac says he helped pull them off Billings's feet in Billings's house after Mrs. Billings was shot. There are tracks leading to the house. These lead from the northwest corner of Reed's garden, next to the fence, on to the hole in the fence, through the hole into Billings's garden, then along the south side of the garden east; then north, cross the garden, over the fence, into the lane, between the Metcalf Office and the buildings north of the lane, which opens into the dooryard. There are tracks leading from the red gate opposite the well, across the corn field, to the bars between the cornfield and the orchard. Across the orchard to the northwest corner of the Reed garden there are no tracks. The orchard was a clover field in which there was a good growth of clover. Now Billings admits making those tracks; but he does not admit making them on his way to shoot his wife. Those in the cornfield, from the red gate to the bars, he claims he made on his way there to find hammer and nails which he believed he had left there. But Garnsey had taken them away. The people claim that Billings knew they had been taken away. There is no direct evidence that he knew it. It is only inferred from the fact that Garnsey placed them where Billings might have seen them."

"Billings claims to have made tracks in the garden after supper and before he went up the lane. Terhune swears he saw Billings in his garden after crossing the garden from the south to the north and that he saw him get over the fence to the west of the office into the lane. Is Terhune to be believed, or is he, as the people say, a suborned witness introduced here to swear away the effect of one of the most important facts in the people's case? I can only make questions; you must answer them. Gilbert found tracks in the Metcalf Office, and the east door of the office was open. The evidence tends to show that the door was hard to open and, therefore, seldom opened. Terhune swears it was not open when he was in it after supper, looking after his paints. The inevitable question for your consideration: was that office entered and the door opened for the purpose of allowing the assassin the opportunity to watch that window and embrace the favorable opportunity, if it should present itself, to fire that shot?"

"Now, gentlemen, upon a careful review of all the testimony, are your minds convinced that there were tracks leading from the Reed flower bed to the oat field at the southwest corner of the cornfield? If so, when were they made? The witnesses speak of them as distinct in several places and as deeply sunken in the ground. You remember the rain and consequent moisture of the earth on Tuesday night. You will reason that the sooner after the rain the tracks were made, the deeper the foot would sink into the soil. By whom were they made? Is the identity of the tracks with the boots of Billings satisfactory to your minds? Put the circumstances all together, and are your minds convinced? It is proper that I should say, in reviewing the evidence in regard to the tracks, that all the other circumstances in the case should be considered. Beginning with every circumstance that preceded that Tuesday night, all that has been said upon the question of motive and in regard to the motive of Billings on that afternoon and evening, all the incidents that surround and follow the shot, should be taken into consideration. These issues will undoubtedly come to mind: who had the motive to make the tracks, and what could he make them for, and why make them at all, and why run? Why did he stop while running, and where was he going? Was he on his way to the old well? Did he place the gun in the old well? The solution of these questions rests upon the force of all circumstances which surround the case.

"These considerations will occur to you. If the gun was used, there would be a motive on the part of the person who used it to conceal it. If the gun had not been used, the motive to conceal it would not exist, unless, as the defense suggests, it was done in order to cast suspicion upon the prisoner. If the gun contained the shell that held the bullet found in Mrs. Billings's head, then it was the gun by which she was shot. Then it was probably thrown in the well by the man who shot her. In order to get to the well, that man made tracks somewhere between the house and well, and he made them sometime after the shot and, therefore, after the heavy rain that softened the ground. If those boots did fit the tracks, and those boots were worn by the prisoner, and the prisoner is shown to have been in that lane opposite that well shortly after the shot, that he drove from it at a 'breakneck speed,' your mind will naturally count all these circumstances together."

"The prisoner's counsel suggests that the gun was put in the well by Sherman. You have seen Sherman on the stand. You have heard others corroborate his testimony that, at the time the shot was fired he was in the store. He has detailed his movements and whereabouts from the time of the shot was fired until the gun was found. Sherman is fully exculpated." With these words, Judge Landon had taken his most definitive position with respect to a witness.

"The People point to the expression of Billings as confirmation of his guilt." The Judge then reviewed the witnesses as to Billings expressions after the murder. The Judge mentioned that Billings had read the paper to a group the day after the murder. He further mentioned Isaac Washburn's testimony in which Billings is described as seeming completely normal when the two talked before his father arrived. Judge Landon also mentioned about Billings's comment to Maggie Mahoney and the description of him at his wife's feet and when he saw her in the coffin.

"I have, in the presentation of the case, already called your attention to the leading points for the defense. The most important and conclusive is alibi. Certainly, if the prisoner was not opposite that window when his wife was shot, he did not shoot her. If you are satisfied that he was at Washburn's, or upon the backside of his farm, or upon the highway, he did not shoot her. He is indicted for killing her himself, and if that charge is not shown to be true, he must be acquitted." In support of the claim that the crime was committed by another, Judge Landon cited the expressions of Jesse Billings on the night of the murder, the men who saw the man running down the tow-path, the finding of the hat, and the seeing of the man crouched down by the fence a few evenings previous to the murder. "This is to say the least, slightest and inconclusive evidence. Why was the man running? Nobody knows. What motive could he have had? Nobody suggests. Why did he run? Nobody can answer. It was upon a public thoroughfare, where many men come and go. True, James A Wilson says he saw tracks in the road near the lumber pile. That too is a public thoroughfare, and it is not strange that Wilson made nothing of them. Suppose the man was here known and bareheaded with this evidence against him; could you for a moment detain him? Do these circumstances contradict, explain or modify a single one of the circumstances which the people adduced to the case? The defense claims that the conduct of Billings was that of an innocent man, sincerely sorry and grieving on account of the great calamity."

"The defense argues the probability that Billings should want to commit this crime. Is it probable that a man of large means, many and widely scattered interests, constant employment, a man of power and influence in his locality, would commit such a crime? Mr. Hughes argues that there is no preparation shown. Further, that it is improbable that Billings should choose that night and that way to commit the crime. Somebody did choose that night, that way and that place.

"The defense further argues that it is improbable that Billings should commit such a crime in the presence of his daughter. The defense asks what beneficial result could accrue to him from the murder or loss of his wife? They point out his wife was a real helpmate. But you will deal with these question as you find them - with human nature, with all its passions, its follies and its crimes as well as with its virtues."

"You have been aided, gentlemen, in a great degree by the representative sides of this case by the counsel. By their labors I have felt my hands greatly strengthened and my labors lightened."

"At this time, gentlemen, the case is for you decide. We thank you in advance for your thoughtful considerations."

With these words the case was left to the jurors. Judge Landon had exhibited throughout the long and difficult trial a presence which showed himself to be a justice worthy of higher courts.

The Daily Saratogian
October 12, 1878.

Billings quietly remarked that he thought more of and was much better interested in the judge's charges than in the four days of scathing remarks hurled like a tornado at him by Moak. He would sooner have Moak talking for him than against him; and if there is anybody who appreciates that fact, it is Jesse Billings Jr. Notwithstanding, his very able counsel have done their level best for their client, and few if any; could have done better. Billings's personal friends have clung to him with remarkable firmness from the moment of his arrest up to the present time, and he undoubtedly appreciates their worth and assistance.

During the first half of the charge, Billings fixed his eyes intently on Judge Landon, listening to every word that was being uttered by the learned justice. After, his eyes would frequently droop and there seemed to be what might be termed a far-away expression to his face. For minutes at a time, he would gaze abstractly in the direction of the floor. At times, he exhibited a nervousness that was unusual for a man of his wonderful nerve. This is but the second time that this has been perceptible during the trial. The first time was when his daughter, Jennie, was upon the witness stand.

The paraphernalia of evidence - carbine, shell, bullets, compasses, cartridges, maps, photographs, were turned over to the jury to assist in the finding of a verdict. There was enough of this evidence to fill a small wagon.

At 4:45 o'clock, the court informed the jury that it could take possession of the courtroom, which was immediately cleared for its exclusive use. Under direction of the court, Sheriff Winney cleared the upper floor of the courtroom of everybody but the jury.

It was learned from an informer that the boat Jones claimed to have borrowed was on blocks being painted on June 4th. Moak had known before the end of the trial but two of his most important witnesses, Finne and Virtue, swore they had launched the boat two weeks previously. If he would put forth the new information, he would discredit his own key witnesses. Moak chose to ignore the material fact.

THE JURY HOLDS THE PUBLIC'S INTEREST

The events that followed were so well covered by the Daily Saratogian that they deserve to be reprinted as the reporter wrote the words. He covered the events and the mood of the people with a style similar to that used today.

From the Daily Saratogian

Ballston Spa, October 11, 11:55 p. m.

There will be no verdict tonight! Judge Landon had told the jury that the court would remain up until 11 o'clock and, if no conclusion had been arrived at by that hour, the court would retire for the night. That hour has passed, and the "jury is still out." The jury had their supper regularly tonight, and an hour or so ago sent down to the American Hotel for

267

their overcoats, thus indicating that their deliberations have temporarily ceased, and that they will devote the balance of the night to needed rest.

During the evening, knots of people could be seen at every hand wrestling with the absorbing topic, "What do you think the verdict will be?" At this hour, the general opinion - whatever that is worth - is that the jury will disagree; while the friends of Billings hope for an acquittal.

Billings received several of his friends and acquaintances in his cell this evening. He was not as talkative as usual, and seemed considerably depressed in spirits. He retired to rest early, saying that he was not feeling very well. Billings spoke of a feeling of faintness in his stomach.

Ballston Spa, October 12, 11:40 a. m.

A large delegation of those who have made this village their home during the progress of the Billings trial returned to their domestic firesides this morning, there to await the news of the coming jury.

The jury is locked in the court room. Listeners on the outside walls claim that the jurors had a spirited discussion late last night and early this morning in regard to the important question before them. The eaves-droppers base this on the grounds that the jury made as much of a "racket as a political caucus."

In the face of the law that prohibits outsiders from approaching the jury for the purpose of ascertaining information in advance, there is a rumor current here this morning that the jury stood ten for conviction and two for acquittal. This is given for what it is worth, as your correspondent can learn nothing in confirmation of it.

The coming of the jury will be announced by the ringing of the courthouse bell. All are on the qui vive for the first echo. After twenty- seven days in a crowded court room, the suspense of waiting for the verdict is becoming almost painful. The monotony is in striking contrast with the stirring scenes enacted in the "temple of justice" during the past month.

Ballston Spa, October 13, 8 p.m.

"The jury is still out," has become a stereotyped response to almost every question here. The jury has now been out fifty one hours, and, as a farmer remarked today: "They have agreed to disagree." Anyway, the Court House bell has not yet rung out that they have reached any sort of verdict. Rumors as thick as leaves in a forest can be heard everywhere. It is now said that, when the jury first retired to the solitude of their council chamber, they stood 8 for conviction to 4 for acquittal. Later in the day the figures were changed to 10 and 2 as against the prisoner; then 7 and 5; afterwards 9 and 3; and the latest makes at 11 and 1, with Billings's only hope clinging to the latter unit. When, where, and how such information leaks from the supposed secrecy of the jury room is not known; but many are inclined to give credence to the figures on the hypothesis that the private workings of the juries have been prematurely divined and corroborated by subsequent facts.

THE BLINDS SIGNALING.

Yesterday evening the sharp-eyed observers on the outside thought that they could detect (from the outside) that some one of the persons in the court room were signaling to parties in or near the American Hotel that the jury stood eleven for conviction and one for acquittal. The three north windows of the court room face the south windows of the American Hotel. The inside blinds in the court room are subdivided into divisions. At one time it was noticed that eleven of these divisions of the east and center windows were turned to admit the passage of light, and that one blind of the division of the west window blinds had also been carefully adjusted in a similar manner. What added to the belief that these blinds had been purposely turned to communicate intelligence was the fact that the Beecher jury had resorted to a similar device, and also that there was a rumor afloat to the effect that "the jury stood 11 to 1."

HIS HONOR RECEIVES NOTES.

About two o'clock yesterday afternoon, Judge Landon, Judge Crane and Justices of the Session Tallmadge and Bogert were seated in Medbery's Hotel waiting for the verdict, when Officer Adsit Newton, one of the officers in the charge of the jury, appeared and handed Judge Landon a sealed letter. The judge perused the letter, which he put in his pocket, and turning to the officer said:

"IT REQUIRES NO ANSWER."

His honor would not divulge the contents of the communication, but it is understood that it, in substance, informed him that the jury was unable to agree; his negative reply to the officer was

269

interpreted as signifying that the jury must continue longer and make an effort to agree on something, as a trial of five weeks and of so much importance could not be disposed of within so short a time, not withstanding the jury had then been out twenty-one hours. The messenger returned to the court house.

KEEP UP A GOOD FIRE.

At 5:40 o'clock yesterday afternoon, Officer Newton again sought Judge Landon and handed him a second communication from the "imprisoned twelve on the hill." As before, the judge scanned and pocketed the note sheet. The purport of the note is believed to have been of similar character to the first, as the Judge said:

"Officer Newton, keep up a good fire in the courtroom and see that the gentlemen lack none of the conveniences that will tend to render them comfortable. The court will remain here over the Sabbath. We will be ready to receive a verdict at any moment up to 11 o'clock tonight, when we will retire. Should no verdict be found up to that hour, the court may be called at any time tomorrow, from 8 o'clock in the morning up to evening, provided an agreement has been reached by the jury." The messenger again returned to his post of duty at the court house. This must have been consoling news to the jurors who had expected to reach home last night.

SUFFERING FOR BLANKETS AND APPLES

That the jury afterwards intended to "make a night of it," may be judged from the fact that, about 9:30 o'clock, Officer Newton, for the third time, appeared before the Judge and stated that the jury desired to know if they could have some "blankets and apples." Judge Landon replied: "Let them have all the blankets and apples they want."

Half an hour later, officers loaded down with blankets and quilts, from the American Hotel, were seen going in the direction of the court house. Apples followed in the same direction.

PILLOWS AND BLACKING.

The jury today made a requisition for "pillows and blacking," and their request was promptly acceded to. To borrow the phraseology of the trial, these are little things - mere trifles - but in the light of all the circumstances, they form a link in the chain of circumstantial evidence showing conclusively that the jury will pass another night without agreeing to anything but blankets and apples, pillows and blacking.

THE APPEARANCE OF THE COURT ROOM

Notwithstanding that no one but the jury is allowed in the courtroom during their deliberations, yet a pen picture of it has been seen. The jury has remained in undisputed possession of it since Friday afternoon at 5 o'clock, when it was in the need of renovation. Since that time, the "official housekeeper" has been excluded and the result may be imagined. The carpeted floor is covered with scraps of paper that almost disguise its colors. Chairs, benches and tables have been turned, twisted, "nobbled and keyholed" into every conceivable shape and form for the purpose of improvising beds. Spittoons, waste baskets and other similar furniture are generally under foot. The hat rack contains a promiscuous wardrobe, while a larger proportion of the jurors sit around in their shirt sleeves.

THE COURT AND COUNSEL

Time has dragged heavily on the hands of the legal gentlemen comprising the court, since Friday afternoon. Not knowing what minute their presence might be demanded by the ringing of the bell, they have lingered along thus far in a kind of listless anxiety, and have almost been talked to death by parties subjecting them to all manner of impossible questions concerning the jury. Judge Landon is stopped at Medbery's hotel. Judge Crane went to Saratoga on the midnight train yesterday. He drove down this morning and returned this evening. Justice of the Sessions Bogert stops at the American and Tallmadge at Medbery's. Capt. Butler was in town today returning home this afternoon. Mr. L'Amoreaux resides here. Messrs. Hughes, Pike, Potter and Ford went home last night, but will return early tomorrow morning.

NIGHT WATCH

Deputy Sheriffs Henry Harrison and Moses Capen are doing night duty in patrolling the grounds in the vicinity of the Court House. They are assisted by Jonathan Deyoe, who represents and has been appointed by friends of Billings.

A BREAK IN THE MONOTONY

Judge Landon announced this afternoon that he would convene the court at 9:00 tomorrow (Monday) morning, that the differences that kept the jury so long might be ascertained, if possible.

271

A STRANGE ADVERTISEMENT.

Among the various forms and devices for advertising, your correspondent has had his attention called to one that is said to have originated in the fertile brain of a Ballstonian, but whether it is worthy of imitation or emulation it is for others to say. It appears that the advertiser has a certain brand of cigars that he desires to exchange for currency, and accordingly he distributes cards - 3 1/2 x 11" - bearing the following words:

Billings's Cigars.
Pure Havana Filler. Northumberland Wrapper
For sale at-

A POLICE JUSTICE PAYS A DETECTIVE'S FINE

Among the witnesses for the prosecution was Thomas McConakey of Waterford. He was a detective employed by District Attorney Ormsby. Yesterday evening, McConakey imbibed rather too freely, and at the hour of midnight he meandered in the direction of the Court House. At 1:20 a.m. today, the Waterford cop was seen hovering rather too close to the county tombs, and Deputy Sheriff Henry Harrison and Jonathan Deyoe, who appear to have been on guard to prevent anyone from breaking into the building and capturing one or more of "the twelve", attempted to arrest McConakey. Deyoe says that McConakey pulled a revolver on him, but the Waterford officer claims that the deadly weapon was nothing more than a broken cigar. After some trouble, McConakey was placed under arrest and put in one of the cells in the jail. He was arraigned this afternoon before Police Justice Drake. As McConakey was passing the cell of Billings, the latter sarcastically exclaimed: "Hello, McConakey, you'd look better in the posy-bed than in jail. What have you been doing?"

McConakey made no reply, but, under charge of Deputy Sheriff Harrison, passed out of the jail and to the office of Police Justice Dake, where, in answer to the unusual interrogatory, he pleaded guilty to being drunk and disorderly.

Court - You are an officer, I believe?

Prisoner - I have been a deputy sheriff up to within a few days since, and was once a constable.

Court - Considering the circumstances under which you have been here in town, I am disposed to make the fine as light as possible. I will fine you $3 and $1.50 cost, making $4.50 in all. Have you the money?

272

The prisoner shook his head.

Court – then I will lend you the money to pay the fine.

"His honor" dove down into his judicial vest pocket and extracting a crumpled $10 greenback, inquired if anybody could change it.

Cummings of the New York Sun, signified that he had sufficient wealth to consummate such a transaction, and passed over two $5's, receiving in exchange the $10.

"His honor" passed one of the $5 over to the prisoner, and the latter immediately liquidated the little obligation by passing the same identical bill back to "his honor."

Such was the manner in which justice was dispensed here on the "the Sunday that the jury was out."

BILLINGS IN HIS CELL

Jesse Billings, Jr., the prisoner, appears in better spirits today than he did yesterday. Notwithstanding the severe mental strain which he must be under, yet he maintains his remarkable self-possession and equilibrium with a tact that is seldom seen in any circumstances that may happen to be. A large number of friends have called upon him today, among them were several ladies. He received with smiles and a friendly grasp of the hand all who called. He has a remarkable nerve.

This Morning's Proceedings– The
Jury Brought into Court and Afterwards
Sent Back for Further Deliberations.

Ballston Spa, Monday, October 14, 11:45 a.m. The arrival of the morning trains again brought their throngs of people interested in the Billings trial. By order of Judge Landon, the courthouse bell rang at 9 o'clock this morning, 64 hours after the time the jury was first sent out. In a few moments the courtroom was again filled, all anxious to gain what information they could. The full court was represented and inside the bar were the respective representatives.

Judge Landon – The recess appointed by the court having expired, the crier may now open the court.

Crier Schureman formally performed the function of his office.

Clerk Horton called the roll of the jury and prisoner.

The following is a verbatim report of the important proceedings:

Clerk Horton - Have you agreed upon a verdict?

Foreman Burr - We have not.

Judge Landon - Mr. Foreman, is there any prospect of your agreeing?

Foreman - I see none.

Judge Landon - You have been discussing this matter among yourselves?

Foreman - We have.

Judge Landon - Is there any difficulty with reference to the law?

Foreman - There seems to be none, I think.

Judge Landon - Is there any matter in which any instructions from the court are desired?

Foreman - There have been none expressed.

Judge Landon - Then it is a difference of opinion among different members of the jury.

Foreman- Yes sir.

Judge Landon - Has that difference of opinion been established or settled for some length of time; in other words, has there been any change? I don't ask you to state how you stand, but has there been any change in your standing from the beginning.

Foreman - There has been a slight change from the first.

Judge Landon - Has there been any change within 24 hours?

Foreman - No sir.

Judge Landon - Within 36 hours, or since Saturday?

Foreman - Not since Saturday night.

Judge Landon - I suppose you have talked and discussed this matter among yourselves as to the importance of this case?

Foreman - Yes, I think we appreciate that fully.

Judge Landon - Is there any juryman who wishes to ask the court anything?

Juror Wiswall - Not unless it would in reference to the tracks and whether we would have a right to suppose things which we don't really agree upon. We don't know hardly how far our suspicions have a right to go. That seems to be the greatest difficulty.

Judge Landon - I don't know as the court has any instructions to give other than what you have already received. If you understood what I said in my charge, I don't know as I have anything further to state. I intended to have you understand that you must be thoroughly convinced as to the result of the evidence. What the evidence satisfies you to be the truth, you act upon. It is a mere question whether your minds are convinced.

Juror Burrs - Perhaps you Honor can give us a little more idea as to what constitutes a reasonable doubt.

Judge Landon - That, perhaps is one of the most difficult things in the world to explain. A reasonable doubt, as I said to you, gentlemen, is doubt for which some reason existed founded upon the evidence. I said to you and repeat that it was not a fanciful or whimsical doubt, such as a man might entertain because he did not see the thing done, or hear the witness testify in regard to it who did see it done, but it is that which exists in the mind after having considered all of the evidence and, as a result of that consideration, the mind remains unconvinced. Do I make myself understood? It is a doubt for which some reason must exist growing out of the evidence; some good, fair reason. I told you the other day, there is nothing in your capacity as jurors which made you act differently from what you would in your capacity as men. It is a simple question whether your minds are convinced. Perhaps it would be well to spend a little time again in considering this matter. It is a case of vast importance and magnitude, and it would be a great burden upon both sides to be compelled to try the case over again. But that circumstance does not require anybody to relinquish his convictions, and every man, of course, may act as his own mind is convinced. But before he firmly makes up his own mind, he ought patiently and candidly to consider whatever his associates adduce. Something may satisfy him that his own convictions are unfounded, or perhaps convince him that his own convictions are true. Your mind should enter into this matter entirely free from - I won't say prejudice - but from that fixedness of determination which would prevent any other conclusion. Perhaps I cannot use any better word than stubbornness to express what I mean. I respect a man's honest conviction of the evidence, and I have no desire to interfere with or remove it unless it can be done by fair and dispassionate reasoning. Gentlemen, you will now retire to the grand jury room for your further deliberation and, when you reach an agreement, have the Court House bell rung. But, perhaps you would prefer to remain here in the court room.

Foreman - We would.

Judge Landon - The court room will now be cleared of all persons but the gentlemen of the jury.

[At the present writing (10:45 a.m.) the ringing of the Court House bell is momentarily expected; but it is possible that many minutes, and perhaps hours, may elapse before the desirable event will occur.]

The Jury Still Out - Anxious Throng
Still Waiting for the Verdict.

Ballston Spa, Monday October 14, 1 p. m.- There seems to be an opinion here that the jury, if it does not arrive at some sort of agreement before 6 p. m. today, will be called in by the court and discharged. This may be mere conjecture on the part of would be knowing ones, but it is given for what it is worth. It is the general opinion here that the jury stands **ten** for conviction to **two** for acquittal. This probably based on the fact that this morning in open court two jurors - Whistle and Burr - made certain interrogatories of Judge Landon, as may be seen by reference to. There are some here who seem firmly convinced that - were the truth known - it would be found the jury stood 11 to 1 against Billings. The friends of Billings concede that the jury stand either 10 to 2 or 11 to 1, but that the majority favor an acquittal. They may have reached the right conclusion, and, if so, it would seem strange that such a small minority, in favor of conviction would stand out so long. The October term will convene here next week, and it is not improbable that several of the witnesses may be brought to the attention of the grand jury. It is understood that the people have at least a dozen witnesses to show Jones committed perjury.

Again the Court House Bell Rings.
- The Jury Disagree and are Discharged.-
Eleven to One.

Ballston Spa, Monday October 14, 1:50 p. m. - The Court House bell has just commenced ringing. In a few moments the courtroom was again filled to overflowing, and the court counsel and prisoner were again in their places.

Judge Landon - Call the roll, Mr. Clerk.

Clerk Horton called the roll.

Judge Landon - Have you agreed upon a verdict?

Foreman Burr - We have not.

Judge Landon - Do you think it impossible that you can agree?

Foreman - We do not.

A brief consultation took place between Judge Landon and the side judges.

Judge Landon - We think that under the circumstances it would not be necessary to keep you together longer. You are discharged.

The jury was formally discharged at exactly 2 p. m.

Gen. Hughes called attention to the statutes giving jurors extra compensation where they have been in the jury box beyond a certain length of time.

The court thought such a thing perfectly proper, and said that the court will certify to additional compensation - $1.50 per day each.

Mr. L'Amoreaux made formal application for bail for the prisoner.

Judge Landon said that if the application was made now it would be entertained; but another court would be in session here in a few days.

Messre. L'Amoreaux and Hughes said they would make application by affidavit in the future.

ELEVEN TO ONE IN FAVOR OF BILLINGS.

District Attorney Ormsby has just stated that the jury stood ELEVEN for acquittal and ONE for conviction.

When the jury went out, it stood 9 to 3 in favor of acquittal, but afterwards changed to 11 to 1 in favor of Billings.

Exceptions to the Judge's Charge.

Ballston Spa, Monday, October 14, 10:30 o'clock -The counsel for the defense have taken exceptions to the charge of Judge Landon, and have received his official signature to them. The following is an extract from the Judge's charge and the portions to which the defense have taken exceptions, as already stated:

"A lady, Mrs. Smith, testified she saw a man some few evenings before looking through Billings's front fence toward the Billings window, but this is, to say the least, very light and inconclusive evidence. Who was the man, nobody knows. What motive could he have had, nobody could guess. Where could he run, nobody could answer."

277

Newspaper Comments on the Billings's Trial

The opinions of those who sat through this long trial can be gained by their reflections. Fortunately, each of the major papers that had correspondents at the trial carried articles reflecting on the findings of the court in Ballston Spa.

New York Sun

The moral effect of the disagreement of a jury in a capital case is not very unlike to that of a Scotch verdict of "Not Proven". The defendant escapes the physical suffering of the execution and of long imprisonment; but he is not wholly absolved from punishment; for it is, in fact, a severe penalty he pays in resting under such a ban the remainder of his days.

We believe in the case of Jesse Billings Jr., this is not wholly unjust. We believe a verdict of guilty would have been wrong, because the evidence did leave room for a reasonable doubt of his guilt; but at the same time there was such a chain of suspicion and circumstance against him that a disagreement of the jury was a very natural result.

Albany Press

The result reached by the jury in the Billings case is equivalent to an acquittal. We have no knowledge how this jury stood at the first vote. There may have been a majority for conviction, but that seems scarcely probable. They were in consultation sixty-nine hours, and, as announced, stood eleven for acquittal and one for conviction. The one juror who stood out against the combined opinion of eleven associates showed the possession of a will remarkable to the last degree. If the testimony was sufficient to convince him that Billings was guilty, one would certainly think that the position taken by the other eleven jurors would raise a doubt in his mind, and, as we know, the prisoner was entitled to the benefit of any doubt. Still this lone juror, under the law, had a right to hold his opinion, and Jesse Billings, Jr. must suffer the consequences.

Albany Evening Journal

When the jury gives such a result, it is idle to try the case in the newspapers or to pronounce a verdict outside. So strong a majority against conviction indicates the force of the "reasonable doubt" which filled the minds of the jurors. If they did not implicitly accept the evidence of alibi, there was enough of it, with the other matters, to restrain them from declaring an adverse verdict. There was no positive and absolute proof. It was a case of circumstantial evidence, and while such evidence is often the most conclusive, there must be no flaw in it. On the one side, there was the motive; the family bitterness; the previous misconduct of Billings; his doubtful relations with another woman; his tracks in the vicinity; the finding of the gun in the old well, and other similar points. On the other side there was the testimony - conclusive if not trustworthy, and raising doubts even if not fully accepted - that Billings was half a mile away when the fatal shot was fired; that the deadly ball must have proceeded from a pistol and not from his gun; that a man was seen running from the yard immediately after the murder; and that others than Billings had a motive for the deed. With these conflicting arguments, the jury went to the room and disagreed. We shall neither sustain its action nor question it. Whether the public judgment fully acquiesces in it or not, it will be accepted as practically closing the case.

The **Daily Saratogian**

That the trial should have been so inconclusive, leaving the public mind as much excited and divided as before it began, is to be regretted, but perhaps it was unavoidable. The great point against the prisoner was that he was the only person who was shown to have any motive to commit the crime which, coupled with many things brought out in the evidence, seemed to single him out as the culprit; while the great point in his favor was the improbability that a man in his circumstances should have been guilty of such a fearful deed, coupled with the evidence tending to establish an alibi for him at the moment the shot was fired. And so it remains as it did before, although not convicted, the prisoner is by no means cleared; although not cleared; he by no means convicted. It is a dark, difficult and mysterious case, but the public good demands that such a monstrous crime should be investigated with utmost and rigid thoroughness, and the innocence or guilt of the prisoner thoroughly established. The first office of a government is to afford protection to its citizens, for this, taxes are

279

levied and courts are maintained, and such a brutal and cold-blooded murder as this should not be allowed to pass unpunished if the culprit can possibly be found. We trust, therefore, that the vigilance and activity of the officers of the law may be in no way relaxed, but that they may rather be increased until all the light which is attainable may be poured in on this dark and horrible tragedy.

New York Tribune

The long trial at Ballston has had a most unsatisfactory conclusion. We do not intend here to discuss the question of guilt of Billings. The evidence that he shot his wife was very strong, and if he did not kill her, it is impossible to conjecture who did. This, however, is not sufficient to justify a verdict of "Guilty"; nor does the opinion of the eleven jurors who believed Billings innocent appear to us at all whimsical. A result of the trial so near to an acquittal has a good deal of the moral effect of a verdict of "Not Guilty." At any rate, the prisoner occupies the same position of presumptive innocence, since the prosecution has failed to prove him otherwise. Indeed, the position is measurably strengthened by the trial; so that it is by no means improbable that the government may decline to enter upon a second trial. A good deal will be said of the obstinacy of the twelfth juror. but it must not be forgotten that under the jury system, usually spoken of as the perfection of human wisdom, Mr. Blood has as good a right to his opinion as the majority of his associates. If he believed that Billings did the deed, and a great many persons so believe, why should he not refuse to be talked or browbeaten out of his conclusions? Whether they were right or wrong, it was his duty to stand by them; after all, they had been honestly arrived at. It is always unfortunate, after an elaborate, prolonged and expensive trial, to be encountered by a disagreement of the jury at last. Both sides will probably experience a feeling of disappointment. The chances of obtaining a verdict upon a second trial are greatly lessened by the failure upon the first, and the legal representative of the people works, at the repetition of the hearing, under great disadvantages.

It is interesting that there was an opinion that there was no other decision possible. The evidence necessary for a conviction was just not there. In contrast, the only person that was shown to have any reason for the murder was Jesse.

Other Verdicts; Other Suspects

THE SECOND JURY

In April of 1880, almost two years after the murder, Jesse Billings, Jr. was tried in Saratoga County Court for a second time. The second trial consumed virtually the same amount of time. The cost, for both the county and Billings, was almost the same as the first trial. It took two attempts, but between the two Billings trials, District Attorney Ormsby was able to win a conviction of George Jones for perjury. The judge in the Jones' trial delayed his sentence until after Billings's second trial. Despite the loss of Jones as a witness, the 1880 jury was unanimous in voting Billings 'not guilty'. Of the twenty-four jurors who heard the case, only one, Blood of Waterford, felt Jesse was proven guilty.

ANOTHER SUSPECT?

On December 3, 1879, the outbuildings on Jesse's home farm including barns, sheds and the carriage house were destroyed by fire. The year's supply of hay and grain stored inside was consumed by the flames. Those neighbors at the scene were able to save the livestock and carriages. At points during the fire, it appeared that Billings's house, lumber shed and store were in peril. It was held by those present that the entire hamlet was saved from being reduced to ashes only because it was a windless night. The newspapers noted the next day noted that the fire was set by someone using an incendiary product. The loss was placed at about $8,000, only part of which was covered by insurance.

The next day, Morris Conery of Schuylerville was arrested on suspicion of starting the fire. Conery was also suspected of being involved in the burning of a building on Jesse's father's farm the previous year. He would appear to have disliked the Billings family immensely.

THE WILL OF DR. BILLINGS

In December 1879, Dr. Jesse Billings died as a result of complications following a buggy accident. For a second time, in as many years, his buggy had turned over. His injuries were not life threatening; however, during his convalescence he developed pneumonia.

Dr. Billings's will indicates who he felt was culpable in the incident.

At the time of his death, Dr. Billings had grandchildren by three of his four surviving children. Dr. Billings left one daughter, Mrs. Ellen Deyoe, whose husband testified in the trial, $4,300, the value of a farm at that time. He left the second daughter, Mary, who was reported to be disabled, the house and farm in which she resided with him. The third daughter, Francis Cramer, was left the farm on which she and her family were residing. Each of Dr. Billings's three grandchildren by his two daughters, Charles Cramer, Mary Deyoe, and Sarah Deyoe received $500. Jesse received all the rest of the estate for use during his lifetime; however, the remainder of Dr. Billings money was to be distributed to those named in the will upon Jesse, Jr.'s death. Jennie was by this time married to John Sherman. Dr. Billings deliberately excluded Jennie from ever receiving any portion of his substantial wealth.

MRS. HARRIS'S BIOGRAPHY

In 1893, Sylvester published the second edition of The History of Saratoga County. This edition included biographies of prominent local persons, among them Jesse Billings, Jr. Six years later The Saratogian published Our County and Its People. Local citizens could have their biographies carried by subscription. Where Mrs. Harris stood on the issue of Jesse's guilt can be seen in the words by which she chose to be remembered:

Harris, Mrs. Mary C., widow of John Harris; the latter was born in 1799, and died on April 24, 1862. They had five children, two now living: John C. Harris of Saratoga Springs, and Gertrude, wife of William Harris of Fort Edward, Washington county. One of Mrs. Harris's deceased children was Mrs. Eliza Harris Billings, who was murdered on the 4th of June, 1878, by being shot through the head while sitting in her room in the company with her daughter and house servant. The murder of Mrs. Billings caused a great sensation at the time and was the means of a long and expensive trial, her husband being accused of the murder. He was finally acquitted after two trials, the first resulting in a disagreement of the jury. Mrs. Harris was born in Oneida County, N. Y., and was the daughter of Joseph A. Clark, an extensive farmer of that vicinity. *She was married to Mr. Harris on August 7, 1831, and went as a bride to Whitehall, where her husband was in general merchandise business. Mr. Harris was the owner of property where the homestead is now located and hither they came the spring following, leaving the business in Whitehall, which was destroyed by fire in 1849. Their first residence was in a dwelling adjoining the present residence. Her mother was Elizabeth Olney, whose people were residents of the village of Quaker Springs in old Saratoga. Mrs. Harris, who has passed the three score years and ten, is one of the liveliest women in the vicinity, conducts her own house, directs the affairs of her farm and exercises a general supervision over the affairs of her large property.*

Mrs. Harris barely mentioned the second jury or the fact that the vote by the first was eleven to one of acquittal. Her bitterness, which it would appear from the testimony had begun before the murder, she carried with her to her death in 1906, one year after Jesse.

JESSE'S RETURN

Jesse left Ballston Spa as soon as he was released by the sheriff. He stopped first at Schuylerville to send a telegraph and to take his mid-day meal. At the time of his arrival the streets were filled with Saturday shoppers. The crowd rushed to shake his hand. He had supper at the Gailey House. After dinner he forced his way through the crowd which had gathered to see him. He entered his buggy and went to his store in Fort Miller. Those at the store were all glad to see Mr. Billings.

Jesse's return to his home in Fort Miller's Bridge was earlier than expected. It was anticipated that he would spend the night at his father's in Bacon Hill. When he arrived at his house, he found that it had missing windows and was deemed to be unsuitable for habitation. He accepted an invitation from Alexander Baucus to stay at his house.

JESSE MEETS WITH JENNIE

On the Monday after his release, Jesse drove up to his brother-in-law's William Harris's to see Jennie. The story below which was printed in the Ballston <u>Journal</u> tells of their encounter.

Jennie, with little Lizzie Hill, came out. Her father asked her for a private interview, which she refused. He then drove to his private bank, and finding Mr. Baucus there, requested him to see Jennie and find out if she intended not to come home, and if she did not she could come and take away everything she wished, as her father was going to start for Buffalo that night and would not return until after several days.

Jennie arrived at her father's house the next morning with two wagons. Later in the Journal the editor listed the items Jennie took from her father's house. She apparently took her father's offer very seriously.

...took all the household goods, embracing the parlor furniture, completely stripping it, even to taking the paper off the fire board; every bed and bedding, except from her father's bedroom; all the plated ware, silver and china ware, glass ware, and best set of white dishes; all the ornaments, pictures, and all the books having her name, her mother's or Harris's; all the mirrors, unless perhaps a small one in her father's room; all the napkins, table linens, towels and toweling; lemon-squeezer, crumb duster, knives and forks, etc. Mr. Baucus told her if she would leave the carpets on the floor, she could get new ones at the store, or their value in money, but she had the best carpets taken up and removed, and also took all the rugs in the house.

This does not stop the bizarre nature of this story. Whether Jesse was one of the most natural public relations persons or not can be debated, but the remainder of the article shows he was outstanding at getting his message across.

Mr. Baucus suggested she could take the parlor organ, a very fine new one, costing $400; and Jennie said she would prize it as a gift from her father, and she would also like the afghan and wolf robe bought last winter. Mr. Baucus said she could take them, as her father had authorized him to give her full liberty. She left the kitchen chairs and common kitchen dishes. She then gave the keys to Mr. Baucus, who locked up the house and left. There were four wagon loads, which gives Jennie a good outfit for her approaching nuptials.

THE NAMING OF THE CHILD

Jennie Billings married John Sherman, her father's former confidential clerk, and a key witness against Jesse, on January 1, 1879. The wedding was held at the home of her grandmother, Mrs. Harris. The date of the marriage is significant, since at this time it was customary to wait at least one year after the death of a parent before being married. The year's wait was considered to be the proper period of mourning; however, as much as Jennie may have cared for her mother she married seven months after her death. Referring back to the article in the Saratoga County Standard, it was noted that they would marry after a "proper time." According to tradition, Jennie should not have married until the following summer. Jennie and her father remained estranged for some time. In 1893, Jennie gave birth to a son, her only child. This was to be Jesse's only heir. Rather than let her father's name die, Jennie named her son Billings Sherman.

Jennie Billings Sherman died July 3, 1900 at the age of 40. She is buried in the Greenwich Cemetery. John Sherman, his second wife and Billings Sherman are all buried with Jennie.

In 1911, John Sherman placed his only son, Billings Sherman in the Rivercrest Sanitarium, Astoria, Long Island. According to the court records, Billings Sherman had always had mental difficulties. He would stand at the end of his bed for hours with his hands extended between his hips and shoulders. He would refuse to eat, and then would eat so rapidly that, if the food were not cut into very small pieces, he might have choked. In 1911, his father bought an automobile in the hopes that traveling around the country side might cause some interest for young Billings Sherman. Instead, he would place his head in his own lap with his hair covering his face as his father drove. By 1947, after the long Depression, Billings Sherman's estate was calculated at $127,000. The majority of the money by this time being in mortgages and bonds. When Billings Sherman died on April 25, 1954, (23 years after his father's death) what remained of Jesse Billings's estate passed from the Billings family to John Sherman's nephew.

EFFECT ON POLITICAL CAREERS

District Attorney Ormsby did not run for reelection in the fall of 1880. After using $30,000 of the taxpayer's money, close to $3,000,000 in today's dollars, perhaps he could anticipate the public's verdict.

General Hughes was reelected to the State Senate in 1880.

Jesse L'Amoreaux ran unopposed for the position of County Judge in 1882. He served from January 1, 1883 to 1889. In 1887 he was unanimously nominated by the Republican Party to serve as Comptroller of the State. The entire ticket was defeated in the general election.

Alexander Baucus, Billings friend, became a State Senator in 1888.

THE LETTER IN THE BILLINGS FILE

The Saratoga County Historian's office is buried in the basement of the building housing the County Clerk in Ballston Spa. Despite its austere location, the people are warm and the information invaluable. In the Billings file are pictures and a letter written by William Bemis in 1938, which is relevant to people knowledgeable about the trial. A portion of the letter is included with its value to be determined by the reader. This letter was part of the effort of one of the previous historians to compile information of human interest. Out of respect for the writer, the grammar was corrected.

Jessie Billings had a sister who married a man by the name of Cramer. They had a son, Charles Cramer, who turned out to be a ne'er-do-well and had a bad reputation among the neighbors of our little hamlet. Just before the murder of Mrs. Billings, he attempted to rob his invalid aunt - his mother's sister - by entering her room in the night through a window. After the murder of Mrs. Billings, a good many people thought he and his uncle, Jessie, held the whole secret. Jessie furnished the means to get him out of the way. Cramer disappeared [shortly after the murder] and was never heard from. I was on a visit to my grandparents, at this time. Charley Cramer was in Wisconsin living under the assumed name of Charles Wood. He was taken sick among strangers and died; the only clue found in his belongings was a letter with Jessie Billings's address. He (Jessie) got a telegram from Wisconsin asking if he knew Charley Wood. He (Jessie) asked them to hold the remains until he arrived. The funeral was held in the same house where Mrs. Billings was shot. I was there on arrival of the remains and attended the funeral, acting as a bearer. He (Cramer) was buried in Bacon Hill Cemetery; the guilt or innocence of the above shows that actions speak plainer than words.

The only important witness, at the first trial of Billings who is living now is George W. Jones, the alibi witness, the lone fisherman. He is living in

Glens Falls, an old man, 86 years old. At the first trial of Billings, the jury's verdict was eleven for conviction and one for acquittal. (in reality the verdict was the opposite.) Billings was admitted to bail for the sum of $50 thousand dollars. In the meantime, Jones was arrested for perjury, tried and convicted. Jones's sentence was deferred, pending Billings second trial. Jones was held in Ballston Jail awaiting the verdict. Billings was acquitted, and Jones was released. So concluded the famous murder trial.

[Further in the letter are these comments regarding Jesse which may give some indication of his personality.]

Jessie Billings and Alvinza Finne were the two leading citizens of our little hamlet. They were sworn enemies. They did not speak to each other, all over the lane that passed through. The well is located on this land; there was a house there that has now been demolished. The fence needed repair. Billings, who was always repairing things, was working on the fence when Finne interfered. They came to blows. In the fracas, Billings grasped a shovel and hit Finne with it. The strike put out one of Finne's eyes. He wore a glass eye after that.

The allegations about Charles Cramer required investigation. The letter indicated that Charles Cramer is buried in Bacon Hill Cemetery. A trip to Bacon Hill established that Charles was buried there, and that his stone noted he died in 1881, at the age of 21. If young Cramer was involved in the murder, and if he was buried by Jesse, as the letter claims, it demonstrates that Billings had a twist for irony. Hugh Thompson Billings, the brother that Jesse shot by accident, and Mary Eliza Harris Billings are buried about twenty feet apart. Charles' is the only body buried in the limited space between the two.

There is also nowhere in the testimony where any witness swears as to Cramer's presence at the time of the murder.

JESSIE BILLINGS'S ESTATE

Jessie Billing, Jr. died on December 3, 1905, without a will. The court appointed his son-in-law, John Sherman, administrator of the estate on behalf of his son, Billings Sherman. In 1910, when young Billings Sherman was 17, his father was executor and still running all the various businesses. John Sherman, asked for, and was granted, control of the estate because his son was "incompetent."

JESSE BILLINGS'S RESTING PLACE

Ultimately, all any person holds against the intrusions of future generations is the place where he is interred. Jesse Billings, Jr. is buried in Prospect Hill Cemetery, which is adjacent to the obelisk known as the Saratoga Monument in Schuylerville. The Billings plot is one of the largest in the cemetery. Jesse's is the only body buried in the plot.

He spends eternity alone.

Sources

This book was written to be read for enjoyment; therefore, the sources are listed for follow up.

Billings File Saratoga County Historians Office, Ballston Spa, New York.

Bemis, Robert; Letter to County Historian;
Peck, Henry; Letter written for historian;
Unsigned article;
Pictures of Billings and Jury.

Local History Books:

Brandow, John Henry: The Story of Old Saratoga and History of Schuylerville, Albany New York, Brandow Printing Company/ Fort Orange Press, 1900.

Dunn, Violet B.: Saratoga County Heritage, New York, Saratoga County, 1974.

Grose, Edward F.: Centennial History of the Village of Ballston Spa including the towns of Ballston and Malta, Ballston Spa, New York, The Ballston Journal, 1907.

Howell and Tenney: History of the County of Albany, N. Y.; With Portraits and Illustrations, New York, From 1609 to 1886, W.W. Munsell and Co. 1886

Johnstone, Jan, with Valarie Collins: Saratoga County Communities an Historical Perspective, Clifton Park, New York, Clifton Park Printing Company, 1980.

Our County and Its People: Descriptive and Biographical Record of Saratoga County New York, Prepared by the Saratogian. The Boston History Company, 1899.

Sylvester, Nathaniel Bartlett, History of Saratoga County, New York, Interlaken, New York, Heart of the Lakes Publishing. 1979.

Sylvester, Nathaniel Bartlett, History of Saratoga County, New York, Gersham Publishing Company: Richmond Ind. 1893.

Spyker, John Howland: Little Lives, New York, Fred Jordan Books/Grosset & Dunlap, 1978.

Vanderwerker, Grace: Early Days In Eastern Saratoga County, Interlaken, New York Heart of the Lakes Publishing, 1994.

Newspapers:
The Ballston Journal: June 1878 through December 1878
Daily Saratogian, the: June 5, 1878 through December, 1878.
The Peoples Journal; June through December 1878.
Republican, Glen's Falls; June 1878 through December 1878.
Saratoga County Standard, the May 9, through December 1878.
Times, The Troy Daily; September 11, through December 1878.

Index

Index

292

Index

Index

Index

Index

Order Form

Deep Roots Publications
P. O. Box 114
Saratoga Springs, NY 12866

Please send _____ copies of <u>To Spend Eternity Alone</u> to:

_____
Name

_____
Address

_____
City   State   Zip

Price $19.95 each
Sales Tax: New York State orders must include 7% sales tax

Shipping: $3.00 for the first book $2.00 for each additional book.

Please remit in check or money order, payable to:

Deep Roots Publications

Total amount included _____